Product Stewardship in Action

The Business Case for Life-cycle Thinking

PRODUCT STEWARDSHIP

IN ACTION

The **Business Case** for **Life-cycle Thinking**

HELEN LEWIS

Routledge
Taylor & Francis Group
LONDON AND NEW YORK

First published 2016 by Greenleaf Publishing Limited

Published 2017 by Routledge
2 Park Square, Milton Park, Abingdon, Oxon OX14 4RN
711 Third Avenue, New York, NY 10017, USA

Routledge is an imprint of the Taylor & Francis Group, an informa business

British Library Cataloguing in Publication Data:
    A catalogue record for this book is available from the British Library.

        ISBN-13: 978-1-78353-390-9 (hbk)
        ISBN-13: 978-1-78353-336-7 (pbk)

Contents

Part 1:
A framework for action

Part 2:
Product stewardship by sector

Part 3:
Conclusions

Figures

Tables

Foreword

Russ Martin

There has been a significant evolution in producer responsibility since I first started following it as a policy analyst in 1990. Then, programmes focused solely on packaging and were Euro-centric: Italy's law requiring separate collection of containers for liquids was taking effect; Switzerland sought to eliminate PVC containers while responding to the introduction of non-refillable beverage containers; and the infamous German Packaging Ordinance was under development but not yet adopted.

What little reliable information was available on programmes and policies at that time was difficult to obtain, especially before widespread internet accessibility. It was usually necessary to seek out the individuals actually involved in developing or implementing the programmes of interest.

Just look at how far we've come since then.

As with sustainability, extended producer responsibility (EPR) and product stewardship have evolved and become more mainstream. It is now generally accepted that companies have some responsibility to reduce the environmental, economic and social impacts of their products, including in their supply chain, during use and at end of life.

Questions increasingly revolve around *how* rather than *whether* producers should demonstrate stewardship, and about the most appropriate roles for government and other stakeholders to support stewardship initiatives. Companies are increasingly prepared to accept some responsibility for their products but seek reasonable levels of control over decisions about funding and implementation.

There is now a multitude of different approaches applied to a vast array of product types and substances (over 380 EPR laws as of 2014, according to the OECD). Finding a great deal of information is now relatively easy. So easy, in fact, that it can appear overwhelming or contradictory.

The Global Product Stewardship Council is an independent, not-for-profit forum that aims to facilitate the development and implementation of effective product stewardship schemes globally. Sharing information is essential to this role, but it must be useful information and understood in context. Therein lies the value of this book.

Helen's work and this book reinforce both the complexity and the value in seeking out independent, objective information on product stewardship and EPR while working with stakeholders to understand the nuanced strengths, weaknesses and circumstances under which the various approaches work best.

There is no "one size fits all" to producer responsibility policy. While consistency among approaches helps to increase efficiency, effective adoption of approaches from other jurisdictions involves an understanding of the particular circumstances that affect programme success and tailoring international approaches to local needs.

For example, recycling revolves primarily around commodities and logistics, both of which affect the relative value of materials and the costs that are ultimately passed on to producers and consumers of the recovered products. Consumer access and convenience help to increase volumes recovered, which in turn helps to reduce transport costs to markets. Programmes cannot just increase the volume of products collected without considering the market options for those recovered products; it's just a matter of basic economics.

Economics is also key to whether product stewardship is best implemented on a voluntary basis or whether a regulatory underpinning may be required. Producers may be willing to incur certain costs to reduce the impacts of their products, but this willingness can be tempered if competitors are also benefiting from an approach without contributing their fair share. Therein lies the distinction between product stewardship and EPR—product stewardship may be voluntary or regulatory, while EPR always has a regulatory underpinning to address potential "free-riders".

This book illustrates the breadth of options for product stewardship policy. Much of the existing literature focuses on mandatory EPR policies rather than the full range of options. However, voluntary programmes can be an effective alternative to regulation, or a useful starting point to engage industry before moving to regulation. This book therefore fills a gap in the literature by highlighting the potential benefits of voluntary initiatives, both for industry and for governments, while being mindful of the circumstances under which they work best and the limits they may have.

Most of the detailed case studies highlighted in this book are from Australia or New Zealand, both of which have had a historical preference for voluntary or at least lightly regulated approaches. This is partly for practical reasons (i.e. the author's direct experience in the region) but also because these initiatives have not featured in other literature and will therefore be new to many readers.

Throughout this book there are many shorter case studies from other parts of the world, including from Europe, North America and South Africa, to highlight the different approaches to product stewardship policies and practices.

This book also makes an important contribution by highlighting the potential for companies to achieved shared value through a strategic approach to product stewardship based on effective stakeholder engagement and a strong knowledge base. We are proud to have had a role in its development and commend its value as a useful resource.

Russ Martin
Chief Executive Officer
Global Product Stewardship Council
August 2016

Acknowledgements

I would like to extend my heartfelt thanks to the many people who have generously shared their time and knowledge in the writing of this book.

First of all, thanks to those I interviewed, many of whom are quoted in the case studies. They provided information, contacts, references and insights, without which this book would not have been possible. My valued "brains trust" included David Perchard, Rose Read, John Gertsakis, Russ Martin, Brett Giddings, Garth Hickle, Michael Waas, Cynthia Dunn, Kathy Frevert, Carmel Dollisson, Janet Leslie, George Gray, Lindsey Roke, Karen Warmen, Elizabeth Kasell, Mike Sammons, Stan Moore, Steve Morriss, Paul-Antione Bontinck, Sophi MacMillan, Carl Smith, Chris Hartshorne and John Webber.

Special thanks to Russ Martin, Chief Executive of the Global Product Stewardship Council, who was enthusiastic about this project from the start and encouraged me along the way.

Thanks also to Patrick Crittenden, who has been a friend and colleague for many years, during which we have collaborated on consulting projects that explored the business case for energy efficiency and packaging sustainability. Some of the ideas in this book emerged from that collaboration and I owe a considerable debt to his insights.

Patrick Crittenden, Rose Read, Brett Giddings, Garth Hickle, David Perchard and Jade Barnaby also peer reviewed chapters and made innumerable suggestions for improvement. Naturally any errors or omissions that remain in the book are mine alone.

Part 1:
A framework for action

1
Introduction: evolution, key concepts and business drivers

> Steward (noun): A person whose responsibility it is to take care of something (Oxford Dictionaries, http://www.oxforddictionaries.com/definition/english/steward).

If you bought a soft drink or a pint of milk in the 1950s, it was sold in a heavy glass bottle. You returned the bottle to a shop, dairy or soft drink bottler and were refunded the deposit you paid with the original purchase. This was typical of the way that many other products were used, reused, repaired or repurposed, a practice Susan Strasser calls "the stewardship of objects".[1]

These practices started to change after the Second World War, when the growing popularity of "disposable" or "throwaway" packaging led to the demise of the refillable glass bottle. An advertisement in 1947 for one of the earliest disposable bottles in the United States, manufactured by Owens-Illinois Glass Company, promoted its convenience for consumers, with the claim that, owing to this new, liberating system, there's "No more bother lugging empties back for refunds!"[2] In Australia, chemical manufacturer ICI claimed in 1967 that its polyvinyl chloride (PVC) bottles were "here to stay" because of their efficiency and convenience: "For the consumer,

---

1   Strasser, S. (1999). *Waste and Want: A Social History of Trash.* New York: Henry Holt and Company, LLC.
2   Rogers, H. (2007). Message in a bottle: mass-scale trash as the outcome of our economic system. In J. Knechtel (Ed.), *Trash* (pp. 113-131). Cambridge, MA: MIT Press, p. 114.

disposability is a strong point in favour of PVC bottles, as normal household incineration will adequately dispose of them ...".[3]

Not everyone shared the industry's enthusiasm for convenience, as new forms of glass, plastic and paperboard packaging contributed to a growing litter problem. In the US there were hundreds of proposals by local and state regulators to restrict the use of disposable containers. The first of these, in Vermont in 1957, "sent shockwaves through the burgeoning disposables industry".[4] Many of these proposals were defeated, at least in part because of intense lobbying by packaging and beverage companies. The industry, led by companies such as the American Can Company, Owens-Illinois Glass Company and Coca-Cola, created a not-for-profit organization—Keep America Beautiful (KAB)—which launched a national anti-litter education campaign. Many of the same companies later supported the development of recycling programmes to divert used containers, particularly glass and aluminium, from landfill.

While criticized at the time and more recently as "greenwashing",[5] anti-litter and recycling campaigns by the packaging and beverage industries were some of the earliest examples of what we would now call "extended producer responsibility" (EPR) or "product stewardship".

1.1 The idea of producer responsibility: history and evolution

By the 1980s solid waste had become a high priority public issue in many developed countries because of declining landfill space, increasing costs of disposal and opposition to new landfills. Those who were actively involved in recycling and waste management at the time realized that the solution needed to go beyond the expansion of recycling systems run by local authorities. In the early 1990s Thomas Lindhqvist, an academic at Lund University in Sweden, proposed an innovative solution that he called extended producer responsibility. The aim of EPR was to reduce the total environmental impact of a product by making the manufacturer "responsible for the entire

3   ICI (1967). Clear to see. In *Polymer* (p. 4). Melbourne, Australia: ICI.
4   Rogers (2007), p. 4.
5   *Ibid.*

life-cycle of the product and especially for the take-back, recycling and final disposal of the product".[6]

EPR is now widely accepted as the basis for product-related environmental policies in the European Union (EU). Beginning with packaging in the late 1980s, producer responsibility policies have now been extended to waste electrical and electronic equipment (WEEE), end of life vehicles (ELV) and batteries. Other countries including Japan, South Korea, Taiwan and many Canadian provinces have followed the European lead by introducing EPR laws for similar groups of products. By 2015 there were more than 90 laws in the United States (US) covering a wide range of products including appliances, batteries, carpets, mobile phones, electronics, mattresses, fluorescent lighting, mercury thermostats, used paint, pesticides and pharmaceuticals.[7]

A related but more inclusive term for producer responsibility is "product stewardship". This is the principle that everyone involved in the manufacture, distribution or consumption of a product shares responsibility for the environmental and social impacts of that product over its life-cycle. Product stewardship tends to have broader scope than EPR: encompassing voluntary action by companies as well as regulated schemes; social as well as environmental impacts; and initiatives at every stage of the product life-cycle.

Producers—often defined to include manufacturers, brand owners and distributors—have a particularly important role to play because of their influence on suppliers, consumers and recyclability at end of life (Fig. 1.1).

Lindhqvist believed that producer responsibility could take many different forms, including economic or physical responsibility for collection, recycling or disposal of the company's products. While acknowledging that the manufacturer, distributor, user, recycler and final disposer all influence the environmental impacts of a product and must be encouraged to do what they can, he argued for a focus on manufacturers because of their unique ability to prevent environmental impacts through environmentally conscious design.[8]

---

6   Lindhqvist, T. (2000). *Extended Producer Responsibility in Cleaner Production* (Doctoral dissertation). The International Institute for Industrial Environmental Economics, Lund University, p. ii.

7   Cassel, S. (2015). The state of EPR in the U.S. In *2015 US Product Stewardship Forum*. Boston, MA: Product Stewardship Institute.

8   See Lindhqvist (2000); Lindhqvist, T. (1992). Extended producer responsibility. Paper presented to an invitational expert seminar, *Extended Producer*

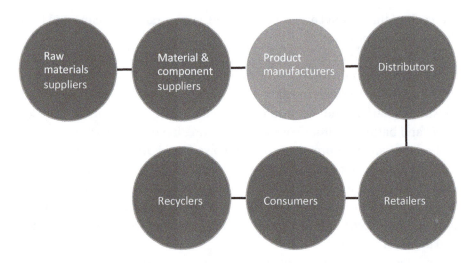

FIGURE 1.1   EPR focuses on the ability of manufacturers to influence the product life-cycle

While originally intended to cover the entire product life-cycle, the term "EPR" has generally been applied to regulatory initiatives that promote producer responsibility for waste management and recycling at end of life. The principle of EPR proposes a reallocation of responsibility for product waste management between industry, consumers and governments:

> EPR *extends* the traditional environmental responsibilities that producers and importers have previously been assigned (i.e. worker safety, prevention and treatment of environmental releases from production, financial and legal responsibility for the sound management of production wastes) to include the management of products at their post-consumer stage.[9]

EPR programmes recognize that the environmental costs of waste management are not reflected in product prices and that these costs should be internalized.[10] However, while the focus of EPR is on post-consumer waste management, there are other benefits. Fishbein noted that:

Responsibility as a Strategy to Promote Cleaner Production, 4–5 May 1992, Troeholm Castle, Sweden.

9   OECD (Organisation for Economic Cooperation and Development) (2001). *Extended Producer Responsibility: A Guidance Manual for Governments.* Paris: OECD, p. 10.

10   Anders, M. (1995). Extended producer responsibility programs. In *Volume 2: Which Policies, Which Tools?* Presentation to *Washington Waste Minimisation*

> ... the post-consumer stage is simply an intervention point ... A producer that responds to EPR by making a less wasteful and more recyclable product will reduce the huge environmental impacts of raw materials extraction ... as well as the impacts of materials and energy use associated with materials' processing and the manufacture of new products.[11]

This supports Lindhqvist's view that a fundamental objective of EPR is to influence product design.

The related concept of product stewardship evolved in North America a decade earlier, with the development of a code of practice by the Canadian Chemical Producers Association (CCPA).[12] A project called "Responsible Care/Product Stewardship" was presented to the industry association in 1981 and its guiding principles were formalized in 1983. Following a serious chemical accident in Bhopal, India in November 1984, the association's board decided that Responsible Care would be developed into a proactive safety audit process "... with particular emphasis on product stewardship".[13]

Responsible Care is now in place in at least 40 countries and contains six codes, including one on product stewardship. Within this context, product stewardship has been defined as "... the set of practices related to reducing risks from chemical and process hazards in a company's supply chain".[14] This interpretation of product stewardship as a risk management process appears to be limited to the chemical industry, particularly in the US.

In its broadest sense the concept of stewardship is even older, having been used in some of the earliest statements about the social responsibilities of business. Bowen argued in *The Social Responsibilities of the Businessman* that "[h]is role is that of steward and he is justified in retaining his social position only if the interests of society, on balance, are best serviced

Workshop. Washington, DC: Organisation for Economic Co-operation and Development.

11 Fishbein, B. (2000). The EPR policy challenge for the United States. In B. Fishbein, J. Ehrenfeld, & J. Young (Eds.), *Extended Producer Responsibility: A Materials Policy for the 21st Century* (pp. 55-112). New York: Inform, p. 62.

12 Lewis, H. (2009, April). *Product Stewardship: Institutionalising Corporate Responsibility for Packaging in Australia* (PhD thesis). School of Global Studies, Social Science and Planning, RMIT University.

13 O'Connor, J.A. (n.d.). *Responsible Care: Doing the Right Thing*. Canadian Chemical Producers Association, p. 5.

14 Snir, E.M. (2001). Liability as a catalyst for product stewardship. *Production and Operations Management*, 10(2), 190-206 (p. 190).

thereby".[15] According to Harré *et al.*, the religious interpretation of the term stewardship, which assumes that the world is made for human beings, has been an important influence on environmental discourse.[16] In the early 1990s it was one of the most common phrases found in corporate environmental policy statements.[17]

Growing levels of municipal waste in the US led to similar policy debates to those in Europe. The preference of regulators, however, was for voluntary approaches rather than legally enforceable EPR. This has been reflected in the use of terminology such as product stewardship or extended *product* responsibility. According to Fishbein, a failed attempt was made in 1992 to include an EPR provision in the reauthorization bill for the Resource Conservation and Recovery Act, thus "ending efforts to enact EPR at the federal level".[18] EPR was introduced by a public interest research group to the President's Council on Sustainable Development (PCSD), a multi-stakeholder group created by President Clinton:

> The subject of EPR was introduced ... and immediately sparked heated debate, with industry representatives strongly objecting to the idea of "producer" responsibility. Ultimately, the PCSD recommended a policy of "extended *product* responsibility", which differs from extended producer responsibility in the following aspects:
> 1. Responsibility is for the environmental impacts of products over their entire life cycle, with no focus on the post-consumer stage.
> 2. Responsibility is shared by consumers, government, and all industry actors in the product chain, with no targeting of specific producers such as manufacturers or retailers.
> 3. Responsibility is not required to be physical or financial; for example, it may simply mean providing consumer education.
> 4. Responsibility is voluntary, not mandatory.[19]

Industry opposition to EPR in the US is gradually being replaced by a more proactive approach to product responsibility. As shown by many of the examples in this book, companies and industry associations are now playing a leading role in the development of product stewardship policies,

---

15   Bowen, H. (1953). *Social Responsibilities of the Businessman*. New York: Harper & Row, pp. 39-40.
16   Harré, R., Brockmeier, J. & Mülhäusler, P. (1999). *Greenspeak: A Study of Environmental Discourse*. London: SAGE Publications, p. 40.
17   UNCTAD (United Nations Conference on Trade and Development) (1993). *Environmental Management in Transnational Corporations*. New York: UNCTAD.
18   Fishbein (2000).
19   *Ibid.*, p. 74.

including underpinning regulations. Despite the lack of action at a national level, many states have introduced their own EPR laws and more are on the way.

1.2 Key concepts

1.2.1 Producer responsibility

While the terms "product stewardship" and "extended producer responsibility" are often used interchangeably, and do overlap, there are important differences. While product stewardship encompasses voluntary and regulated approaches, EPR is generally regarded as a mandatory type of product stewardship.[20]

A common theme is that, while responsibility is shared between many different actors, manufacturers have the most important role to play because of their influence on the product life-cycle. Scott Cassel, Director of the US-based Product Stewardship Institute (PSI), described this in more colourful terms when he referred to "the more nuanced framing of the product stewardship movement as having a lead actor with a strong supporting cast".[21]

For the remainder of this book, product stewardship refers to the principle that manufacturers, retailers and other organizations involved in a product supply chain have a responsibility to minimize the environmental and social impacts of that product over its life-cycle. It encompasses government policies that mandate EPR in some form, as well as individual or collective industry programmes that aim to improve the environmental or social sustainability of a product. The responsibilities of consumers, while important,[22] are not the focus of this book.

---

20   For example, see Product Policy Institute, Product Stewardship Institute, and California Product Stewardship Council (2012). *Product Stewardship and Extended Producer Responsibility: Reducing Economic, Environmental, Health and Safety Impacts from Consumer Products.* Athens, GA.

21   Casell, S. (2011, November 29). In search of honest dialogue: Six stages of industry grief. *The PSI Blog.* Retrieved from https://productstewardshipinstitute. wordpress.com/2011/11/29/honest-dialogue/

22   Lane, R., & Watson, M. (2012). Stewardship of things: The radical potential of product stewardship for re-framing responsibilities and relationships to products and materials. *Geoforum,* 43(2012), 1254-1265.

The idea that individual products have their own "life-cycle" is a relatively new one, but it is now widely accepted in business and policy fields.[23] While the concept merits more critical analysis,[24] life-cycle thinking provides a useful way of conceptualizing the total impacts of a product. It encourages companies to think outside the physical boundaries of their manufacturing facility and the conventional legal boundaries of product responsibility; to understand and minimize impacts in their supply chains and at end of "life".

The concept of "shared responsibility" is widely accepted by product stewardship practitioners, although the allocation of responsibilities is often contested. A report published by ANZRP, an industry group collecting waste electrical and electronic waste ("e-waste" or WEEE) in Australia, called for local government and retailers to assume a greater role in funding or facilitating collection.[25]

John Gertsakis has argued that practitioners and policy-makers need to revisit the original goals of product stewardship and EPR.[26] In his view these concepts have increasingly been interpreted as producer-funded recycling programmes: "simplistic end-of-pipe solutions that are overtly focused on collecting 'rubbish' and primitive materials recovery". Gertsakis suggests that a more useful approach is to target relevant stages of the product life-cycle to intervene with necessary environmental measures, for example through design, cleaner production, supply chain management or public education.

This book aims to clarify the scope of product stewardship by addressing four key areas of activity for companies (Fig. 1.2):

- **Policies** that establish goals and targets for product sustainability

- **Design** processes that consider sustainability impacts over the entire product life-cycle

23   Heiskanen, E. (2000). *Translations of an Environmental Technique: Institutionalization of the Life Cycle Approach in Business, Policy and Research Networks* (PhD thesis). Helsinki School of Economics and Business Administration, ACTA Universitatis Oeconomicae Helsingiensis.

24   Bio Intelligence Service (2014). *Development of Guidance on Extended Producer Responsibility (EPR)*. Report to European Commission—DG Environment.

25   The Economist Intelligence Unit (2015). *Global E-waste Systems: Insights for Australia from Other Developed Countries*. Report for the Australia New Zealand Recycling Platform. Melbourne.

26   Gertsakis, J. (2014, May 12). The product stewardship 2.0 imperative. *Infoactiv blog*. Retrieved from http://infoactiv.com.au/the-product-stewardship-2-0-imperative/

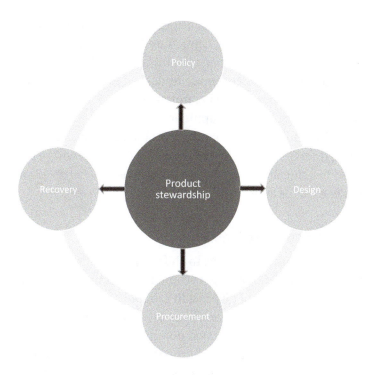

FIGURE 1.2   Four key elements of producer responsibility

- **Procurement** policies and guidelines that impose minimum sustainability standards for suppliers

- **Recovery** of products at end of life; fully or partially funded by producers

When Thomas Lindhqvist originally conceived the idea of EPR he envisaged a broad range of initiatives to achieve product-related goals.[27] In practice, its implementation by governments has focused on laws that make producers responsible for the costs of recycling. These have had only limited success in promoting design for environment or more sustainable supply chains.

A more sophisticated understanding of product and packaging life-cycles and the potential trade-offs between different environmental impacts (for example between material and energy consumption and recyclability) is prompting government policy-makers and companies to look for integrated approaches to policy and practice. The EU, which led the development of

27   Lindhqvist (2000).

EPR policies in the 1990s, now considers waste management within the context of its Sustainable Consumption and Production Policy.[28] This policy seeks to improve product sustainability through a more coordinated approach that includes environmental design, consumer labelling, green procurement and voluntary retailer initiatives.

Consistent with a life-cycle approach to product stewardship, policymakers need to clearly understand their objectives and identify the most appropriate intervention point. For example, complementary policies may be required to achieve specific design objectives such as the elimination of particular hazardous substances.

1.2.2 Products and sustainability

The original objective of EPR was to shift responsibility for post-consumer waste management from local government (and ratepayers) to producers. By internalizing the costs of disposal in product prices, this was expected to provide companies with an incentive to design less wasteful and more recyclable products. Over time its stated objectives have moved beyond waste, for example a recent report to the European Commission claimed that EPR should "... provide an incentive for producers to take into account environmental considerations along the product's life-cycle, from the design phase to their end-of-life".[29]

Discourses on product stewardship have generally focused on a broader range of issues than EPR, particularly in the chemical industry where health and safety are as important as environmental management. Under the Responsible Care programme, product stewardship is defined as "... the responsibility to understand, manage and communicate the health and environmental impacts of chemical products".[30]

The term product stewardship is now widely used by companies to describe policies and initiatives that aim to reduce the environmental and social impacts of products at different stages of their life-cycle. Packaging manufacturer and recycler Visy describes what this means:

28   Commission of the European Communities (2008). *Communication from the Commission on Sustainable Consumption and Production and Sustainable Industrial Policy Action Plan.* Brussels. Retrieved from http://eur-lex.europa.eu/legal-content/EN/NOT/?uri=CELEX:52008DC0397
29   Bio Intelligence Service (2014), p. 10.
30   American Chemical Council (2012). *Responsible Care Product Safety Code of Management Practices.* Washington, DC: American Chemical Council, p. 1.

In simple terms [this means] that we take responsibility for all the stages of our products' lifespans. It's only by really understanding how our products will be made, used and disposed of that we can minimise their environmental and social impact. So we look at the bigger picture to work out where we can improve.

Product stewardship at Visy involves everything from stipulating conditions to suppliers, to documenting and controlling our internal processes. Basically, we influence everything we can to improve disposal, reuse and recycling systems.[31]

In its broadest interpretation product stewardship implies that manufacturers have a responsibility to ensure that their products and services are as sustainable as possible throughout their life-cycle. In most cases the ideal of a "sustainable product" is not realistic, but companies can and should look for solutions that minimize negative and maximize positive sustainability impacts—economic, environmental, social and ethical—across the full life-cycle.[32]

This book is primarily interested in the strategies that companies are taking to reduce the *environmental* impacts of their products, particularly at end of life. Many social issues in the product supply chain, such as human rights abuses, child labour and unsafe working conditions, are also being addressed by companies as part of their broader commitment to corporate social responsibility, but are beyond the scope of this book.

1.3 Understanding the business case

There has been very little critical analysis of product stewardship from a business perspective. For example:

- Why *should* producers take responsibility for the environmental and social impacts of their products, many of which are outside their direct control?

- What drives individual companies to implement product stewardship initiatives?

- How can product stewardship help to create business value?

31   Visy (2015). Sustainability. Retrieved from http://www.visy.com.au/about/ sustainability/#header-title

32   Charter, M., & Tischner, U. (2001). Introduction. In M. Charter & U. Tischner (Eds.), *Sustainable Solutions* (pp. 17-22). Sheffield, UK: Greenleaf Publishing.

The first question is often answered by academics and pressure groups through reference to business ethics, social obligation and a company's "licence to operate".

The second question relates to the *actual* behaviour and motivation of practitioners in business rather than theories about what should or should not be done. Individuals involved in product stewardship initiatives are more likely to link these to particular stakeholders, such as highly motivated employees, the expectations of customers or the threat of government regulation, than to abstract ideas about business ethics and social responsibility.

The third question starts to focus on successful strategies for business. How can practitioners identify the most important sustainability issues for their products? Which product stewardship initiatives are most likely to create value for their stakeholders *and* their business? There is some evidence that a strategic approach to design, for environment, sustainable procurement and recycling, can help to improve a company's competitive position.

These three questions represent different ways of looking at the business case for product stewardship. Is it a social obligation, a stakeholder management issue, a source of competitive advantage, or all three? Each option is explored further below and then used to develop a more integrated approach to product stewardship.

From a public policy perspective, product stewardship can also be seen as a way of internalizing the social and environmental costs of consumption, including pollution, resource depletion, waste and litter. This approach, which draws on economic theories about "market failure", aims to improve efficiency by ensuring that prices reflect true (social) costs. This perspective is important but outside the scope of this book, which focuses on the business of product stewardship rather than its public policy benefits.

1.3.1 Product stewardship as an ethical or social obligation

Discourses on product stewardship and producer responsibility suggest that companies have a moral or social responsibility to address the environmental and social impacts of their products. But what is this based on?

From a business perspective product stewardship can be justified on the basis of "corporate social responsibility" (CSR): the principle that companies have obligations to society that go beyond legal compliance. Many early writers on CSR tried to define the scope and limitations of these responsibilities.[33] Economic rationalists, for example, argued that the only social responsibility of a corporation is to maximize profits for shareholders within the constraints of the law. The most famous advocate was Milton Friedman, who argued that:

> there is one and only one social responsibility of business—to use its resources and engage in activities designed to increase its profits so long as it stays within the rules of the game, which is to say, engages in open and free competition, without deception or fraud.[34]

Others took a broader view of social responsibility, arguing that the business institution as a whole, as well as individual companies, will only survive if they operate in accordance with social values and expectations. Davis and Blomstrom called this the "Iron Law of Responsibility", which is that "in the long run, those who do not use power in a manner which society considers responsible will tend to lose it".[35] CSR is therefore consistent with self-interest:

> Of the many arguments favoring social responsibility, one of the most prevalent is that of the long-run self-interest of business. This concept rationalises that society expects business to accomplish a variety of social goods, and it must accomplish these goods if it expects to profit in the long-run.[36]

This view is embodied in "legitimacy theory", the idea that in order to operate successfully, corporations have to work within the bounds of socially acceptable behaviour.[37] Societal obligations are constantly changing and therefore businesses need to implement strategies that make them responsive to societal demands.[38] CSR is particularly important during the "zone of

---

33 Wood, D. (1991). Corporate social performance revisited. *Academy of Management Review*, 16(4), 691-718.

34 Friedman, M. (1962). *Capitalism and Freedom*. Chicago: University of Chicago Press, p. 133.

35 Davis, K., & Blomstrom, R.L. (1971). *Business, Society, and Environment*. New York: McGraw-Hill, p. 95.

36 Davis, K. (1973). The case for and against business assumptions of social responsibilities. *Academy of Management Journal*, 16(2), 312-322 (p. 313).

37 O'Donovan, G. (2002). Environmental disclosures in the annual report: extending the applicability and predictive power of legitimacy theory. *Accounting, Auditing & Accountability Journal*, 15(3), 344-371.

38 Sethi, S.P. (1979). A conceptual framework for environmental analysis of social issues and evaluation of business response patterns. *Academy of Management Review*, 4(1), 63-74.

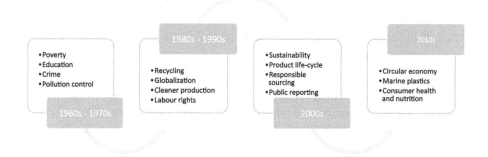

FIGURE 1.3   Evolution of corporate social issues

discretion"—the period during which something is neither required by law nor entirely voluntary.[39]

Swanson and Niehoff provide a strong cautionary note about society's expectations of business, observing that "[w]hat is required, expected or desired of business will depend on the issue at hand and whether economic and ecological responsibilities are seen as mutually reinforcing or conflicting" and "[g]roups in society often disagree on what constitutes required, expected or desired corporate conduct".[40]

The issues that companies are expected to address voluntarily change over time (Fig. 1.3). By the 1970s corporate responsibilities had shifted from social issues external to the corporation, such as poverty, to those more directly linked to a business's operation, such as pollution.[41] Many of the issues that were voluntary or discretionary "social responsibilities" in the 1960s and 1970s, such as product safety and pollution control, have been institutionalized through legislation and are now considered a prerequisite for doing business.

Product waste and recycling became government priorities in the 1980s, although the perception that these were also *corporate* responsibilities only became widespread towards the end of the 20th century. The 1990s saw the

39   Ackerman, R. (1973). How companies respond to social demands. *Harvard Business Review*, 51, 88-98.
40   Swanson, D., & Niehoff, B. (2001). Business citizenship outside and inside organisations: an emergent synthesis of corporate responsibility and employee citizenship. In J. Andriof & M. McIntosh (Eds.), *Perspectives on Corporate Citizenship* (pp. 104-116). Sheffield, UK: Greenleaf Publishing, pp. 107-108.
41   Ackerman, R., & Bauer, R. (1976). *Corporate Social Responsiveness*. Reston, VA: Reston Publishing Company.

emergence of activist pressure around issues related to globalization and outsourcing, including human rights abuses, labour rights, corruption and environmental degradation.[42]

The social issues that need to be addressed by a particular business also depend on their industry sector, including public visibility, degree of government scrutiny, competitive structure and culture.[43] Wood summed this up when she noted that:

> Businesses are not responsible for solving all social problems. They are, however, responsible for solving problems they have caused, and they are responsible for helping to solve problems and social issues related to their business operations and interests.[44]

1.3.2 Product stewardship as a stakeholder management strategy

These broad notions of corporate social responsibility help to explain the public interest in product stewardship. They are less useful, however, when applied to the behaviour of individual firms. Porter and Kramer argue that the use of moral arguments to support CSR (i.e. that companies have a duty to be good corporate citizens) is not very helpful.[45] It fails to recognize the complex choices that companies have to make when balancing competing values, interests and costs.

The "licence to operate" principle is more pragmatic because it provides a way for a business to identify the social issues that matter to its stakeholders and to make decisions about them.[46] The concept of a licence to operate "derives from the fact that every company needs tacit or explicit permission from governments, communities and numerous other stakeholders to do business".[47] Understanding and responding to stakeholder expectations is therefore important to most managers.[48]

42   Waddock, S. (2004). Parallel universes: companies, academics, and the progress of corporate citizenship. *Business and Society Review*, 109(1), 5-42.
43   Jones, M. (1999). The institutional determinants of social responsibility. *Journal of Business Ethics*, 20(2), 163-179.
44   Wood (1991), p. 697.
45   Porter, M., & Kramer, M. (2006, December). Strategy and society: the link between competitive advantage and corporate social responsibility. *Harvard Business Review*, reprint pp. 1-16.
46   *Ibid.*
47   *Ibid.*, p. 5.
48   Clarkson, M. (1995). A stakeholder framework for analyzing and evaluating corporate social performance. *Academy of Management Review*, 20(1), 92-117.

The international standard for social responsibility acknowledges that stakeholder identification and engagement is integral to social responsibility:

> Social responsibility is the responsibility of an organization for the impacts of its decisions and activities on society and the environment, through transparent and ethical behaviour, that:
> - contributes to sustainable development
> - takes into account the expectations of stakeholders
> - is in compliance with laws and consistent with international norms of behaviour
> - is integrated throughout the organization and practiced in its relationships.[49]

In this context, the standard defines "activities" to include "products, services and processes". The standard notes that organizations are under increasing scrutiny by their various stakeholders, and the perception of an organization's performance on social responsibility can influence, among other things, their competitive advantage, reputation, ability to attract workers and customers, employee productivity, the view of investors, and relationships with governments, suppliers, the media, peers and local communities in which they operate.[50]

There is an extensive literature on "stakeholder theory" that helps to clarify *to whom* a business is responsible.[51] It reduces the abstract idea of "society" to the stakeholders who are related to the firm's interests, operations and actions. Tomer has argued that stakeholder theory is consistent with commercial self-interest.[52] This is because companies that take a longer-term view are willing to sacrifice some short-term profit to minimize "legitimacy costs" which they might incur if they fail to meet stakeholder expectations. These could include the higher costs of meeting regulatory requirements if governments decide they have to legislate, or damage to corporate reputation which might result from external pressure on the organization.[53]

Some writers on stakeholder theory have attempted to categorize stakeholders according to their salience to the firm. For example, companies are likely to give priority to stakeholders that provide critical resources and are

49   ISO (International Organization for Standardization) (2010). *Guidance Standard on Social Responsibility, ISO 26000 (Extracts)*. Geneva: ISO.

50   *Ibid.*

51   Wood (1991).

52   Tomer, J.F. (1994). Social responsibility in the human firm: towards a new theory of the firm's external relationships. In A. Lewis & K. Warneryd (Eds.), *Ethics and Economic Affairs* (pp. 125-250). London: Routledge.

53   *Ibid.*

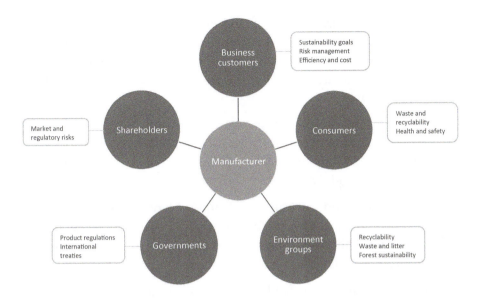

FIGURE 1.4   Product stewardship within a stakeholder framework

therefore important to the survival of the company.[54] Clarkson distinguished between "primary stakeholders"—those who are involved in transactions with the corporation including employees, shareholders and customers—and "secondary stakeholders"—those who can influence, or are influenced by, a corporation but are not engaged in transactions with it.[55]

Mitchell *et al.* argued that the attention paid by a corporate manager to the demands of a stakeholder group will depend on how that manager perceives the legitimacy and power of the group as well as the urgency of their claim.[56] The most legitimate, powerful and urgent corporate stakeholders are those who are critical to the commercial success of the organization, including suppliers and customers.[57]

The application of stakeholder theory to product stewardship is illustrated in Figure 1.4. From this perspective, product stewardship is driven by the concerns of stakeholders; for example:

54   Hill, C., & Jones, T. (1992). Stakeholder-agency theory. *Journal of Management Studies*, 29(2), 131-154.
55   Clarkson (1995).
56   Mitchell, R., Agle, B., & Wood, D. (1997). Toward a theory of stakeholder identification and salience: defining the principle of who and what really counts. *Academy of Management Review*, 22(4), 853-886.
57   *Ibid.*

- Many product manufacturers and retailers impose environmental requirements on their global suppliers. Dell has standards for carbon, water, waste, worker health and safety, and human rights and dignity that all suppliers have to meet, and regularly audits supplier performance.[58]

- Laws that mandate producer responsibility for waste and recycling are already widespread for packaging and electronics, and are increasingly being adopted for batteries, paint and other hazardous household products.

- Community and environmental groups have targeted product manufacturers in high profile campaigns on issues such as poor working conditions in developing countries, paper fibres harvested from old growth forests, or low recycling rates.

Stakeholder perceptions can have a negative or a positive impact on a business. Consumers, for example, may change their purchasing choices based on product recyclability or a company's reputation for responsible environmental management. Product manufacturers may de-select suppliers that fail to meet their environmental standards.

Responding positively to stakeholder concerns about a particular issue can generate business benefits. Between 2004 and 2009 Greenpeace campaigned against Kimberly-Clark's use of paper fibre from Canadian forests. In 2009 the company signed an agreement with Greenpeace to work together to increase the use of "environmentally preferred" fibres in the company's products. Reflecting on the five-year anniversary of the agreement, Lisa Morden (global sustainability leader for Kimberly-Clark Professional) noted that the partnership with Greenpeace gave them a deeper understanding of environmental issues and insights into ways to improve the sustainability of their supply chains.[59]

Stakeholder theory helps to explain some of the business drivers for product stewardship by linking it to the expectations of stakeholders, particularly those who are critical to commercial success. However, it continues to frame corporate social responsibility as a response to external demands.

---

58   Dell (2012). *Dell 2020 Legacy of Good Plan*. Retrieved from http://i.dell.com/sites/doccontent/corporate/corp-comm/en/Documents/2020-plan.pdf

59   Morden, L. (2014, October 6). What Kimberly-Clark learned from 5 years with Greenpeace. *GreenBiz.com*. Retrieved from http://www.greenbiz.com/blog/2014/10/06/kimberly-clark-and-ngos-building-sustainable-supply-chain

This ignores the potential for companies to address social problems more strategically as a source of competitive advantage.

1.3.3 Product stewardship as a source of competitive advantage

> CSR can be much more than a cost, constraint, or charitable deed. Approached strategically, it generates opportunity, innovation, and competitive advantage for corporations—while solving social problems (Porter and Kramer).[60]

Porter and Kramer have argued that most businesses take a reactive approach to CSR that fails to connect with corporate strategy.[61] In their view this represents a tremendous lost opportunity. Instead they advocate a strategic approach to CSR based on "shared value": the principle that companies should choose strategies that create a meaningful benefit for society while adding to the company's bottom line. By looking at every business decision through a shared value lens, companies can unlock new sources of productivity growth.[62] Excess packaging, for example, is a cost to business and the environment. By reducing the amount of packaging and improving efficiencies in distribution, companies can save money in packaging and transport while reducing greenhouse gas emissions and solid waste.

A number of thought leaders in academia and industry have continued to develop the concept of shared value as a practical business tool. A "how-to guide" on creating shared value notes that leading companies are starting to look at social responsibility through a new lens.[63] They realize that they can maximize the benefits of their social investments by aligning them with their core business interests, expertise and influence. A simple representation of this idea is shown in Figure 1.5.

McDonald's has started to use this approach as the framework for its sustainability strategy, describing it as "[g]rowing our business by making a

---

60 Porter & Kramer (2006), p. 1.

61 *Ibid.*

62 Porter, M., & Kramer, M. (2011, January–February). Creating shared value: how to reinvent capitalism—and unleash a wave of innovation and growth. *Harvard Business Review*, January–February 2011.

63 Bockstette, V., & Stamp, M. (2011). *Creating Shared Value: A How-to Guide for the New Corporate (R)evolution.* FSG, p. 3. Retrieved from http://www.fsg.org/publications/creating-shared-value-how-guide-new-corporate-revolution

Figure 1.5　Creating shared value

Source: Based on Bockstette and Stamp (2011), p. 4

positive difference in society".[64] Case studies are starting to be published to demonstrate how shared value is being created by companies such as Alcoa, HP, GE and Nestlé.[65] Alcoa, for example, built a new recycling facility for aluminium cans in the US to reduce its energy costs and greenhouse gas emissions. To ensure that it has enough material to feed the recycling plant, Alcoa is leading industry efforts to increase the recycling rate for aluminium cans in North America, with initiatives ranging from social marketing and education through to investments in collection infrastructure. While the campaign is still at an early stage, the recycling rate is starting to improve.[66]

In an influential article for *Harvard Business Review*, Porter and Kramer identified three ways in which shared value is created: by reconceiving products and markets; by redefining productivity in the value chain; and by enabling local cluster development.[67] Some examples that show how these categories might be applied to product stewardship are shown in Table 1.1.

Stuart Hart suggests that effective environmental management strategies can provide a competitive advantage for companies in two primary ways:

64　McDonald's (2014). *Our Journey Together for Good: McDonald's Corporate Social Responsibility & Sustainability Report 2012–13*, p. 7. Retrieved from http://corporate.mcdonalds.com/content/dam/AboutMcDonalds/2.0/pdfs/2012_2013_csr_report.pdf

65　See Bockstette & Stamp (2011); Shared Value Initiative (2016). *About Shared Value*. Retrieved from http://sharedvalue.org/about-shared-value

66　Bockstette & Stamp (2011).

67　Porter & Kramer (2011).

TABLE 1.1 Creating shared value through product stewardship

Opportunities to create shared value*	Product stewardship examples
Reconceiving products and markets	• Redesigning products and packaging to reduce their environmental impact (e.g. by reducing the amount of material or designing for reuse), while increasing sales to environmentally aware consumers • Developing new products to grow the business while addressing an environmental problem (e.g. energy- or water-saving products) • Replacing physical products with virtual ones (e.g. selling e-books online or a movie subscription service rather than books and DVDs)
Redefining productivity in the value chain	• Eliminating unnecessary packaging • Using more efficient logistics to save energy and emissions in transport • Taking back used products or components from consumers to meet regulatory requirements or to build customer loyalty • Replacing virgin materials with recycled materials to reduce costs and environmental impact and improve security of supply
Enabling local cluster development	• Investing in a local infrastructure for recycling to reduce waste and address reputational risks from poor practices (e.g. developing standards and supporting e-waste recycling businesses in developing countries) • Training farmers to adopt more sustainable farming practices in developing countries, in order to reduce environmental impacts and improve reliability of raw material supplies

* The three categories are from Porter and Kramer (2011)

- By gaining preferred or exclusive access to important resources

- By establishing rules, regulations or standards that are uniquely tailored to the firm's capability[68]

He also proposes that competitiveness relies on both internal (competitive) resources and external (cooperative) strategies, as both are essential for social legitimacy (Table 1.2). The case studies described throughout this book include internal business processes, such as changes to product or packaging design, as well as collaborative projects undertaken with external stakeholders. End-of-life strategies such as litter management or product recovery can be difficult to implement as an individual business, but more achievable through collaborative efforts.

68   Hart, S. (1995). A natural-resource-based view of the firm. *Academy of Management Review*, 20(4), 986-1014.

TABLE 1.2   Strategies that build capabilities in product stewardship

Internal (competitive) strategies	External (cooperative) strategies
• Integrate life-cycle assessment in the product development process • Manage suppliers to minimize environmental impacts in the supply chain • Ensure close collaboration between environmental staff, marketing staff and customers to integrate environmental considerations in product design and procurement • Integrate the views of external stakeholders including environmentalists, community leaders, the media and regulators in product design and development	• Involve external stakeholders in the development of product stewardship strategies, e.g. through an advisory group • Collaborate with regulators on the development of new rules, regulations or standards

Source: Based on Hart (1995)

There is no conclusive empirical research on links between product stewardship and competitive advantage. However, there are numerous case studies that demonstrate the potential business benefits. Interface, for example, has reduced the environmental impacts of its carpet tiles through dematerialization (lightweighting), use of post-consumer recycled content and product take-back and recycling initiatives. These strategies have contributed to a steady increase in market share.[69]

Product recycling will increasingly be driven by the need to control the supply of raw materials. Resource scarcity has been identified as one of the six megatrends of the 21st century as a result of a growing population and economic development.[70] Increased demand for resources and supply constraints will lead to higher prices and increasing price volatility.

In future the most successful companies will be those that integrate resource efficiency and recycling into their business model. Nestlé Waters North America has supported EPR laws for packaging because it believes that this is the best way to increase the supply of recycled plastics for its bottles. The company's former Director of Sustainability Michael Washburn described this as a risk management strategy:

---

69   Hensler, C.D. (2014). Shrinking footprint: a result of design influenced by life cycle assessment. *Journal of Industrial Ecology*, 18(5), 663-669.

70   Hajkowicz, S., Cook, H., & Littleboy, A. (2012). *Our Future Our World: Global Megatrends That Will Change the Way We Live*. Australia: CSIRO.

And why we want to do that is, frankly, a risk reduction strategy around our materials. The cost of oil can be volatile, as we're seeing in the headlines, and that has a direct impact on our cost and consequently our pricing.[71]

Consumer demand for more sustainable products and services will be another source of competitive advantage for manufacturers and retailers. Many consumers expect companies to be socially responsible, and this is becoming more important to brand reputation. "Guilt-free consumption" was identified as one of the seven key consumer trends in 2014.[72] Consumers are increasingly aware of the damage done by their consumption to the planet, society or themselves, and this creates opportunities for new products and services.

A proactive approach to product stewardship looks for business opportunities that respond to increasing resource scarcity, consumer demand for more sustainable products, and other social and environmental trends. It builds new capabilities in business to identify and reduce environmental and social impacts of products through product innovation, multistakeholder collaborations and new business models.

1.4 Purpose and outline of the book

This book focuses on the actions that practitioners can take to minimize the life-cycle impacts of their products while achieving positive outcomes for their business. It builds on different perspectives on product stewardship—as a social responsibility, a response to stakeholder expectations and a source of competitive advantage—to provide a structured and systematic framework for action by organizations in the product supply chain.

The framework that underpins the remainder of the book has three components to guide the development of an effective product sustainability programme (Fig. 1.6). It must be based on a good understanding of the material issues for each organization (the "drivers" for product stewardship). Building on this information, alternative responses ("strategies") can then be identified and evaluated by analysing the potential outcomes ("benefits")

71   Thomas, J. (2012, February 24). Exclusive: Nestle Waters on EPR. *Resource Recycling*. Retrieved from http://resource-recycling.com/print/2531
72   Trendwatching.com (2013, November). *Guilt-free Consumption*. Trend Briefing 2013. Retrieved from http://trendwatching.com/trends/guiltfreeconsumption/

Drivers
- Social legitimacy, linked to the expectations of stakeholders
- Evidence of product impacts
- Business priorities and targets

Strategies
- Corporate policy, goals & targets
- Strategies for design, procurement, recovery

Benefits
- Sustainability outcomes
- The business benefits for individual firms (cost savings, market access, reputation etc.)

FIGURE 1.6   Framework for product stewardship

for both the organization and external stakeholders. This approach will help to build internal support for the programme and maximize its effectiveness.

While government regulations are very important, the emphasis here is on actions that are either voluntary or go "beyond compliance". These are more useful as a guide to product stewardship because they tend to achieve multiple business benefits as well as positive environmental and social outcomes. Examples of voluntary stewardship also highlight the potential for alternative, "light touch" policy options for governments, particularly where there is a high degree of industry commitment. From a business perspective, an industry-led approach tends to be less costly and more flexible than a government-led approach as long as the costs associated with free-riders can be managed.

Chapter 2 focuses on the first two elements of the framework. It explores the many ways that stakeholders including governments, consumers and supply chain partners are driving product stewardship within firms. It describes the types of policies, goals and targets that companies have adopted to guide their product-related sustainability programmes, and three of the most important strategies being implemented to achieve these: design for sustainability, supply chain management (procurement) and product recovery.

This is followed by three case study chapters that focus on product stewardship for packaging (Chapter 3), electrical and electronic equipment (Chapter 4) and batteries (Chapter 5). These draw on real-world case studies to identify some of the practical issues and strategies for companies in each sector. Each chapter explores three questions from a business perspective:

- **Why should I care?** The drivers for product stewardship are linked to the expectations of stakeholders and evidence of product impacts.

- **How should I respond?** The strategies that companies pursue to minimize product-related impacts throughout their life-cycle.

- **What's in it for us?** No matter what the original driver was, companies normally find additional benefits along the way.

Examples are used throughout the book to provide real-world examples of the drivers, strategies and benefits of product stewardship, and more detailed case studies are appended to Chapters 2 to 5.

Chapter 6 draws on these examples and case studies to identify some of the lessons learned by organizations involved in successful design for environment or recycling initiatives. These include internal strategies, such as listening and responding to stakeholder concerns, taking a life-cycle approach and aligning product sustainability initiatives with business priorities, and external strategies, such as pilot projects that allow an organization to "learn by doing".

Finally, Chapter 7 draws on interviews with industry practitioners and policy-makers to explore some of the policy and market trends likely to influence the future of product stewardship.

It is hoped that the information and case studies provided here will both encourage and guide the actions of those with an interest in making their products more sustainable. The book's primary objective is to reinforce the importance of a structured, evidence-based approach that connects an organization's product sustainability strategy to its core activities, expertise and influence. In doing so it aims to reframe product stewardship as an essential business strategy rather than an environmental programme.

Practitioners who are new to the topic can use this book to understand why product stewardship is important to their business and how to integrate it into policy and practice. Others will benefit from the more specific, product-related information, strategies and case studies for packaging, e-waste and batteries. While much of the material is written for a business audience, it will also be of value to government policy-makers, academics and activists in non-government organizations who are working with business to promote more sustainable management of products and packaging.

2
A strategic approach to product stewardship

2.1 Introduction

Product stewardship is no longer a discretionary activity confined to businesses that want to "do the right thing". There is growing government and consumer interest in the social and environmental impacts of products, from their supply chain through to end of life. This represents both a risk and an opportunity for businesses that make, sell or recover products.

Most product stewardship programmes are a reaction to regulations or pressure from external groups. Responsiveness to stakeholder expectations on issues such as worker safety, hazardous substances and recycling can be beneficial, for example by improving a company's reputation. A more proactive and strategic approach, however, is to look for opportunities that create "shared value": that simultaneously achieve social and environmental objectives while building long-term competitiveness.[1]

The approach outlined in this chapter, and used as a framework for analysis throughout the book, is based on the idea of shared value. It draws on successful examples of "product stewardship in action" to show how companies that take a strategic, systematic approach can reduce the life-cycle impacts of their products while building business value, for example by reducing costs, improving access to raw materials or building customer loyalty.

---

[1] Porter, M., & Kramer, M. (2011). The big idea: Creating shared value. *Harvard Business Review*. Retrieved from https://hbr.org/2011/01/the-big-idea-creating-shared-value

FIGURE 2.1   Framework for product stewardship

This framework has three elements (Fig. 2.1):

- The **drivers** for product stewardship. These include the expectations of stakeholders, evidence of product impacts, and the business case for individual organizations.

- The **strategies** that businesses pursue to manage the environmental and social impacts of their products, including design, procurement and recovery at end of life. These are guided by corporate policies, goals and targets for product sustainability.

- The **benefits** of product stewardship for the organization, for stakeholders and for the natural environment. Understanding and promoting these outcomes can help to build internal and external support for product stewardship.

This chapter presents a strategic approach to product stewardship from a corporate perspective. It draws on the experience of leading companies and stewardship organizations. These include detailed case studies appended to this and later chapters. The two very different examples in this chapter highlight some of the drivers, strategies and benefits of product stewardship for an individual company and a collective industry programme:

- New Zealand paint manufacturer Resene (Case study 2.6.1) introduced a recycling programme for leftover paint and packaging to reduce the environmental impacts of its products. Funded by the company, a levy on consumers and start-up contributions from local councils, the successful PaintWise programme has added to Resene's reputation as an environmentally responsible manufacturer and helped it to win high profile awards.

- The Australian polyvinyl chloride (PVC) industry's Product Stewardship Program (Case study 2.6.2) was developed in response to external pressure from Greenpeace and purchasing guidelines that discriminated against PVC on environmental grounds. The pro-gramme, funded by companies at every stage of the value chain, has addressed many of the original stakeholder concerns and changed perceptions of PVC in key markets.

2.2 Drivers for product stewardship

While product stewardship is often driven by stakeholder perceptions or expectations about a particular issue in the product life-cycle, a more strategic approach also considers the available scientific evidence and how stakeholder concerns interact with business priorities. As Porter and Kramer argue, stakeholder views are important, but:

> … these groups can never understand a corporation's capabilities, competitive positioning, or the trade-offs it must make. Nor does the vehemence of a stakeholder group necessarily signify the importance of an issue—either to the company or to the world.[2]

In practice most companies are driven to take action by a combination of factors, including stakeholder expectations, evidence of product impacts, and business goals and priorities. A systematic approach to product stew-ardship involves careful evaluation of all three drivers to guide decision-making within firms (Fig. 2.2).

One reason why this is important is that it helps to overcome individual bias or group decisions based on uninformed assumptions and the influ-ence of particular stakeholders (internal or external). To maximize the busi-ness benefits and to achieve "shared value", practitioners need to ensure that their product sustainability strategies are based on evidence and care-ful analysis rather than perception or personal values.

The following section considers each of the three drivers for product stewardship individually: stakeholders, product research and business priorities.

---

2   Porter, M., & Kramer, M. (2006, December). Strategy and society: the link between competitive advantage and corporate social responsibility. *Harvard Business Review*, 1-16 (p. 8).

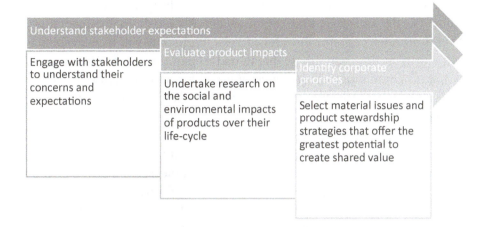

Understand stakeholder expectations

Engage with stakeholders to understand their concerns and expectations

Evaluate product impacts

Undertake research on the social and environmental impacts of products over their life-cycle

Identify corporate priorities

Select material issues and product stewardship strategies that offer the greatest potential to create shared value

FIGURE 2.2   Three steps towards a product stewardship strategy

2.2.1 Stakeholder engagement

Stakeholders are defined by the Global Reporting Initiative as:

> … entities or individuals that can reasonably be expected to be significantly affected by the organisation's activities, products and services; and whose actions can reasonably be expected to affect the ability of the organisation to successfully implement its strategies and achieve its objectives.[3]

Ongoing stakeholder engagement through surveys, workshops or informal dialogue is essential to the success of many of the product stewardship initiatives described in this book. Most of the initiatives were developed in response to pressure from environment groups or regulators. In the 1990s Greenpeace International campaigned to stop companies using chlorine-containing products, including PVC plastic. In Australia, following similar developments in Europe, resin suppliers and converters responded by developing a comprehensive environmental programme in consultation with stakeholders. This included a voluntary phase-out of heavy metal additives and support for collection and recycling of PVC products (Case study 2.6.2).

In contrast, the Call2Recycle battery recycling programme (Case study 5.7.2) was set up by battery manufacturers in the US to avoid product bans and recycling laws. In 1991 the Environment Protection Agency announced

---

3   GRI (2013). *G4 Sustainability Reporting Guidelines: Implementation Manual.* Amsterdam, The Netherlands: Global Reporting Initiative, p. 9.

that rechargeable nickel cadmium batteries would be classified as a haz-ardous waste and delegated responsibility to the states for regulation. After a number of states introduced laws mandating producer responsi-bility for recycling, and others threatened to ban the sale of mercury and cadmium-containing products, including rechargeable batteries, the indus-try established a voluntary national recycling scheme to avoid any further regulation.

Over time these organizations, and many others like them, have shifted from a reactive and defensive approach to a more proactive engagement strategy. The Vinyl Council of Australia, for example, seeks input to its pro-gramme through an external Technical Steering Group that meets quarterly and a larger stakeholder round table every two to three years. Some of the significant changes that have been made in response to stakeholder feed-back include a commitment to open disclosure of material components and actions to address climate change.

Companies can minimize the risks associated with negative stakeholder perceptions and influence by taking steps to engage with groups that are important to their business. The most appropriate engagement tools will vary depending on the purpose: for example whether stakeholders are being approached to help identify corporate social responsibility priorities; to guide product development and marketing strategies; or to inform prod-uct take-back programmes.

2.2.1.1 Stakeholder mapping

A useful starting point is the development of a "stakeholder map". This can take many different forms, ranging from a simple diagram to a matrix show-ing the potential importance of each stakeholder to the business. Regulators and customers are generally given a high priority because of their poten-tial to negatively impact the business if their concerns are not addressed. Non-compliance with a government directive, for example, could result in a financial penalty or (more importantly) a loss of corporate reputation.

A hypothetical stakeholder mapping exercise for a battery producer is shown in Table 2.1. The outcome of an exercise like this could be a list of product-related impacts categorized as either a high, medium or low priority for the organization. A structured, methodical approach allows a company to prioritize stakeholder interests and influence, and through this process to identify the most effective strategies. An alternative (reactive) approach might respond to pressure from the most vocal or powerful stakeholders.

TABLE 2.1   Example of a hypothetical stakeholder analysis for a battery manufacturer

Stakeholder	Issue of concern	Potential influence on the business	Priority for the business
Environmental regulator	• Poor recycling rate • Toxicity in landfill	• EPR regulations • Restrictions on the use of hazardous substances	High
Environmental groups	• Poor recycling rate • Toxicity in landfill	• Negative campaign in social media • Consumer boycott • Influence on government regulations	Medium
Customers (retailers and consumer electronics manufacturers)	• Sustainability of their supply chain • Reputation and brand value • Added service to consumers	• De-selection based on sustainable procurement criteria	High
Shareholders	• Product-related risks to corporate sustainability	• Shareholder activism, e.g. motions at Annual General Meetings • De-selection based on sustainable investment criteria	High
Consumers	• Lack of convenient, free recycling facilities • Toxicity in landfill	• Boycott products in favour of those with a product stewardship programme	High
Battery recyclers	• Poor collection and recycling rate • Potential business opportunity	• Service provider	Low
Industry associations	• Industry reputation • Avoiding onerous regulations	• Negotiating unsuitable regulations with government	Medium

Risks of this include the potential to miss emerging issues and stakeholders, or cause unintended consequences such as upsetting another stakeholder.

According to Carl Smith, CEO of Call2Recycle, addressing stakeholder expectations is never a simple process, and requires a "delicate balance" between competing interests:

> Stewardship is a complex concept that involves maintaining a delicate balance among stakeholders with different priorities, opposing constraints and diverse definitions of success … No stewardship program can fully satisfy the needs of all stakeholders. A successful product stewardship program cost-effectively balances their interests while minimising risk. The key is balancing the sometimes conflicting and overlapping issues among the groups and recognising that the needs are constantly changing. The greater the common ground, the more influence, credibility and impact the recycling organisation has on its stakeholders.[4]

In practice a firm's stakeholders are never equally important, and their issues and expectations need to be prioritized. Business for Social Responsibility (BSR) has developed a list of five criteria to guide this process:

- **Contribution (value)**. Does the stakeholder have information, counsel or expertise on the issue that can be helpful to the company?

- **Legitimacy**. How legitimate is the stakeholder's claim to engagement?

- **Willingness**. How willing is the stakeholder to engage?

- **Influence**. How much influence does the stakeholder have, and on whom?

- **Necessity of involvement**. Is this someone who could derail or de-legitimize the process if they are not included?[5]

Canon regularly surveys its stakeholders to identify material issues for its business. The company's corporate philosophy, *Kyosei*, embodies the idea of living and working together for the common good, and this underpins its interactions with stakeholders (Fig. 2.3).[6]

---

4   Smith, C. (2015, June 18). Industry stewards: the hidden benefactors of recycling. *Environmental Leader*. Retrieved from http://www.environmentalleader. com/2015/06/18/industry-stewards-the-hidden-benefactors-of-recycling/
5   BSR (2011). *Stakeholder Mapping*, p. 2. Retrieved from http://gsvc.org/ wp-content/uploads/2014/11/Stakeholders-Identification-and-Mapping.pdf
6   See Figure 2.1 in Canon Oceania (2013). *Sustainability Report 2013*. Sydney, Australia: Canon Australia.

FIGURE 2.3 Canon Oceania's stakeholders linked to the corporate philosophy of *Kyosei*

Source: Canon Oceania (2013), pp. 7-8

Canon, like many other leading global brands, places a high priority on stakeholder engagement. It seeks to "understand stakeholder opinion in order to continually improve its CSR activities", and one of the ways it does this is through an annual global survey.[7] The target groups for this include consumers, suppliers, investors and analysts, non-government organizations, academics, and national and local governments in Japan, the Americas, Europe and Asia.

A global survey is likely to identify some different stakeholder concerns in different countries. This requires a flexible approach that may combine consistent global strategies for design and procurement with localized strategies for product return and recycling. At a regional business level Canon Oceania has established processes to facilitate dialogue with stakeholders, including formal and informal, qualitative and quantitative measures. These include customer surveys, social media, conferences with partners, an employee engagement survey, tenders, media, community events and participation in regulatory consultation processes.[8] Each year the company compiles a list of "material issues" for the business, by:

- Analysing the outcomes of the various stakeholder engagement processes

7   Canon (2015). *Canon Sustainability Report 2015*. Tokyo: Canon Inc, p. 8.
8   Canon Oceania (2013).

- Inviting key people from all of the different parts of the business, including those with direct contact with external stakeholders, to a workshop to identify the most significant issues raised by stakeholders

In 2014 Canon Oceania identified six priority issues, and these were used as the structure for the company's sustainability report. One of these was "*Environment*—preparing for a low carbon, recycling-oriented society".[9] The business has pledged to "reduce the environmental burden at all stages of the product lifecycle", and is actively engaged in initiatives to recover computers, printer cartridges and batteries.[10]

2.2.1.2 Engaging with consumers

A successful product stewardship strategy requires a good understanding of consumer attitudes and behaviour. Consumers can influence the environmental impact of products in several ways:

- Through their purchasing decisions: for example whether or not to buy a "green" or environmentally improved product

- Through the way they use products: for example whether they choose to wash clothes with hot or cold water

- Through their disposal decisions: for example whether to give something away when they no longer want it, recycle it, or put it in a rubbish bin

For these reasons individual companies, stewardship organizations and government environment agencies often undertake market research to inform their environmental programmes.

Numerous surveys have been undertaken on consumer attitudes to the environment, their purchasing preferences and their willingness to buy more sustainable products. These often identify a gap between consumers' expressed concerns about social and environmental issues and their willingness to reflect these concerns in their purchasing behaviour.[11]

BBMG, GlobeScan and SustainAbility surveyed over 6,000 consumers in six international markets (Brazil, China, Germany, India, United Kingdom

9   Canon Oceania (2014). *Sustainability Report 2014*. Sydney, Australia: Canon Australia, p. 7.
10   *Ibid.*, p. 33.
11   Belz, F.M., &, Peattie, K. (2009). *Sustainability Marketing: A Global Perspective*. Chichester, UK: John Wiley & Sons.

and United States) and identified strong demand for more sustainable products.[12] Almost two-thirds of respondents (65%) said that they "feel a sense of responsibility to purchase products that are good for the environment and for society".[13] When asked about which social and environmental issues were most important for companies to address as part of their products, services or operations, there was universal agreement in all markets that "safe drinking water" was the most important issue overall, followed by several other social issues such as healthcare and jobs. Waste reduction was supported by 85% of respondents, which made it the highest ranking environmental issue on the list.[14]

In the same survey, a majority of consumers (75%) agreed that they would "purchase more products that are environmentally and socially responsible" if they "performed as well as, or better than, products they usually buy". This clearly presents a marketing opportunity for companies with the ability to change their product mix or redesign products to reduce their environmental or social impacts.

Individual companies often undertake their own market research to guide product design and marketing strategies. Through customer surveys Nutrimetics identified that its customers were concerned about excess packaging and the recyclability of its packaging. This helped managers justify the investment in new packaging approaches.[15] Nutrimetics sells skincare, makeup and body care products through an extensive network of independent "consultants". In 2012 the company surveyed its customers on waste and recycling, and found that:

- 30% disposed of their primary packaging (e.g. jars and tubes) with general rubbish

- 9% disposed of their cartons with general rubbish

- 31% were dissatisfied with the existing recycling information provided by Nutrimetics

- 36% thought Nutrimetics products contained excessive packaging

12 BBMG, GlobeScan, & SustainAbility (2012). *Re: Thinking Consumption: Consumers and the Future of Sustainability*. Retrieved from http://www.globescan. com/component/edocman/?view=document&id=46&Itemid=591

13 *Ibid.*, p. 7.

14 *Ibid.*, p. 15.

15 Lewis, H., & Crittenden, P. (2014). *The Business Case for Packaging Sustainability: Nutrimetics*. Sydney: Australian Packaging Covenant.

This research informed the design brief for Nutrimetics' new skincare packaging, which specified greater efficiency as well as design for recycling. Significant environmental benefits were achieved. For example, the 30 ml jar uses 46% less material than the previous jar and is more recyclable. The previous jar could not be recycled because it had two material components (acrylic and polypropylene (PP)) that could not be separated. The new design consists of two recyclable materials—polyethylene terephthalate (PET) and PP—that can be separated by the consumer. It also achieved significant business benefits. Packaging costs were reduced because all of the components are smaller and use less material, and the simpler design saved money on tooling.[16]

Market research on consumer behaviour during use and at the end of a product's life is critical for recycling programmes. The Australian Mobile Telecommunications Association (AMTA), for example, has undertaken numerous market surveys over a ten-year period to inform its mobile phone recycling programme (Case study 4.7.4). The first survey, in 2004, revealed that the programme had a poor public profile, with only 46% of consumers being aware that they could recycle their phone. This led to a rebranding and re-launch of the programme under its new name, MobileMuster. Since that time AMTA's surveys have continued to investigate consumer use, storage and disposal behaviours to refine their collection and marketing strategies. A review of ten years of consumer research by AMTA highlighted continuing challenges, including "hoarding" of unwanted phones by consumers instead of recycling.[17]

Battery stewardship organization Call2Recycle (Case study 5.7.1) also uses market research to guide its strategic planning and communication with stakeholders. Research commissioned by Call2Recycle in 2012 investigated a range of issues including awareness of the programme, motivations for recycling, behaviour when recycling at retail and barriers to recycling among non-recyclers.[18] This generated a number of insights: for example the research found that:

- The availability of a recycling service for batteries and phones in retail stores makes most consumers feel more positive about the retailer (49–80% of consumers, depending on the store)

16   *Ibid.*
17   AMTA (2015). *Australia's Mobile Decade: 10 Years of Consumer Insights into Mobile Use and Recycling.* Sydney: Australian Mobile Telecommunications Association.
18   Ipsos Marketing (2012). Understanding consumer recycling behaviour. *Report to Call2Recycle* (unpublished). Atlanta, GA: Ipsos Marketing.

- While not a key driver of store traffic, recycling does increase the frequency of store visits
- Recyclers typically shop or browse the store when dropping off batteries or phones

This type of feedback is important because it reinforces the business case for retailers that provide a recycling collection point. The Call2Recycle survey also asked "non-recyclers" what would motivate them to recycle their unwanted phones or batteries, and they cited incentives (31%), information (20%), convenience (19%) and advertising (15%).[19]

2.2.2 Understanding product impacts

Additional research is often required to test stakeholder perceptions or to gather further information on product impacts. The PVC industry in Australia, for example (Case study 2.6.2), commissioned a literature review from Australia's pre-eminent scientific organization, the Commonwealth Scientific and Industrial Research Organization (CSIRO), to investigate stakeholder claims that PVC was more hazardous than other building materials and should be avoided in construction of infrastructure for the 2000 Olympic Games in Sydney.

CSIRO's report concluded that PVC building products were generally sound from an environmental perspective but there were issues that could be addressed to improve their performance.[20] The findings of this study and a later update have helped to shape the industry's product stewardship programme.[21] The programme's environmental achievements include a reduction in vinyl chloride monomer (VCM) emissions from manufacturing, elimination of cadmium and hexavalent chromium additives, and an improved recycling rate for PVC containers.

2.2.2.1 Life-cycle mapping

A literature review is useful to investigate specific issues raised by stakeholders. A visual "life-cycle mapping" exercise can also provide insights into

---

19   *Ibid.*
20   Smith, R. (1998). *The Environmental Aspects of the Use of PVC in Building Products.* Report by CSIRO Molecular Science for the Plastics and Chemicals Industries Association. Clayton, Australia.
21   Coghlan, P. (2001). *A Discussion of Some of the Scientific Issues Concerning the Use of PVC.* Report by CSIRO Molecular Science and Australian National University, a report to the Vinyl Council of Australia. Canberra, Australia.

the product life-cycle and some of the sustainability benefits and impacts associated with each stage. This can be as simple as a hand-drawn flow chart, compiled by a cross-functional and knowledgeable group of people within the company, showing the different stages in the product life-cycle and some of the inputs and outputs at each stage. An exercise like this has a number of advantages compared with a literature review:

- It is specific to a particular company, product and supply chain

- A visual map, particularly when undertaken as a group exercise, can identify materials, components or activities that may have been overlooked

A more detailed explanation and step-by-step guide to developing a life-cycle map is found in Verghese and Lockrey.[22]

2.2.2.2 Life-cycle assessment

Life-cycle assessment (LCA) is an internationally recognized method for evaluating the environmental impacts of a product over its total life-cycle. LCA is useful when an organization needs to evaluate the environmental impacts of a product or system with a high degree of accuracy, for example to support product claims.[23] Nestlé, for example, commissioned an LCA to calculate the environmental benefits of a new laminated pouch for coffee, and the results were promoted on the label. The LCA found that the pouch used 73% less non-renewable energy, 66% less water and emitted 75% less greenhouse gas emissions over its entire life-cycle than a glass jar, challenging a common perception that glass is superior to plastics from an environmental perspective.[24]

An LCA can also make an important contribution to understanding and managing environmental problems, for example by revealing "blind spots"

22   Verghese, K., & Lockrey, S. (2012). Selecting and applying tools. In K. Verghese, H. Lewis, & L. Fitzpatrick (Eds.), *Packaging for Sustainability* (pp. 251-283). London: Springer.

23   Verghese, K., & Carre, A. (2012). Applying life cycle assessment. In K. Verghese, H. Lewis, & L. Fitzpatrick (Eds.), *Packaging for Sustainability* (pp. 171-210). London: Springer.

24   RMIT (2015). *Life Cycle Assessment of Nestle NESCAFE Gold Packaging*. Retrieved from http://www.rmit.edu.au/about/our-education/academic-schools/architecture-and-design/research/research-centres-and-groups/centre-for-design-and-society/research-areas/sustainable-products-and-packaging/projects/life-cycle-assessment-of-nestl-nescaf-gold-coffe

in the knowledge base.[25] While batteries are often perceived as a hazardous waste issue, for example, there are also significant issues in raw materials extraction and processing.[26] One of the benefits of an LCA is that it generally highlights a range of different impacts that may require trade-offs in the selection of appropriate strategies.

The cost of an LCA can be a valuable and worthwhile investment if it helps to generate new business opportunities. Interface Carpets, for example (Box 2.1) used an LCA to identify and promote design improvements, such as the use of lower yarn weights, which gave the company a competitive advantage. The PVC industry in Australia has used LCA data to demonstrate the environmental attributes of the material and to avoid de-selection in the building industry (Case study 2.6.2).

There are a number of LCA software tools which are available to assist practitioners.[27] These include publicly available inventory data and also allow the user to add their own product-specific data to improve its accuracy and therefore value.

Box 2.1 Strategic use of LCA by Interface to build market share

Interface Inc. manufactures carpet tiles and broadloom carpet, primarily for the commercial market. The company's headquarters are in Atlanta, Georgia in the United States. Connie Hensler's case study, summarized here, explains how product design at Interface has been influenced by LCA results.[28]

Drivers

Interface founder Ray Anderson experienced an "environmental epiphany" in 1994, inspired by Paul Hawken's book, *The Ecology of Commerce*. Anderson challenged his company to become a leader in industrial ecology. The company has pursued multiple strategies to achieve its sustainability goals, including changes in design and recovery of products at end of life.

---

25 Grant, T., & MacDonald, F. (2009). Life cycle assessment as decision support: a systemic critique. In R. Horne, T. Grant, & K. Verghese (Eds.), *Life Cycle Assessment: Principles, Practice and Prospects* (pp. 33-41). Melbourne: CSIRO Publishing.

26 Olivetti, E., Gregory, J., & Kirchain, R. (2011). *Life Cycle Impacts of Alkaline Batteries with a Focus on End-of-life*. Report by Massachusetts Institute of Technology for the National Electrical Manufacturers Association. Retrieved from http://www.epbaeurope.net/documents/NEMA_alkalinelca2011.pdf

27 Verghese & Lockrey (2012).

28 Hensler, C.D. (2014). Shrinking footprint: a result of design influenced by life cycle assessment. *Journal of Industrial Ecology*, 18(5), 663-669.

Strategies

LCA was used to identify the key areas of environmental impact in carpet manufacturing, beginning in earnest in 2000. LCA results showed that yarn production was a major contributor to environmental impact, providing the impetus for designs with lower yarn weights. Average yarn weights have fallen from over 1,000 g/m^3 to approximately 700 g/m^3, resulting in significantly lower carbon emissions (measured as global warming potential or GWP).

Interface has worked closely with suppliers to change some of its material inputs. For example the company put pressure on fibre producers to incorporate recycled content into carpet yarns. This was first done with Universal Fiber Systems (UFS) for nylon yarn. Interface partnered with UFS by separating the yarn from carpet returned through its ReEntry® programme (the backing is also recycled to make new carpet tiles). As the relationship with UFS was initially exclusive it enabled Interface to be the first to market with the "highly preferable" post-consumer yarn.

Interface played an active role in the development of LEED (Leadership in Energy and Environmental Design) certification, created by the US Green Building Council in 2000. In 2008 it was the first company in the US building sector to publish self-declared environmental product declarations (EPDs), which included LCA results.

Benefits

The initial driver for change was Ray Anderson's goal of becoming a "zero waste manufacturer", but the environmental initiatives resulted in multiple business benefits.

Reductions in environmental impact almost always went hand in hand with cost savings. For example, the reduction in yarn weights led to significant cost savings. This was not specific to Interface but it did make carpet tiles more competitive compared with broadloom carpets.

The company's market share also increased as a direct result of its environmental improvements. The commercial carpet industry mainly supplies the architectural and design community, which is sensitive to environmental issues and welcomed Interface's initiatives to reduce its environmental impacts. Interface was able to capitalize on its status as an early mover. For example, Hensler notes that "... Interface's leadership in transparency was rewarded by market advantage when LEED introduced credits for products with EPDs. Specifiers preferentially purchase products that provide LEED credits ...".[29]

Source: Based on Hensler[30]

2.2.3 Identifying priority issues and strategies

Stakeholder engagement and product research can both help to identify social issues that could be considered "material" to a business. These have been defined as issues that:

29   *Ibid.*, p. 664.
30   *Ibid.*

- Reflect the organization's significant economic, environmental and social impacts or

- Substantially influence the assessments and decisions of stake-holders[31]

Businesses are not responsible for all of society's problems; nor are they always in the best position to address them (many issues are better addressed by governments or civil society actors). Porter and Kramer advise companies to select social issues that intersect with their particular business interests:

> The essential test that should guide CSR is not whether a cause is worthy but whether it presents an opportunity to create shared value—that is, a meaningful benefit for society that is also valuable to the business.[32]

The principle of shared value underpins Fuji Xerox's approach to CSR. To select its strategic priorities for CSR, Fuji Xerox identified, from a wide range of social issues, those that were considered most important to address "in light of factors such as the nature of our business and our management goals".[33] These were categorized as either "offence" (creating new value) or "defence" (guarding corporate value). The medium-term, high priority CSR themes for Fuji Xerox include "strengthening environmental management". This issue was categorized as one that helps to create new value, for example through carbon dioxide reduction in the value chain or by providing customers with resource and energy-saving products and services.

Porter and Kramer distinguish between three types of issues: generic social issues; those directly related to a company's value chain; and social issues in the external environment that affect competitiveness (Table 2.2).[34] To maximize the overall benefits of a CSR programme, the authors recommend that companies choose CSR strategies that either transform their value chain activities to benefit society and improve competitiveness at the same time, or change aspects of the external environment to improve the "competitive context" in which they operate. External issues that affect productivity include the availability of raw materials and labour, the nature

---

31   GRI (2013), p. 11.
32   Porter & Kramer (2006), p. 10.
33   Fuji Xerox (2014). *Sustainability Report 2014*. Tokyo: Fuji Xerox. Retrieved from https://www.fujixerox.com/eng/company/sr/booklet/2014e.pdf, p. 13.
34   Porter & Kramer (2011).

TABLE 2.2   Prioritizing social issues

Generic social issue	Value chain social impacts	Social dimensions of competitive context
Social issues that are not significantly affected by a company's operations nor materially affect its long-term competitiveness	Social issues that are significantly affected by a company's activities in the ordinary course of business	Social issues in the external environment that significantly affect the underlying drivers of a company's competitiveness in the locations where it operates

Source: Porter and Kramer (2006), p. 9

of regulations and standards, demand from local consumers and access to firms in related fields.[35]

This framework for strategic CSR can also be used to identify material issues and priorities for product stewardship. Changes to products or packaging to reduce material consumption, eliminate toxic components or improve recovery can transform a company's value chain in ways that achieve both societal and business benefits. Walmart, for example, has worked with suppliers to eliminate or reduce packaging components, and in the process achieved a range of benefits for the retailer, its consumers and the natural environment.[36] In the early 1990s deodorant was normally packed in a plastic or steel primary pack, and then in a cardboard box. When Walmart asked its suppliers to remove the box, the change was so successful it became the new industry norm. The cost savings from less packaging and more efficient transport, which Walmart typically shares with consumers, have been significant. When the elimination of boxes from the entire deodorant market is taken into account, the savings in the United States from this one change alone is estimated to be in the hundreds of millions of dollars. In addition, "millions of trees were not cut down, acres of cardboard were not manufactured only to be discarded, one billion deodorant boxes didn't end up in landfills each year";[37] a perfect example of shared value.

Other product stewardship initiatives have focused on changing the external environment, for example by improving the infrastructure for product recycling:

35   Porter & Kramer (2006).
36   Fishman, C. (2006). *The Wal-Mart Effect.* London: Penguin Books.
37   *Ibid.*, p. 2.

- Vinyl Council of Australia (Case study 2.6.2) is working with a wide range of stakeholders to improve systems for recovery of medical and building products

- Call2Recycle (Case study 5.7.1) has established a national recycling programme for mobile phones and batteries, and is also working with state regulators to mandate producer responsibility

- Through their financial contributions to The Closed Loop Fund in the US, manufacturers are helping to fund public and private investments in the infrastructure for packaging recycling

2.3 Product stewardship policy and strategies

To be effective, product stewardship needs to be considered in every aspect of a business; from corporate policy and targets through to the product portfolio, design, procurement and distribution. It has implications for every function within the business (Fig. 2.4).

This section outlines some of the strategies that companies are commonly using to manage the environmental and social aspects of their products. It

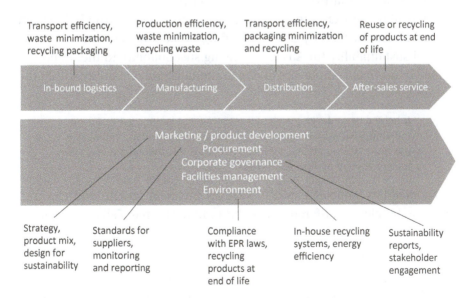

FIGURE 2.4   Product stewardship linked to business function

Policy	Design	Procurement	Recovery
• A policy outlining sustainability values and objectives • Sustainability targets for products or packaging	• Life-cycle assessment to identify opportunities • Design for sustainability embedded in product development processes	• Industry standards for supply chain performance • Guidelines for suppliers • Supply chain auditing and transparency	• Take-back of products at end of life • Funding recycling infrastructure • Influencing regulations and standards

FIGURE 2.5   Examples of product stewardship strategies

focuses on four key areas of activity: corporate policy (leadership), design, procurement and product recovery (Fig. 2.5).

2.3.1 Policy

Many businesses have a CSR or sustainability policy that outlines their corporate values and objectives. These should reflect the knowledge and insights gained through stakeholder engagement and product research.

To be effective, a sustainability policy must be relevant and meaningful to employees and customers. With many of its products manufactured from paper, Kimberley-Clark (K-C) has placed a high priority on sustainable sourcing of its fibre, for example by aiming to reduce its use of wood fibre from natural forests by 50% by 2025. According to Jacquie Fegent-McGeachie, head of sustainability for Australia, linking sustainability to the brand has helped to motivate employees and operationalize sustainability within the business:

> It helped us to develop a shared meaning and language around sustainability within our business. This has been particularly valuable as the term "sustainability" can be sometimes misunderstood and can mean a myriad of different things.[38]

Sustainability policies can also support business growth and competitiveness by clearly differentiating the brand. Thomas Falk, K-C's global

---

38   WME Magazine (2015, February). K-C in Australia: a story worth telling. *WME Magazine*, pp. 14-15 (p. 15).

Chairman and CEO, believes that "great customers want to do business with companies that operate in a transparent, responsible and ethical manner".[39]

2.3.1.1 Product goals and targets

Sustainability or CSR policies provide a broad framework for action, but more specific product goals and targets are needed to guide product stewardship strategies in design, procurement and recovery. Foodstuffs New Zealand for example, has a goal to ensure that all of its own-brand packaging is recyclable (Case study 3.7.1). This has helped to guide the development of environmentally improved packaging, including the launch of a new recyclable plastic meat tray in 2015. Foodstuffs uses around 100 million meat trays a year, and previously these were all manufactured from non-recyclable foamed polystyrene. The new tray is made from recyclable PET, which can be collected through municipal recycling programmes.

The achievement of product-related policies, goals and targets must be supported by procedures to ensure that these are implemented in everyday practices including design and procurement (explored further below).

Within the marketing function, a strategic approach to product stewardship integrates sustainability objectives in the product portfolio, the product development process and the marketing mix. In their book, *Sustainability Marketing*, Belz and Peattie suggest two important questions that need to be answered:

- Which markets should we compete in?

- Within each of our markets, how shall we compete?[40]

They argue that the choice of products will depend on a range of factors, including the perceived attractiveness of the market and the potential strength of the company's competitive position within it. The process of strategic portfolio planning involves decisions about which products the company should withdraw from as well as those it will invest in, and sustainability considerations may influence these decisions.[41] BASF, for example, is evaluating the sustainability of its entire product portfolio to identify opportunities for improvements (Box 2.2).

---

39   Kimberly-Clark (2013). *Leading the World in Essentials for a Better World.* Retrieved from http://www.sustainabilityreport2013.kimberly-clark.com/files/K-C_2013_Sustainability_Report.pdf

40   Belz & Peattie (2009).

41   *Ibid.*

Marketing practitioners need to consider when and how sustainability can be a source of competitive advantage. This can be generated in a number of ways, including:

- By using superior environmental or social performance to differentiate a business and its products from competitors

- By using environmental strategies to reduce costs and prices

- By identifying, occupying and defending a particular market niche.[42]

Box 2.2 Evaluating the product portfolio at BASF

Chemical manufacturer BASF is repositioning its brand and product portfolio to reflect its commitment to sustainability and CSR. This commitment is clearly stated in a mission statement on the home page of its website:

At BASF, we create chemistry—and have been doing so for 150 years. As the world's leading chemical company, we combine economic success with environmental protection and social responsibility. Through science and innovation we enable our customers in nearly every industry to meet the current and future needs of society.[43]

Consistent with this philosophy, BASF has developed a system to systematically review and evaluate the sustainability aspects of products in the company's portfolio, called the "Sustainable Solution Steering" method. This is used to show how a product contributes to cost effectiveness, resource conservation and health and safety. By 2014 BASF had already analysed more than 80% of its portfolio of around 50,000 product applications. Products are sorted into four categories:

1. **Accelerators** make a substantial contribution to sustainability in the value chain

2. **Performers** are products that meet the standard market requirements for sustainability

3. For **Transitioners**, specific sustainability issues have been identified and action plans developed

4. **Challenged** products are those for which there is a significant sustainability concern. BASF is developing action plans for these products to find improved solutions

The Sustainable Solution Steering method aims to increase the number of "Accelerators" in the portfolio to further improve the sustainability profile of BASF and its customers. This means that the product portfolio is under constant review.

42   *Ibid.*

43   BASF Corporation (2014). *Welcome to BASF.* Retrieved from https://www.basf.com

BASF sees this approach as a significant business opportunity driven by the expectations of customers. The Chairman of the Board, Dr Kurt Bock, stated that:

It is becoming increasingly important to our customers to be able to combine economic, environmental and societal demands. We see this development as a business opportunity for BASF, and intend to seize it in a targeted manner. This approach forms an integral part of our corporate purpose: we create chemistry for a sustainable future.

Source: BASF Corporation[44]

2.3.2 Design

While environmental impacts occur at every stage of a product's life-cycle, most of these impacts are "locked-in" at the design stage.[45] The specification of materials, for example, will determine where resource impacts occur, whether toxic substances will be released during manufacture, and whether or not the product is recyclable. Impacts such as energy and water consumption during use, or recycling rates at end of life, are also influenced by consumer behaviour, and may require alternative strategies (Fig. 2.6).

"Design for sustainability" means thinking about the environmental and social impacts of a product during the design process. Implementing design for sustainability requires new skills and capabilities, including life-cycle thinking. A simple life-cycle mapping exercise, common sense and a good understanding of the supply chain will almost always identify opportunities for improvement. Many larger companies, such as Interface (Box 2.1), also use LCA to inform product development.

To maximize its effectiveness, design for sustainability must be integrated in product development procedures and undertaken as early as possible. Nestlé has a detailed policy on environmental sustainability, which outlines its corporate values and how its environmental goals will be integrated in every aspect of the business, including product development:

In order to have sustainability being more and more built into our products, our *Sustainability by Design Programme* systematically

44   BASF Corporation (2014). *BASF's Product Portfolio Evaluated for Sustainability*. Retrieved from https://www.basf.com/en/company/news-and-media/news-releases/2014/09/p-14-322.html

45   Lewis, H., Gertsakis, J., Grant, T., Morelli, N. & Sweatman, A. (2001). *Design + Environment: A Global Guide to Designing Greener Goods*. Sheffield, UK: Greenleaf Publishing.

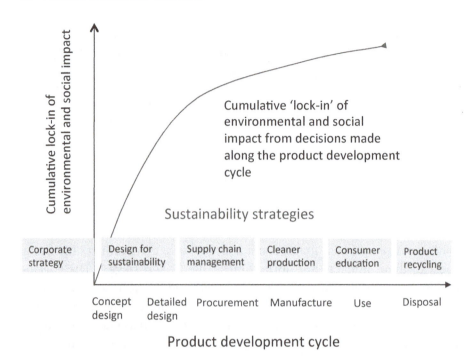

FIGURE 2.6   Environmental "lock-in" over a product's development cycle

Source: Adapted from Lewis *et al.* (2001), p. 14

assesses and optimizes environmental performance across the entire value chain at the earliest stage in the development of new and reno-vated products.[46]

A commitment to product stewardship in the design process can gener-ate a range of business benefits. Resene (Case study 2.6.1) reformulated its products to meet the "Environmental Choice" eco-labelling standard for decorative paints, which restricts the use of pigments, solvents, additives and volatile organic compounds that are environmentally damaging or haz-ardous to human health.[47] Initiatives such as this have helped to build a pos-itive reputation for the company with commercial markets and specifiers.

46   Nestlé (2013). *The Nestlé Policy on Environmental Sustainability.* Retrieved from http://www.nestle.com/asset-library/documents/library/documents/environ mental_sustainability/nestl%c3%a9%20policy%20on%20environmental%20 sustainability.pdf

47   The New Zealand Ecolabelling Trust (2015). *Licence Criteria for Paints EC-07-13.* Auckland, NZ. Retrieved from http://www.environmentalchoice.org.nz/ assets/Specifications/ec-07-15-paints-specification.pdf

Many other examples are provided in later chapters. Mobile phone manufacturers, for example, have shifted away from nickel cadmium and lead batteries to less hazardous chemistries such as lithium-ion. This has saved materials in manufacture, made them more energy efficient, and eliminated the pollution associated with toxic components such as cadmium and lead (Case study 4.7.4).

2.3.3 Procurement

Companies are increasingly being held accountable for the social and environmental impacts of products and materials in their supply chain. Many of these impacts are outside the direct control of a product manufacturer or brand owner, but there are a number of ways that companies can influence or control the actions of suppliers. These include:

- The development of voluntary or mandatory industry standards in collaboration with industry peers

- Specifying minimum standards in procurement guidelines and contracts

- Collaborating with suppliers to develop more sustainable materials or products

2.3.3.1 Industry-wide guidelines and standards

Media coverage of a factory fire in Bangladesh in 2013 revealed that many well-known clothing brands were being manufactured in unsafe conditions. As a direct result of the fire, Walt Disney Company announced that it would no longer allow the manufacture of its branded merchandise in Bangladesh.[48] However, labour groups suggested that Western companies should "stay and fix the problem" rather than leave. The outcome was the development of the legally enforceable "Accord on Fire and Building Safety in Bangladesh", which has been signed by over 100 international brands and retailers; local and global labour unions; and non-government organizations.[49]

48   Greenhouse, S. (2013, May 1). Some retailers rethink role in Bangladesh. *New York Times*. Retrieved from http://www.nytimes.com/2013/05/02/business/some -retailers-rethink-their-role-in-bangladesh.html?pagewanted=all&module= Search&mabReward=relbias%3As

49   Clean Clothes Campaign (n.d.). *Frequently Asked Questions (FAQs) about the Bangladesh Safety Accord*. Retrieved from http://www.cleanclothes.org/issues/ faq-safety-accord/#1---what-is-the-accord-on-fire-and-building-safety-in -bangladesh-

Other sustainability issues are being addressed in response to actions by government. The Conflict-Free Sourcing Initiative was developed by consumer electronics manufacturers after President Obama signed the Dodd-Frank Consumer Act into law.[50] The resources available through the initiative help companies to comply with a requirement to verify and report on their use of "conflict minerals" that may be contributing to conflict or human rights abuses.

2.3.3.2 Procurement policies and processes

Many companies are taking action to integrate sustainability goals and standards in their procurement processes. Nike, for example, exerts control over its packaging supply chain by requiring that suppliers comply with its "Packaging restricted substances list and packaging design requirements".[51] Many of Nike's requirements, including bans on PVC and foamed plastics, go beyond legal compliance.

In the electronics sector most leading brands also have documented policies and procedures to ensure that suppliers comply with minimum sustainability standards. Dell has supplier standards for carbon, water, waste, worker health and safety, and human rights and dignity.[52] The company audits supplier performance and works with them to share best practices.

2.3.3.3 Collaboration with suppliers

Collaboration with suppliers is essential to the achievement of many product stewardship objectives, particularly those for raw materials and components. The PVC Product Stewardship Program (Case study 2.6.2) involves manufacturers of PVC products as well as their resin suppliers. This is essential given that some of the most important impacts for stakeholders occur early in the material life-cycle, including emissions generated during the resin production process.

---

50   Conflict Free Sourcing Initiative (2013). *Reasonable Practices to Identify Sources of Conflict Minerals: Practical Guidance for Downstream Companies.* Electronic Industry Citizenship Coalition and the Global e-Sustainability Initiative. Retrieved from http://www.conflictfreesourcing.org/media/docs/news/CFSI_DD_ReasonablePracticesforDownstreamCompanies_Aug2013.pdf

51   Nike Inc. (2015). *Packaging Restricted Substances List and Packaging Design Requirements: Update Log.* Retrieved from www.nikeincchemistry.com/restricted-substance-list/prsl-pdr-3.0-feb-2015.pdf

52   Dell (2012). *Dell 2020 Legacy of Good Plan.* Retrieved from http://i.dell.com/sites/doccontent/corporate/corp-comm/en/Documents/2020-plan.pdf

2.3.4 Recovery

One of the most important goals of product stewardship is the recovery of used products at end of life for reuse or recycling. To achieve this goal companies are implementing a range of strategies including take-back, support for recycling infrastructure, and the development of industry-wide recycling standards (Fig. 2.7).

Take-back programmes may be implemented by an individual company or undertaken collectively by a group of companies in the same sector to achieve economies of scale. Collective industry programmes can be further categorized as either industry-led, as is the case for most producer responsibility organizations (PROs); provided by a more conventional waste management service provider on behalf of an industry sector; or entrepreneur-led, where a company such as RED Group (Case study 3.7.2) develops a programme and then works with industry stewards to implement it.

2.3.4.1 Take-back

Extended producer responsibility (EPR) laws shift financial and/or physical responsibility for recycling from local government to producers. Most regulations give producers a choice of complying individually or collectively, which means they can either implement their own take-back and recycling programme or join a collective PRO. Many of these are discussed in detail in

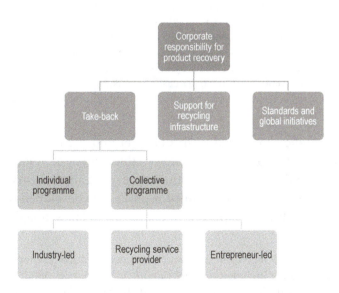

FIGURE 2.7   Producer responsibility strategies for product recovery

the following chapters for packaging, electrical and electronic equipment (EEE) and batteries.

In certain circumstances a company might choose to implement its own individual programme: for example if it has an efficient reverse logistics system; if it thinks it could do it more cost effectively than an established PRO; or if it wants more control. There are indications that some companies are reviewing whether their objectives could be better serviced by fulfilling their EPR obligations individually; not as part of a collective scheme.[53]

Individual producer responsibility (IPR) programmes have also been introduced for many products and in different jurisdictions on a voluntary basis. In New Zealand two companies—paint manufacturer Resene (Case study 2.6.1) and appliance manufacturer Fisher & Paykel (Case study 4.7.2)—have both chosen to implement collection and recycling programmes despite the absence of a regulatory driver. Both organizations collect products other than their own in order to provide a convenient service to their customers. While both programmes were initiated for environmental reasons, additional business benefits have been achieved along the way. Fisher & Paykel's commitment to recycling has provided the company with a marketing advantage over competitors.

Janet Leslie from Canon Oceania supports collective industry schemes, such as the "Cartridges 4 Planet Ark" programme (Case study 4.7.1), because of their cost effectiveness:

> I'm a strong believer in a multi-vendor approach. Before Cartridges 4 Planet Ark [C4PA] was developed we used to have a take back program for our own business products. Consumers would wrap their cartridges and post them back to us. Each one cost us about $12, so it was really expensive. That's why we saw CP4A as a much more efficient multi-vendor approach. It's easier for customers, cheaper for us, and we collect a lot more cartridges, so it's better for the environment too.[54]

The case studies appended to this chapter and the following chapters on packaging, EEE and batteries, represent three different models for takeback. The first and most common is the industry-led and industry managed model, which usually involves a not-for-profit PRO developed by a group of companies with the purpose of meeting compliance obligations. The

53   Bury, D. (2010). Policy forum: should extended producer responsibility programs use eco-fee-included pricing? *Canadian Tax Journal*, 58(4), 927-950.
54   Personal communication (interview) with J. Leslie, Manager Sustainability, Canon Australia, 13 November 2013.

TechCollect programme for televisions and computers in Australia (Case study 4.7.3) is one example.

The second collective model involves a waste management or logistics company providing a compliance service to producers, with the total cost shared between a number of different companies. In Australia, for example, logistics supplier DHL was competing with TechCollect to provide a compliance service for TVs and computers (DHL has since withdrawn from this activity).

The third option for a collective programme is one initiated by an entrepreneurial organization in response to a perceived need rather than a compliance obligation. RED Group, for example, developed a national retail recycling initiative for "soft plastics" (bags and film) with the support of food and consumer product manufacturers (Case study 3.7.2). This was driven by its founder, Liz Kasell, who had become concerned about the amount of soft plastic packaging going to landfill. She convinced retailers and manufacturers to support her vision for an industry-funded recycling programme called REDcycle. Through a similar approach, Close the Loop's founder Steve Morriss convinced equipment manufacturers to support a national programme to recover used printer cartridges (Case study 4.7.1).

2.3.4.2 Other options to support product recovery

Where product take-back is not regulated, some companies have chosen to support recycling of their products in other ways, for example by providing financial support for collection or recycling infrastructure. The Closed Loop Fund in the US, which is supported by consumer goods manufacturers, provides financial support for packaging collection, sorting, reprocessing and manufacture into new products.[55]

Another way in which companies support recovery of their products is through global initiatives. Dell, for example, is working with the United Nations Industrial Development Organization (UNIDO) to facilitate the development of appropriate e-waste regulations in developing countries (see Chapter 4).

---

55 Closed Loop Fund (n.d.). *About the Closed Loop Fund*. Retrieved from http://www.closedloopfund.com/page/about

TABLE 2.3   Product stewardship case studies and their shared value outcomes for producers

Case study	Environmental or social outcomes	Additional business benefits to the company or members	Case study number
Resene PaintWise	Elimination or reduction of hazardous materials, donation of recycled materials	Support for corporate/brand reputation	2.6.1
PVC Product Stewardship Program	Elimination or reduction of hazardous materials in production, increased recycling	Market differentiation/ competitiveness; protection of key markets	2.6.2
Foodstuffs packaging design	Reduced waste to landfill, resource recovery	Support for corporate/brand reputation, reduced material or packaging costs; reduced waste disposal costs, increased customer loyalty	3.7.1
REDcycle soft plastics recycling	Reduced waste to landfill, donation of recycled materials	Support for corporate/ brand reputation; additional service to customers	3.7.2
Glass Packaging Forum	Reduced waste to landfill, resource recovery	Avoided regulation	3.7.3
Close the Loop cartridge recycling	Reduced waste to landfill, resource recovery	Access to business intelligence data, meeting customer procurement specifications, maintaining access to raw materials	4.7.1
Fisher & Paykel appliance recycling	Reduced waste to landfill	Market differentiation and competitiveness	4.7.2
TechCollect TV and computer recycling	Diversion of hazardous materials from landfill, resource recovery, reduced waste	Regulatory compliance, support for corporate reputation	4.7.3
MobileMuster phone and battery recycling	Diversion of hazardous materials from landfill, resource recovery	Meet CSR policies or commitments, avoiding costly or less favourable regulations	4.7.4
Call2Recycle phone and battery recycling	Diversion of hazardous materials from landfill, resource recovery	Regulatory compliance, avoiding costly or less favourable regulations, increased customer loyalty/ service to customers	5.7.1
Battery World	Diversion of hazardous materials from landfill, resource recovery	Increased foot traffic in stores, enhanced brand value	5.7.2

2.4 Product stewardship benefits

The detailed case studies described in the chapter appendices highlight the potential for product stewardship to achieve shared value outcomes, i.e. environmental or social benefits, as well as direct business outcomes. They also reinforce the importance of a strategic approach that positions product stewardship as a business opportunity rather than a corporate social responsibility.

Business benefits that have been achieved by companies involved in these initiatives include lower costs, improved brand reputation, avoided regulation, market intelligence and protection of key markets (Table 2.3).

2.5 Conclusions

Companies that take a strategic and knowledge-based approach to product stewardship seek to understand the perceptions and expectations of their stakeholders; investigate sustainability issues over the total life-cycle of their products; and use this knowledge to identify material issues and priorities for their business. Successful product stewards create "shared value": reduced environmental or social impacts and a range of business benefits.

The following chapters use this framework as a starting point to explore stakeholder expectations and product impacts in three product categories: packaging (Chapter 3), electrical and electronic equipment (Chapter 4) and batteries (Chapter 5). Real-world examples and case studies are used to highlight some of the strategies being pursued by industry leaders and the potential benefits of a strategic approach.

2.6 Case studies

Case study 2.6.1   Resene PaintWise

> Our vision is to be respected as an ethical and sustainable company
> and acknowledged as the leading provider of innovative paint and col-
> our technology (Resene Paints Ltd).[56]

2.6.1.1 Summary

Resene is a privately owned paint manufacturer based in Wellington, New
Zealand. In 2004 the company launched a paint and paint container recycling programme called "Resene PaintWise", which collects any brand of
paint through company-owned stores and municipal depots. The programme is jointly funded by Resene and a 15 cent a litre levy on consumers,
with additional start-up support from municipal partners. The voluntary
initiative was accredited by the Ministry for the Environment in 2011.

By 2014 the environmental benefits had included the recovery of over
600,000 kg of packaging and almost 700,000 litres of paint. While there are no
direct commercial benefits to Resene, the stewardship programme reinforces
its reputation in New Zealand as an environmentally responsible brand.

2.6.1.2 Drivers for product stewardship

Resene has always tried to "do the right thing" from an environmental perspective. The company's vision is to become an "ethical and sustainable
company", and its Environmental Statement notes that "environmental
responsibility is embedded as a key principle for our organization".[57]

Marketing Manager, Karen Warman, notes that in the 1950s Resene was
the first company in Australasia to sell water-based paints, and in the mid-
1990s reformulated its products to meet the "Environmental Choice" environmental labelling standard:

> If the product works just as well but with lower impact, why wouldn't we
> do it? A product that lasts longer and causes least harm is the best option
> … It was about doing the right thing. New Zealand is a green country,
> and we wanted to produce products that our families could use.[58]

56   Resene Paints Ltd (n.d.). *Development of Resene Paintwise*. Retrieved from
     http://www.resene.co.nz/comn/envissue/paintwise_development.htm
57   Resene Paints Ltd (2007). *Environmental Statement*. Wellington, NZ. Retrieved
     from http://www.resene.co.nz/pdf/environmental-policy.pdf
58   Personal communication (interview) with K. Warman, Marketing Manager,
     Resene, 21 November, 2014.

Photo 2.1   Paint collected by Resene PaintWise

Photo: Resene

According to Warman, the logical next step was to look at product waste:

> So then we had greener products, and we thought "what else can we
> do?" One of the things we looked at was what could be done with paint
> at end of life …

The company's website promotes the Resene PaintWise programme as "an extension of Resene's environmentally responsible culture ensuring that we are minimizing the impact on the environment in everything from product formulation and production to responsible recovery and disposal".[59]

In addition to recycling waste, Resene takes a responsible attitude to the way it sells paint in the first place. For example, the company focuses on getting customers to buy the right amount for their project of the right paint, rather than "upsize" deals such as 25 litres for the price of 20 litres, as this might encourage people to buy far more than they need. Most promotions are a straight percentage off the normal selling price.

59   Resene Paints Ltd. (n.d.).

2.6.1.3 Stewardship strategies

Resene's involvement in recycling began with paint cans in 1999:

> Some councils took back paint cans and some didn't, so we started to
> educate councils about how to recycle paint cans. No-one was tak-
> ing back cans with paint, so we thought we could take back our paint
> for recycling, Then we thought, that only solves part of the problem;
> maybe we should take back all brands. So within two months we went
> from paint can recycling to taking back everyone's paint.[60]

The programme evolved slowly, beginning with a trial in one store, one
day a month, for six months in 2004. This didn't work from a practical perspective as the store was getting too much paint on one day and it wasn't
convenient for consumers. There was clearly demand for a service, however. Resene and product stewardship specialist 3R Group took the lessons
from the trial and developed them into a plan for an ongoing programme,
which 3R was appointed to manage.[61]

The programme was gradually rolled out region by region, starting in the
Upper North Island around Auckland in 2005 and extending to the South
Island in 2007. Customers pay a 15 cent per litre levy when they purchase
a can of Resene paint, which enables them to return any unwanted paint
or packaging to a Resene store. Other brands of unwanted paint are also
accepted at Resene stores for a small fee, and some local councils pay for
collection of paint from their waste depots.

After collection the paints are separated into solvent-based and water-
based paints for decanting. Solvent-based paints are sent to a recycler where
the solvents are recovered and the remaining solid waste goes to landfill.
Water-based paints are recovered in several ways:

- Because steel cans are decanted mechanically the paint is mixed
  into a generic grey colour. The grey paint is donated to community
  groups and local councils for use where quality is not as important,
  for example to cover graffiti.

- Paint in plastic pails is decanted manually with some colours batch
  processed together (cream, green, brown, grey and off-white) and
  donated to community groups.

---

60   Personal communication with K. Warman, Resene.
61   3R Reimagineers (n.d.). *Case study Resene PaintWise.* Hastings NZ. Retrieved
     from http://3r.co.nz/wp-content/uploads/2014/06/3R-Group-Case-Study-
     Paintwise.pdf

- Resene and 3R have also found an additional market for unwanted paint as a concrete additive. After five years of testing by the University of Auckland they developed a new product, PaintCrete™, which improves the performance of certain types of concrete.

The recovered packaging is recycled. Steel cans are sent to a metal recycler, while plastic pails are recycled locally to manufacture new, 100% recycled pails for Resene.

The ongoing costs of Resene PaintWise are financed through The Resene Foundation charitable trust with money from the company, the point-of-sale levy, fees for recycling other brands and service fees from local councils who use the Resene PaintWise collect service. According to Karen Warman, the original motivation for the trust was to enable other manufacturers to join a collective scheme that would share the costs of recycling. This is developing slowly, with a number of non-Resene outlets using the Resene PaintWise programme to recycle paint.

In 2011 the programme was accredited by the Ministry for the Environment under the Waste Minimization Act 2008. Warman believes that this adds to its credibility with the community:

> Resene PaintWise is still relatively new in some ways. Accreditation says it's above board and all the paint is being handled responsibly. It shows we're doing it right; it's a bona fide initiative.[62]

2.6.1.4 Shared value outcomes

Over a 10-year period to 2014 the environmental and social benefits of the programme have included:

- Over 2 million separate items collected for recycling

- Over 400,000 kg of steel and 200,000 kg of plastic recovered

- Over 500,000 litres of solvent-based paint sent to solvent recovery

- Over 190,000 litres of paint donated to social projects[63]

Karen Warman is unaware of any direct business outcomes of PaintWise, although she believes that the programme has helped to build the company's brand reputation. The company surveys its customers through a feedback form given to consumers with every sale, and these indicate that

---

62   Personal communication with K. Warman, Resene.
63   3R Reimagineers (n.d.), p. 2.

PHOTO 2.2   Paint pails collected by Resene PaintWise

Photo: Resene

consumers appreciate the recycling service. Feedback from the commercial market and specifiers has also been positive.

Resene PaintWise has also helped the company to win various awards that add to its reputation as an environmentally sustainable company. These include the Sustainable Business of the Year Award at the National Sustainable Network Awards in 2010. Resene also won an Award for Excellence in the Environmental Packaging Awards in 2005.

Case study 2.6.2 PVC Product Stewardship Program

2.6.2.1 Summary

During the 1990s polyvinyl chloride (PVC or "vinyl") was under attack by Greenpeace International through a campaign that threatened key markets for PVC in packaging and building products. In Australia, resin suppliers and converters responded by developing a comprehensive stewardship programme in consultation with stakeholders. Shared value outcomes have included reduced emissions from manufacturing; the complete elimination of cadmium additives and near complete elimination of lead additives; increased recycling; and the development of best practice environmental standards for PVC products in the building industry.

2.6.2.2 Drivers for product stewardship

In the early 1990s Greenpeace International began to campaign against products and materials linked to the chlorine industry. One of its targets was PVC, because at the time PVC consumed around 25% of global chlorine production. Greenpeace's primary concern was the emission of organochloride compounds including:

- Vinyl chloride monomer (VCM, which is carcinogenic) during the resin manufacturing process

- Potential dioxin emissions if PVC ended up being burned in an open fire such as backyard burning, in a building fire, or in a poorly managed waste incinerator

Greenpeace also argued that lead stabilizers in PVC building products and plasticizers in flexible PVC products such as cable, could leach into the environment during use or in landfill.

Greenpeace Australia helped to draft the environmental guidelines that formed a part of Sydney's bid to host the 2000 Olympic Games. These guidelines called for "minimizing and ideally avoiding the use of chlorine-based products (organochlorines) such as PCB, PVC and chlorinated bleached paper". According to Sophi MacMillan, Chief Executive Officer of the Vinyl Council of Australia, this "had very deep ramifications for PVC building products in particular, since about two-thirds of the PVC consumed in Australia was in the building sector".[64]

2.6.2.3 Stewardship strategies

The PVC industry's first response was to commission a report in 1996 from Australia's leading scientific organization, CSIRO. Based on a detailed literature review, CSIRO concluded that PVC building products were generally sound from an environmental perspective but there were issues that could be addressed to improve their performance (the report has since been updated).[65] In 1998 resin manufacturers and compounders formed an industry association, the Vinyl Council of Australia ("Vinyl Council"), to develop an effective response. The Vinyl Council enlisted other representatives across the supply chain, including compounders, additives providers and service providers in logistics.

The PVC industry was facing similar pressures in other countries. In Europe the industry launched a voluntary sustainable development initiative called "Vinyl 2010". Its aim was "… to progress the PVC industry towards sustainability by minimizing the environmental impact of PVC production, promoting responsible use of additives, supporting collection and recycling schemes, and encouraging social dialogue between all of the industry's stakeholders and beyond".[66]

The Vinyl 2010 plan brought together four industry groups, each representing a part of the PVC supply chain. It provided a model for the Vinyl Council, already representing the key parts of the supply chain, to build on. Council members were able to agree a set of objectives and commitments that addressed issues across the full PVC life-cycle, from resin manufacture through to disposal. These included, among others:

- Targets for minimizing VCM emissions during manufacturing and VCM levels in the finished product to global best practice levels

---

64   Personal communication with S. MacMillan, Chief Executive, Vinyl Council of Australia, 3 June 2015.
65   Coghlan (2001).
66   Vinyl 2010 (2011). *Vinyl 2010: 10 years.* Brussels, p. 4. Retrieved from http://www.plasticseurope.org/documents/document/20110422155920-vinyl2010_progress_report_2011.pdf

- Target dates for the phase out of cadmium and lead stabilizers

- Development of recycling programmes for recovery and recycling of PVC products at end of life.

The PVC Product Stewardship Program ("the programme") was launched in 2002 "to recognise and address all environmental issues facing the Australian PVC industry".[67]

Effective stakeholder engagement has always been critically important for programme development. When the programme was initially developed, the Vinyl Council approached federal and state government environment agencies for input. Sophi MacMillan notes that the broad membership of the council also helped to establish an ambitious but practical programme:

> One of the things that was really important, was that we had the whole supply chain engaged as members ... In Europe they have separate associations, one for the resin manufacturers, one for the converters, one for the additive industry ... it makes it a lot more complex for them to reach agreement. We had everyone sitting around the table together, and that was really important when it came to discussing things like the phase-out of lead stabilisers. We had the suppliers of lead stabilisers sitting at the table with the converters discussing technical and commercial feasibility of how that phase-out could happen. I think that was really important. Still today, having the different parts of the supply chain involved really adds to the discussion and facilitates how individual companies can proceed and meet their commitments.[68]

Ongoing stakeholder input is achieved through a Technical Steering Group comprising representatives from industry, government and other stakeholder groups. The group meets four times a year to refine and clarify commitments and develop new ones. A larger stakeholder round table is held every two or three years following publication of the annual progress report. According to MacMillan these have been very useful and constructive:

> We've had people there who have held quite strong views about PVC but have provided really valuable input, and it has resulted in changes to the program.

67   Vinidex (2013). *Product Stewardship*. Retrieved from http://www.vinidex.com.au/sustainability/product-stewardship/

68   Personal communication with S. MacMillan, Vinyl Council of Australia.

Since 2002 the programme has been updated many times in response to feedback from signatories and external stakeholders. MacMillan again:

> The program has evolved continuously. We've not set it in stone. We've allowed it to evolve as commitments have been met and we want to continually improve. [For example] ... the original program had nothing on energy efficiency or greenhouse gas emissions and that was seen by stakeholders four or five years ago as a bit of a gap given the current policy climate.
>
> We also introduced a commitment on open disclosure, where convertors or manufacturers of a product will provide the ingredient list for their products. That was introduced probably eight years ago ... directly as a result of stakeholder feedback that said, essentially, that "while it's great that you're phasing out lead and telling us about plasticiser use, what else do you have in your products that we don't know about?" So there is [now] an open disclosure commitment and mercury avoidance.

The programme includes commitments to improve the recycling rate for PVC products, but it is unusual among stewardship programmes in its focus on the *total* life-cycle of PVC rather than just recovery at end of life. This approach has been driven by stakeholder concerns and expectations that cover impacts during resin production and use as well as disposal.

The emphasis on a life-cycle approach extends to the actions of individual members. A new commitment to consider whole-of-life impacts in the development of new products was added in 2007, with signatories encouraged to attend training on life-cycle thinking. The Vinyl Council has contributed PVC data to the Australian life-cycle inventory, and is now starting a process to help members prepare Environmental Product Declarations. According to MacMillan, life-cycle assessment (LCA) has been a useful tool for the council and its members:

> Our position in the industry, and at the Vinyl Council, has always been that products should be selected based on their merit in terms of fitness for purpose, life cycle cost and environmental performance using credible life cycle assessments. We have always been very supportive of the use of LCA. We encourage industry to undertake LCAs of their products, not only to use them internally to look at where they can improve the environmental footprint for their own products, but also to use LCA to understand the benefits of PVC products versus others, and where they might not be as strong.

In 2007 Russ Martin from the Product Stewardship Council (now the Global Product Stewardship Council) suggested that external verification should be considered to improve transparency and credibility. This was accepted by the Vinyl Council. An annual progress report outlines the progress made by signatories in meeting their commitments, and is independently verified by a third party.

Verification also includes examination of data provided to the Vinyl Council by signatories, and whether or not the signatory is compliant with the intention of the commitment. This usually involves site visits to a number of signatories and follow-up by phone and email. Reporting is mandatory for all signatories, and failure to do so can lead to delisting. Verification is taken seriously, with one company delisted as a signatory in 2011 for failing to report on progress towards meeting its commitments. The council noted on its website that "While it is regrettable that a company is delisted, it is imperative that the integrity of the Product Stewardship is maintained for the benefits that are derived by the industry and its stakeholders".[69] Two other companies had previously been delisted for non-reporting.

Failure to comply with commitments can also lead to delisting, if there is no genuine effort to comply. This is a last resort only, and has not yet happened. The Vinyl Council prefers to help companies that struggle to meet their commitments rather than delisting them (if they are willing to comply). Delisting is clearly a last resort. Generally when the auditors identify a commitment that is proving difficult to meet, the Vinyl Council develops tools and methodologies to help companies achieve it.

2.6.2.4 Shared value outcomes

The programme has been successful in changing perceptions of PVC in the building industry and therefore protecting important markets for PVC pipe, cable, flooring and fittings. While Greenpeace is no longer campaigning directly on this issue, MacMillan notes that the reputational damage to PVC that resulted from the original campaign "still permeates and [is] picked up by other organizations". An example was the Green Building Council of Australia's (GBCA) Green Star building rating tool, which originally adopted the PVC minimization clause from the green guidelines for the Sydney Olympics. The Vinyl Council argued that this approach discriminated against PVC products that had already addressed many of the environmental and health issues previously associated with the material.

As a result of approaches from the council, and following a comprehensive LCA and literature review, GBCA updated its Green Star tool. A building design can now earn points for use of PVC products in a building that have

69 Vinyl Council of Australia (2015).

been independently verified as compliant with new best practice guidelines for PVC in the built environment.[70] These guidelines include a range of practices including low emissions, no lead stabilizers, no mercury in production and end of life product stewardship.

MacMillan believes that this result could not have been achieved without the PVC Stewardship Program. Data collected through the programme was able to demonstrate that the industry had made significant progress, and that "PVC products today are quite different to the PVC products of 15 or 20 years ago".[71] The programme's record of transparency and stakeholder engagement was also important in building credibility with GBCA.

MacMillan also points to other benefits for signatories, which include:

- Product innovation including improved additives such as stabilizers and pigments

- Differentiation in the market through their ability to meet the Green Star best practice guidelines, or by being a signatory to the PVC Stewardship Program

- Cost savings through energy efficiency initiatives

- Educational and networking benefits for those involved in the Technical Steering Group

- The sense of pride that companies and their employees get from being seen as responsible manufacturers

The programme has reduced the health and/or environmental impacts of PVC in a number of ways. VCM is no longer manufactured in Australia, but the commitment to only use VCM or vinyl manufactured from "mercury-free" processes is helping (along with regulatory developments in Europe) to drive change in the global supply chain. Emissions of VCM by the Australian producer of suspension PVC (S-PVC) resin have fallen to 20.1 grams per tonne of PVC, which is below the programme's target of 30 g/t and represents global best practice. For companies using resin manufactured abroad, or companies importing PVC products to Australia, commitments on VCM emissions and residual VCM in resin also help drive change throughout the global supply chain.

---

70   GBCA (2010). *Literature Review and Best Practice Guidelines for the Life Cycle of PVC Building Products.* Sydney: Green Building Council Australia.
71   Personal communication with S. MacMillan, Vinyl Council of Australia.

PHOTO 2.3   Collection bins for flexible PVC hospital waste

Photo: Vinyl Council of Australia

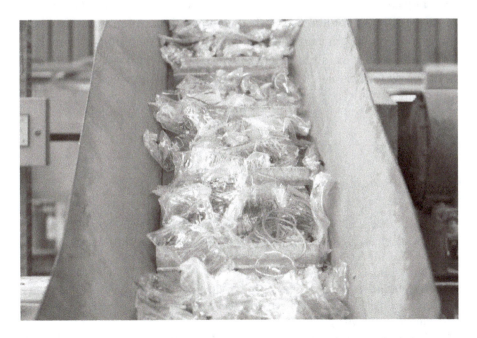

PHOTO 2.4   PVC hospital waste on a conveyor belt at the recycler

Photo: Vinyl Council of Australia

Cadmium and hexavalent chromium additives have been eliminated by programme signatories, while the use of lead stabilizers and pigments by signatories had fallen by 99.8% by 2014.[72] This is consistent with overseas initiatives and trends. Again there is a flow through effect, as the commitment applies to products imported to Australia.

Product innovation facilitated by the programme has delivered business benefits for members. Chemson Pacific, one of the world's leading manufacturers of PVC stabilizers, committed to phasing out lead additives by 2008. Chemson developed new calcium/zinc stabilizers, which have superior physical properties such as higher hoop-strength in pressure pipes compared with alternatives. Chemson relocated to a new lead-free facility, which avoided stringent and costly procedures that were required to protect workers from lead exposure.[73]

Progress has been made towards the achievement of the Vinyl Council's Industry Recycling Strategy. In the earlier years of the programme there was a strong focus on recycling of packaging because of the limited options available for consumers. By 2007, as a result of initiatives by the Vinyl Council and resin manufacturers to support kerbside recycling, 90% of the Australian population were able to add PVC bottles to their kerbside recycling containers, with a recycling rate of around 50% for PVC bottles.[74] More recently the council has worked with individual members to facilitate increased recycling for a range of different products. With support from Baxter Healthcare, for example, a recycling programme has been implemented in hospitals for flexible PVC products such as oxygen masks, IV fluid bags and tubing.

72   Vinyl Council of Australia (2015). *PVC Stewardship Program 2014*. Laverton North, Victoria. Retrieved from http://www.vinyl.org.au/images/Product_Stewardship/VCA_PSP2014Report.pdf

73   Vinyl Council of Australia (n.d.). *PVC Stewardship Case Study: Best Practice in PVC Additives*. Melbourne, Australia. Retrieved from http://members.vinyl.org.au/images/Chemson_Best_Practice_additives_DRAFT_mod_JDK_GH_JS_edit_for_web_V02.pdf

74   Vinyl Council of Australia (2007). *5 Year Evaluation Report of the PVC Industry's Product Stewardship Program*. Retrieved from http://www.vinyl.org.au/images/Product_Stewardship/PVCPSP5YearEvaluationReport.pdf

Part 2:
Product stewardship by sector

3
Packaging

The business case is clear. The more we reduce our packaging and the less waste that goes to landfill, the greater the cost savings in materials, energy, transport and disposal. The more we can design in a circular way, the more value we can create for our company and for others (Unilever's Sustainable Living Plan).[1]

3.1 Introduction

Chapter 2 suggested that a successful product stewardship strategy is based on a good understanding of stakeholder expectations and product impacts, and aligns with corporate priorities and capabilities. This chapter considers some of the strategic issues for packaging from a business perspective. It begins by describing several packaging trends that may either support or constrain a company's ability to achieve sustainability improvements.

This is followed by an overview of stakeholder groups and their perceptions of packaging, or expectations for product stewardship. Packaging was the first sector to be subject to producer responsibility regulations as a result of stakeholder concerns about waste. Over time the focus for packaging sustainability has broadened to other issues including the source of raw materials and impacts on food waste.

Leading companies are taking action to reduce the life-cycle impacts of their packaging. The final section provides examples of initiatives in

1   Unilever (2015). Waste and Packaging. Retrieved from https://www.unilever.com/sustainable-living/the-sustainable-living-plan/reducing-environmental-impact/waste-and-packaging/

corporate policy, design for sustainability, procurement strategies and packaging recovery. Three more detailed case studies at the end of the chapter demonstrate some of the common drivers, strategies and benefits of voluntary packaging stewardship initiatives:

- Foodstuffs New Zealand is working to ensure that all of the packaging used for its private label products is recyclable. This case study describes two successful design projects that reduced waste and delivered multiple business benefits.

- RED Group collects soft plastics (bags and film) for recycling through supermarkets, with the support of food and consumer product brand owners. Their programme is an example of industry collaboration to address a common problem, facilitated by an entrepreneurial small business.

- The Glass Packaging Forum is a supply chain collaboration. Originally developed by an industry association in response to government concerns about the lack of local markets for recovered glass, it now undertakes a wide range of activities to reduce waste and litter.

3.2 Background: packaging and market trends

3.2.1 Overview

There are several significant trends driving the quantity of packaging on the market and its environmental impacts. The amount of packaging coming on to the market in developing and emerging economies is increasing rapidly to meet the needs of a growing and more affluent population. This has implications for every stage of the life-cycle, from the need to source more raw materials for production to a growing volume of waste that must be managed at end of life.

Increasing production is being moderated to some extent by the drive for greater efficiency in product supply chains. Product stewardship regulations and cost pressures are prompting companies to look for savings by using less packaging to deliver the same amount of product. This has positive benefits for sustainability by reducing demand for raw materials and reducing waste and emissions throughout the packaging life-cycle. In Europe and North America the amount of packaging being consumed and thrown away appears to have decoupled from economic growth.

Another significant trend is the increasing use of plastics packaging at the expense of more traditional materials such as glass and metals. Plastics can be more efficient and offer additional functionality, but most are made from non-renewable fossil fuel resources and some are more difficult to sort and recycle. Consumer and stakeholder expectations for sustainable packaging are driving the development of new polymers from plant-based materials that are renewable and either recyclable or compostable.

3.2.2 Increasing production

Demand for packaged goods is closely linked to population size. The global population is expected to reach 9.5 billion in 2050 and 10.8 billion by 2100.[2] Most of this growth will occur in less developed countries in Africa and Asia, and the global distribution of packaging consumption will follow. Asia accounted for 36% of the packaging market by value in 2012, and this is expected to grow to 41% by 2018. Increasing affluence is helping to drive packaging demand, particularly in China, India, Brazil, Russia and other emerging economies.[3]

In contrast, the quantity of packaging placed on the market in the EU (by weight) has stabilized.[4] The total quantity of packaging waste generated (i.e. disposed or recycled) in the EU-27 increased between 2005 and 2008 from 78.6 million tonnes to 81.3 million tonnes, before falling during the economic slump in 2009. While it has since recovered, the quantity of waste generated in 2012, at 78.9 million tonnes, showed very little change over the previous seven years.

3.2.3 Increasing efficiency

The trend to lighter weight and more efficient packaging (less packaging for the same amount of product) has been under way for at least 20 years. This has been primarily driven by brand owners and retailers trying to reduce costs. In his book on the history of Walmart, Charles Fishman uses an anecdote on deodorant packaging to demonstrate the company's influence on the market:

2   UN (2013). *World Population Prospects: The 2012 Revision*. Retrieved from http://esa.un.org/unpd/wpp/Documentation/publications.htm
3   Smithers PIRA (2013). *Global Packaging Market to Reach $975 Billion by 2018*. Retrieved from http://www.smitherspira.com/news/2013/december/global-packaging-industry-market-growth-to-2018
4   Eurostat (2016). *Packaging Waste Statistics*. Retrieved from http://ec.europa.eu/eurostat/statistics-explained/index.php/Packaging_waste_statistics

> Starting in the early 1990s, a change swept through a line of 'ducts that most Americans use every day. Until then, nearly every brand and style of deodorant … came in a paperboard box … In the early 1990s, [Walmart], among other retailers, decided the paperboard box was a waste. It added nothing to the customer's deodorant experience. The product already came in a can or a plastic container that was at least as tough as the box, if not tougher. The box took up shelf space. It wasted cardboard. Shipping the weight of the cardboard wasted fuel. The box itself cost money to design, to produce … With the kind of quiet but irresistible force that [Walmart] can apply, the retailer asked deodorant makers to eliminate the box.[5]

Deodorants are no longer packed in boxes in Walmart, or anywhere else. A similar process has been under way within the company ever since: "A wasteful routine, often long entrenched, is detected and eliminated, establishing a new standard of efficiency, lowering costs for everyone, especially ordinary customers".[6]

The US-based Grocery Manufacturers Association (GMA) has observed that a culture of continuous improvement within the food, beverage and consumer goods sector means that companies are always looking for new and innovative ways to optimize packaging. A survey of their members in 2011 concluded that more than 1.5 billion pounds (680,000 tonnes) of packaging has been avoided between 2005 and 2010, and another 2.5 billion pounds (1.1 million tonnes) was expected to be avoided between 2011 and 2020.[7]

There are different views on whether product stewardship regulations have also played a part in eliminating or reducing packaging. Evaluations of the German Packaging Ordinance have used product case studies and consumption and recycling data to assess its effectiveness in changing packaging practices.[8] All of these studies concluded that the policy had resulted

---

5   Fishman, C. (2006). *The Wal-Mart Effect*. London: Penguin Books, p. 1.
6   Fishman (2006), p. 3.
7   GMA (2011). *Reducing Our Footprint: The Food, Beverage and Consumer Products Industry's Progress in Sustainable Packaging*. Washington, DC: Grocery Manufacturers Association, p. 2. Retrieved from http://www.gmaonline.org/file-manager/Sustainability/ReducingOurFootprint.pdf
8   See DSD (1992). *Ecological Optimization of Packaging*. Bonn: Duales System Deutschland (DSD); Michaelis, P. (1995). Product stewardship, waste minimization and economic efficiency: lessons from Germany. *Journal of Environmental Planning and Management*, 38(2), 231-243; OECD (2001). *Extended Producer Responsibility: A Guidance Manual for Governments*. Paris: Organisation for Economic Cooperation and Development.

in significant changes in design to reduce packaging and to make it more recyclable.

There is an alternative view that these packaging changes were the result of continuous improvements in design that had been occurring throughout the global packaging industry, and could not be attributed to the Packaging Ordinance.[9] A report prepared for GMA compared packaging use and gross domestic product in the EU and the US between 1998 and 2008, and undertook detailed analysis of packaging formats for selected product categories.[10] The report concluded that packaging use had increased slowly in the EU, where there are widespread EPR laws for packaging, and had remained flat or declined in the US, where EPR for packaging was *not* regulated. Packaging use had effectively decoupled from economic growth in both regions.

3.2.4 More plastics

Paper and board continue to be the most commonly used packaging materials, but glass, steel and aluminium are losing market share to plastics. In Europe (EU-15 countries) for example, plastics made up 22% of packaging sold in 2011, by weight (Fig. 3.1). Between 2003 and 2011 consumption of plastics packaging per capita increased from 26 to 33 kg, while consumption of glass packaging fell from 40 to 36 kg per capita, and metal packaging from 12 to 10 kg.[11]

The trend to use more plastics in packaging is driven by a range of factors including increasing demand for soft drinks and bottled water in PET; substitution of traditional metals, glass and paper-based materials; increased use of packaging for fresh foods such as meat, fish and poultry; and rising consumption of ready-meals and other convenience foods.[12] Many of the newer packaging materials, such as multi-layer films and bags, are more difficult to recycle than more traditional materials.

9   Sinclair, A.J. (2000). Assuming responsibility for packaging and packaging waste. *Electronic Green Journal*, 1(12). Retrieved from http://escholarship.org/uc/item/3g08m7jp#page-25

10   SAIC (2012). *Evaluation of Extended Producer Responsibility for Consumer Packaging*. Report to the Grocery Manufacturers Association (GMA): Washington, DC.

11   EUROPEN (2014). *Packaging and Packaging Waste Statistics 1998–2011*. Brussels, Belgium. Retrieved from http://www.pac.gr/bcm/uploads/europen-packaging-packaging-waste-statistics-1998-2011.pdf

12   World Packaging Organization (2008). *Market Statistics and Future Trends in Global Packaging*. Brazil: World Packaging Organization.

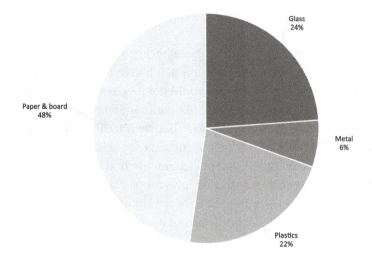

FIGURE 3.1   Consumption of packaging by material, per capita (kg), 2011, EU-15

Note: Data excludes wood packaging.

Source: Based on EUROSTAT data in EUROPEN (2014), pp. 20-27

3.3 Stakeholder expectations

This section reviews the expectations of five key stakeholder groups: consumers, product and packaging manufacturers (producers), government regulators, environmental groups and municipalities. It looks at some of the drivers for product stewardship and the issues of most concern to each group. These are summarized in Table 3.1, although there are likely to be significant differences between stakeholder interests and levels of engagement within and between countries.

3.3.1 Consumers

Companies need to understand and engage with consumers as both purchasers and waste managers. Their first role—as the ultimate end-consumer of a product—puts them at the very centre of company decisions about product design and marketing. Their second role, as waste managers in the home, is important if companies wish to promote a preferred end-of-life option for their packaging: for example whether the consumer is being asked to reuse, refill, recycle, compost or dispose of it with other rubbish. Disposal decisions by consumers have a significant influence on the total environmental impact of packaging.

TABLE 3.1   Stakeholder interests in packaging and product stewardship

Stakeholder	Interests
Consumers	• Functionality, including product protection and ease of use • Over-packaging • Recyclability
Product and packaging manufacturers	• Corporate reputation and sustainability goals • Reduction in packaging • Recyclable or compostable packaging • Preference for voluntary stewardship or EPR led by industry • Cost of product stewardship compliance schemes • Uniform global standards and metrics for packaging sustainability • Paper-based packaging from certified sustainable sources
Government regulators	• Quantity of packaging waste • Conservation of non-renewable resources (linked to the goal of a "circular economy") • Ecological impacts of packaging in litter, e.g. plastic grocery bags and take-away food packaging
Environment groups	• Quantity of packaging waste • Use of non-renewable resources • Non-refillable and non-recyclable packaging • Ecological impacts of packaging in litter, e.g. plastic grocery bags and take-away food packaging • Ecological and social impacts of packaging from plants, i.e. paper fibre from rainforest timber or biopolymers from food crops
Municipalities	• Local government involvement in planning and implementation • Costs of waste management to ratepayers • Maintaining or improving the level of recycling service

A survey of 2,000 consumers in the US found that packaging plays a significant role in consumer purchasing behaviour, brand loyalty and product satisfaction. The majority of consumers considered the followed attributes of packaging to be extremely or very important:

- Protects the product from tampering and contamination (77%)

- Does not contain harmful materials or substances (83%)

- Keeps products fresh/effective (77%)

- Prevents spillage/breakage (82%)

- Sustainable and environmentally friendly (65%)[13]

---

13   Westrock (2016). Packaging Matters Report. Retrieved from https://www.westrock.com/-/media/pdf/insights/packaging-matters-report-vfinal-pdf, pp. 4-7.

The report concluded that consumers value brands that balance sustainability and function: "Brands should not use less packaging, but just the right amount of packaging—for the product, for the supply chain and for the retail environment".[14]

Many consumers react negatively to perceptions of "over-packaging". A survey of consumer attitudes to packaging in the UK has observed an increase in negative perceptions.[15] In 2008 79% of respondents agreed with the statement that products are over-packaged, compared with 68% in 1997; 82% agreed that "packaging is a major environmental problem" in 2008 compared with 71% in 1997.

Consumer perceptions of the "environmental friendliness" of packaging materials are often linked to their perceived recyclability. In a New Zealand survey, for example, consumers were asked to rate the environmental friendliness of packaging types and then rate their recyclability, and there was a strong relationship between the two. Paper bags and cardboard boxes rated among the most environmentally friendly and the most recyclable, while polystyrene rated lowest for both questions.[16]

A more recent report from the Association of Packaging and Processing Technologies identified recyclability and reusability as one of the three main trends affecting the global packaging market.[17]

These results are consistent with a customer survey undertaken by Nutrimetics, a manufacturer of personal care products, which highlighted customer concerns about excess packaging and recyclability. The company responded by reducing the size of its skincare packs and making them more recyclable.[18]

The strong link in consumers' minds between the amount of packaging, recyclability and environmental friendliness poses a challenge for

14   *Ibid.*, p. 7.
15   IPSOS Mori (2008). *Public Attitudes to Packaging 2008*. Report to INCPEN and Valpak: London, p. 3.
16   New Zealand Paperboard Packaging Association (2005). *Attitudes to Packaging, Recycling and the Environment*. Lower Hutt, New Zealand: New Zealand Paperboard Packaging Association, p. 14.
17   APPT (2015). *What's Happening in Packaging Around the Globe?* Retrieved from http://packexpolasvegas.com/files/packexpo/2015/Infographic_Global_Packaging_Trends.pdf
18   Lewis, H., & Crittenden, P. (2014). *The Business Case for Packaging Sustainability*. Sydney: Australian Packaging Covenant. Retrieved from http://www.helenlewisresearch.com.au/category/publications/selected-reports-handbooks-and-guidelines/

marketers.[19] In some cases more rather than less packaging may be required to minimize product waste, particularly for food. In some cases, a light-weight pack such as a laminated pouch may deliver more environmental benefit from a life-cycle perspective, even if it means that the packaging cannot be recycled.[20]

Research on consumer behaviour at end of life also helps to inform the way that companies communicate with their customers on disposal and recycling, for example through labelling. In a survey by the Institute of Scrap Recycling Industries and Earth911 in the US, a surprising 65% of respondents said they didn't understand which plastics are acceptable in kerbside recycling.[21]

3.3.2 Product and packaging manufacturers

Most of the leading brands that manufacture packaged goods, particularly in the food, beverage and consumer goods sector, have a policy to reduce the environmental or sustainability impacts of their packaging. This is driven by a range of factors, including compliance with regulations, customer (retailer) expectations and a desire to protect their corporate reputation. Environmental priorities for manufacturers include reducing the amount of packaging, using recyclable or compostable materials, and sourcing paper and paperboard from certified sources.

Retailers around the globe are using their power in the supply chain to influence packaging sustainability. UK retailers including Tesco, Sainsbury's and Marks & Spencer have all committed to packaging initiatives, as have Carrefour (France) and Walmart (US). Sainsbury's had a target to reduce the weight of its own-brand packaging, relative to sales, by 33% by 2015 against a 2009 baseline. It also committed to work with all stakeholders to make more of its packaging recyclable.[22]

19   Lewis, H., & Stanley, H. (2012). Marketing and communicating sustainability. In K. Verghese, H. Lewis, and L. Fitzparrick (Eds.), *Packaging for Sustainability* (pp. 107-153). London: Springer.

20   *Ibid.*

21   McTigue, L. (2014, July 14). Confused consumers toss out plastic packaging instead of recycling: poll. *Packaging Digest*, 2014. Retrieved from http://www. packagingdigest.com/sustainable-packaging/confused-consumers-toss-out -plastic-packaging-instead-of-recycling-poll140731

22   J Sainsbury plc (2010). *Sainsbury's Corporate Responsibility Report 2010*. Retrieved from http://www.j-sainsbury.co.uk/investor-centre/reports/2010/ corporate-responsibility-report-2010/

Manufacturers and retailers are collaborating at national and global levels to develop uniform guidelines and standards for packaging sustainability. Influential groups driving these developments include the Sustainable Packaging Coalition in the US, EUROPEN in Europe and the global Consumer Goods Forum (CGF). In 2013 the CGF developed guidelines on pulp, paper and packaging to support its commitment to achieve "zero net deforestation" by 2020. The fact that these were developed in response to stakeholder concerns about unsustainable forestry practices is illustrated by frequent references in the guidelines to the need to avoid "controversial sources" of pulp, paper and packaging.[23] The high profile campaign by Greenpeace in 2010 to stop Mattel using fibre from Indonesian rainforests in its packaging is just one example of the controversy that CGF members are trying to avoid (this is discussed further below under Environment groups).

From a policy perspective producers tend to support voluntary initiatives over regulation. In the US, where there is a strong push from some stakeholders to introduce EPR laws for packaging,[24] the GMA has argued for alternative policies that focus on government rather than producer responsibility:

> States and municipalities already have at their disposal a suite of non-EPR policies that are both effective and efficient in terms of raising recycling rates. Together, they can achieve high recycling rates, without excess cost or administrative burden that results from EPR.[25]

The alternative policy mechanisms mentioned in the GMA report include disposal bans, recycling rewards or rebates, "pay-as-you-throw" disposal pricing and mandatory recycling standards.[26] GMA members include over 300 food, beverage and consumer products manufacturers, but their views

---

23   Consumer Goods Forum (2013). *CGF Pulp, Paper & Packaging Guidelines.* Issy-les-Moulineaux, France. Retrieved from http://www.theconsumer goodsforum.com/files/Publications/Pulp_Paper_and_Packaging_Guidelines_ June_21.pdf

24   Laskow, S. (2015, February 9). Who will pay America's $1.5 billion recycling bill? *Next City.* Retrieved from http://nextcity.org/features/view/cost-of-recycling -america-extended-producer-responsibility-cities

25   GMA (2012, September 12). *New Study Shows Alternatives to Extended Producer Responsibility Achieve High Recycling Rates with Less Cost and Administrative Bureaucracy.* Retrieved from http://www.gmaonline.org/news-events/ newsroom/new-study-shows-alternatives-to-epr-achieve-high-recycling -rates-with-less/

26   SAIC (2012).

are not representative of the sector as a whole. A notable exception is Nestlé Waters North America (NWNA), a Connecticut-based bottled water company, which has advocated a regulated EPR approach to the recovery of used packaging. The company's then Director of Sustainability, Michael Washburn, outlined the rationale in an interview in the *Resource Recycling* journal:

> We have an interest in putting more recycled plastic back into our bottles. And why we want to do that is, frankly, a risk reduction strategy around our materials. The cost of oil can be volatile, as we're seeing in the headlines, and that has a direct impact on our cost and consequently our pricing. It really makes no sense that we're putting tremendous amounts of valuable material into the ground.[27]

According to Washburn, EPR is "a 21st century solution to a very old problem". The company's preference is for industry-run EPR schemes that are run independently of government because this is likely to be the most cost-effective approach:

> ... our preference would be for US models to have an industry-managed program where a producer responsibility organisation, comprised of brand owners, would take the fiduciary and managerial obligations of running the program. Through that we hope that we can create a lower administrative burden consistent with how businesses ought to behave and a more equitable cost structure that is driven by performance goals ...[28]

Where EPR laws are already in place, producers tend to support more direct industry control of packaging recovery programmes. In contrast to the GMA, the European Organization for Packaging and the Environment (EUROPEN) argues that industry-run programmes are likely to be more efficient and less costly that those that are heavily regulated or managed by municipalities:

> As industry has the legal responsibility, industry must be entitled to take an active role in fulfilling these obligations and to control compliance costs. This means being enabled to control how separate collection, sorting and recycling/recovery are organized and to drive cost-efficiency to ensure the lowest sustainable cost to consumers and society.[29]

27 Thomas, J. (February 24, 2012). Exclusive: Nestlé Waters on EPR. *Resource Recycling*. Retrieved from http://resource-recycling.com/print/2531
28 *Ibid.*
29 EUROPEN (2013). *EUROPEN Position on Extended Producer Responsibility for Post-Consumer Packaging in the EU*. Brussels, Belgium, p. 6. Retrieved from http://www.europen-packaging.eu/policy/9-extended-producer-responsibility.html

For similar reasons some producers in Canada are promoting competition among producer responsibility organizations (PROs) rather than one state-sanctioned service provider. In 2014 a new "producer responsibility corporation", StewardChoice, announced its plan to launch a packaging and printed paper compliance service in British Columbia. At that stage Multi-Material British Columbia (MMBC) was the only PRO with an approved plan. According to StewardChoice there are many benefits of a competitive approach:

> Producers who have spoken with StewardChoice like the idea of "choice" in the marketplace because it raises the level of service; spurs innovation and collaboration across the recycling supply chain; increases valuable material collection and waste diversion across the province and minimizes the cost burden for producers and consumers.[30]

In Europe, while EPR was originally seen as a "natural monopoly", most of the newer member states allowed competition from the beginning and the original EU-15 countries are now being opened up to competition.[31]

3.3.3 Government regulators

Product stewardship laws for packaging were among the first to be implemented and are now widespread. The most common policies are:

- EPR laws that make producers partially or fully responsible for packaging recovery

- Container deposit legislation ("bottle bills")

- Design requirements including restrictions on heavy metals

- Packaging bans or restrictions

- Packaging taxes or levies

A summary including the typical goals of each policy and regions and countries where they are in place is provided in Table 3.2. While they share many common objectives, such as a desire to reduce waste and litter and to encourage design for recycling, governments have chosen very different

---

30   StewardChoice (2015). *Producers Value Choice*. Retrieved from http://stewardchoice.ca/producers-value-choice/

31   Personal communication (email) with D. Perchard, Managing Director, Perchards Limited, 9 February 2016.

approaches. These range from highly regulated EPR schemes, found in many European countries and Japan, for example, to more flexible, industry-led approaches such as those in Australia and New Zealand.

According to Russ Martin, CEO of the Global Product Stewardship Council, while Germany was the first country to implement EPR on a significant scale, Italy was the first to introduce a law making producers financially responsible for recycling:

> A lot of people tend to associate the start of EPR with the German Packaging Ordinance [1991], but we feel that it started with Italy's law number 475 in November 1988. The law required separate collection of containers for liquids from kerbside, starting in 1990. Local authorities were responsible for collection but all local manufacturers and importers had to join material specific consortia to work with authorities on recycling. Consortia members contributed a levy to cover their operating costs.[32]

Most of the earliest laws aimed to reduce packaging waste. In Japan, for example, the Containers and Packaging Law (1995) was introduced in response to diminishing waste disposal sites and the increasing ratio of packaging in municipal waste.[33] Mandatory deposits and taxes on single-use containers were introduced in some jurisdictions to force beverage companies to keep (or return to) refillable bottles. EPR laws were designed with a broader objective—to internalize the costs of packaging waste management and, by doing so, provide companies with an incentive to design less wasteful and recyclable packaging.

Another important objective of EPR is to shift waste management costs from taxpayers to producers and consumers. When they were introduced most countries already had an established recovery system for packaging, for example through kerbside collection or drop-off points, but policymakers wanted to shift some or all of the cost burden to producers. The Canada-wide strategy for sustainable packaging, for example, states that:

> EPR provides an effective tool for shifting the costs of end-of-life management onto those responsible for the packaging; improving end-of-life management of packaging; and providing an incentive

32 Personal communication (interview) with R. Martin, CEO, Global Product Stewardship Council, 16 December 2013.
33 Ori, A. (2014). Experience from Japan: containers and packaging recycling law. In *Global forum on Environment: Promoting Sustainable Materials Management through Extended Producer Responsibility*. Tokyo, Japan.

TABLE 3.2   **Examples of product stewardship laws and policies for packaging**

Type of regulation	Detail	Purpose	Examples
Extended producer responsibility	Producers are physically or financially responsible for recovery of packaging at end of life.	To shift the costs of recycling from taxpayers to producers and consumers; to increase levels of recycling; to promote design of recyclable packaging by internalizing disposal and recycling costs.	• Asia: Japan, South Korea • Europe: most EU member states (excl. Denmark), Norway • Canada: five provinces (Ontario, Manitoba, British Colombia, Quebec and Saskatchewan)
Bottle bill/ Container deposit legislation	A deposit on beverage containers is paid by consumers and redeemed when they return the container to a retailer, waste collection depot or reverse vending machine.	Originally introduced to encourage producers to use refillable containers. Their current purpose is generally to promote return by consumers and to achieve higher recycling rates for beverage containers.	• Europe: Denmark, Estonia, Germany, Lithuania, Netherlands, Sweden • US: ten states (California, Connecticut, Hawaii, Iowa, Maine, Massachusetts, Michigan, New York, Oregon and Vermont) • Canada: 12 of the 13 provinces and territories (the exception is Nunavut) • Australia: one state (South Australia) and one territory (Northern Territory), with others to follow in 2017 (New South Wales) and 2018 (Queensland)
Design requirements	Either prescriptive regulations that focus on particular outcomes, e.g. a maximum number of layers or restrictions on hazardous components; or requirements for companies to implement design for environment processes.	To reduce the environmental impacts of packaging at end of life (landfill or incineration); to reduce the amount of packaging waste; to promote design for reuse or recycling.	• Asia: China (Excessive Packaging Law), Japan • EU member states ("Essential Requirements" in the Packaging and Packaging Waste Directive) • US: 19 states have implemented the "Toxics in Packaging" model bill; several specify recycled content in plastic containers (Oregon, California, Wisconsin)

Type of regulation	Detail	Purpose	Examples
Packaging tax	A tax on the sale of certain types of packaging (weight or volume)	To encourage producers to reduce the amount of packaging or use refillable containers; or to pay for waste or litter programmes.	• Asia: Taiwan • Europe: Denmark, Norway
Ban or levy on plastic checkout bags	A ban on the sale of certain types of lightweight plastic checkout bags, or a mandatory levy	To change consumer behaviour, e.g. to reduce consumption of disposable plastic bags by encouraging use of reusable shopping bags; or to finance recycling.	• Asia: Bangladesh, China, Hong Kong • Oceania: four Australian states (South Australia, Tasmania, ACT, Northern Territory) • US: California; other cities and counties • Europe: Ireland, Italy, Malta, UK (England, Wales, Scotland, Northern Ireland) • Africa: South Africa, Togo, Kenya
Voluntary or co-regulatory agreements with industry	Voluntary agreements or plans supported by back-up regulation. These generally include funding for recycling as well as design requirements.	To reduce waste and increase recycling.	• Australia

for producers to incorporate environmental considerations into the
design of their products.[34]

Governments are becoming more focused on the role of recycling in
conserving resources to achieve economic as well as environmental goals.
In the EU, for example, more ambitious packaging targets have been proposed to support the drive towards a "circular economy", which is considered essential to achieve "smart, sustainable and inclusive growth" for the
region.[35] These targets include a minimum 65% of packaging prepared for
reuse and recycling by 31 December 2025 and 75% by 2030 (the current
target is 55%).[36] For similar reasons the Japanese Government's EPR laws
are designed to create a sustainable economic system based on the "3Rs"
(reduce, reuse, recycle).[37]

Litter continues to be a priority for many governments. Some have
responded to the problem by introducing mandatory deposits on beverage
containers, which are the third-most common item found in land-based
marine litter surveys.[38] Australian research concluded that South Australia's
container deposit legislation appears to have reduced the number of beverage containers in marine litter by a factor of three when compared with
states without deposits.[39]

Other jurisdictions have restricted the use of lightweight plastic shopping bags, which are the sixth-most littered item in marine and freshwater

34   CCME (2009). *A Canada-wide Strategy for Sustainable Packaging.* Winnipeg, MB,
       Canada: Canadian Council of Ministers of the Environment, pp. ii-iii. Retrieved
       from http://www.ccme.ca/files/Resources/waste/packaging/pn_1501_epr_
       sp_strategy_e.pdf
35   European Commission (2014). *Towards a Circular Economy: A Zero Waste Pro-
       gramme for Europe.* Brussels, Belgium: EC.
36   European Commission (2015). *Proposal for a Directive of the European Par-
       liament and of the Council Amending Directive 94/62/EC on Packaging and
       Packaging Waste.* Brussels, Belgium. Retrieved from http://ec.europa.eu/
       environment/waste/target_review.htm
37   Ministry of Economy, Trade and Industry (2008). *Towards a 3R-Oriented Sus-
       tainable Society: Legislation and Trends.* Retrieved from http://www.meti.
       go.jp/policy/recycle/main/data/pamphlet/pdf/handbook2008_eng.pdf
38   Ocean Conservancy (2014). *Turning the Tide on Trash.* Washington, DC: Ocean
       Conservancy.
39   Hardesty, B.D., Wilcox, C., Lawson, T., Lansdell, M., & van der Velde, T. (2014).
       Understanding the Effects of Marine Debris on Wildlife. Report by CSIRO for
       Earthwatch Australia: Australia.

TABLE 3.3   Developments in product stewardship regulations for packaging

European Union	In December 2015 the European Commission put forward proposals to amend the Packaging and Packaging Waste Directive, with changes including higher targets and alignment of definitions with the Waste Framework Directive, and new rules for EPR compliance systems.
United States	Between 2012 and 2014 there was a renewed push by environment groups and municipalities for EPR regulations, driven by concerns that municipalities will be unable to invest sufficient funds to improve recycling rates. The movement lost some impetus in 2015 as legislative proposals in some states, such as Rhode Island, failed to get support.
Canada	EPR is being implemented by provincial and territorial governments in accordance with the *Canada-wide action plan for extended producer responsibility* (2009). Most programmes are based on a shared responsibility model, with local government responsible for collection.
Australia	In 2015 the future of the Australian Packaging Covenant (APC) was in doubt as environment groups and other stakeholders pushed for a national container deposit scheme (CDS, or "bottle bill").

environments.[40] Restrictions are likely to become more widespread, with the European Commission agreeing to introduce a new Directive to cut plastic bag use.[41] Member states can either introduce mandatory pricing of bags or binding targets to reduce the number of bags used per person per year from the current 191 to 40 in 2025. One of the main objectives of the measure is to reduce the impact that plastic bags have when they accumulate in the environment, especially in the form of marine litter.[42]

Some of the key developments in product stewardship regulations around the world are summarized in Table 3.3.

3.3.4 Environment groups

Following the introduction of single-use beverage containers in the 1970s, non-government organizations (NGOs) began to campaign for increased government regulation of packaging. The original objective of many NGOs was to force manufacturers to retain (or reintroduce) refillable bottles, but over time their focus has shifted to policies that promote waste reduction or

40   Ocean Conservancy (2014).

41   Nelson, A. (2014, November 21). EU set to approve historic deal to cut plastic bag use. *The Guardian*. Retrieved from http://www.theguardian.com/environment/2014/nov/20/eu-set-to-approve-historic-deal-to-cut-plastic-bag-use

42   European Commission (2013). *Green Paper on a European Strategy on Plastic Waste in the Environment.* Brussels, Belgium: EC.

recycling. In more recent years environment groups have campaigned for EPR laws in the US and container deposits in Australia that force producers to take more responsibility for packaging waste management. In Australia, for example, around 30 environment groups have joined the campaign by Boomerang Alliance for a national container deposit scheme ("cash for containers") to reduce waste and litter.[43]

As You Sow, a non-government environmental group based in the US, targets companies more directly through dialogue and shareholder advocacy. Its campaign on consumer packaging encourages manufacturers to adopt EPR policies through research, engagement and shareholder resolutions.[44] The group's arguments against packaging waste include the financial value of discarded materials, the increasing cost to taxpayers of waste management, its contribution to greenhouse gas emissions, over-reliance on non-renewable resources, and increasing plastic pollution in marine environments.[45]

In the US, EPR is also being promoted by UPSTREAM (previously the Product Policy Institute). On packaging its goals are to develop and advance sustainable packaging through state and corporate policies. The organization has formed a coalition of public interest groups to promote EPR for packaging.[46] Its principles for producer responsibility stress that EPR should not undermine existing recycling systems, container deposits laws or local ordinances relating to packaging (such as bans on plastic bags or polystyrene).

Many environment groups place a high priority on the recyclability of packaging, which can pose a reputational risk to companies that pursue other design strategies such as lightweighting through the use of plastic bags or pouches. Kraft Foods, for example, introduced a recycling programme for its drink pouches in the US through a partnership with TerraCycle. The programme has been criticized by As You Sow as nothing more than a "stop-gap" measure:

43 Boomerang Alliance (2014). *Cash for Containers*. Sydney, Australia: Boomerang Alliance.

44 As You Sow (2015). *Consumer Packaging*. Retrieved from http://www.asyousow. org/our-work/waste/consumer-packaging/

45 MacKerron, C. (2012). *Unfinished Business: The Case for Extended Producer Responsibility for Post-consumer Packaging*. Oakland, CA: As You Sow.

46 The Cradle2 Coalition (2013). *Public Interest Principles of Producer Responsibility for Reducing, Reusing and Recycling Packaging*. UPSTREAM The Cradle2 Coalition.

> This is more beneficial than landfilling, but is generally very limited in the volume of materials gathered and re-used and achieves only a temporary reprieve since the laminate is disposed after its second useful life has ended.[47]

As You Sow has identified "recyclability and materials use" as one of the four pillars of product stewardship (the other three are source reduction, recycled content and "boosting materials recycling"). They argue that "[m]aterials that are very difficult to recycle, like flexible laminate pouches (e.g. juice pouches) should be avoided in favor of readily recyclable packaging".[48] This argument ignores the significant life-cycle environmental benefits that may be achieved using lightweight packaging formats such as the plastic pouch compared with heavier but recyclable containers (Nestlé's Smart Pack is an example—see Photo 3.2, below).

Some environment groups have a very specific regulatory objective, such as a ban on plastic grocery bags, to address litter impacts. Others have worked with manufacturers and other stakeholders to stop the use of paper-based packaging from "old growth" or environmentally sensitive forests. Greenpeace chose the world's largest toy manufacturer, Mattel, and its iconic Barbie and Ken dolls, as the face of its creative campaign against deforestation.[49] Research by the NGO linked the packaging used by Mattel and other large toy manufacturers to Sinar Mas Group's Asia Pulp & Paper (APP), which sources pulp from tropical rainforests in Indonesia. The "Barbie, it's over" campaign included an interview with Ken, a Twitter feud between the couple, and photos of Barbie with a chain saw. This resulted in a considerable amount of media attention and 500,000 emails were sent to Mattel from people asking the company to stop buying pulp and paper from APP.[50]

There are many new polymers on the market or under development that are being marketed for their environmental benefit compared with conventional plastics. These include polymers made from plants, which are

47   MacKerron (2012), p. 7.
48   MacKerron, C. (2015). *Waste and Opportunity 2015: Environmental Progress and Challenges in Food, Beverage and Consumer Goods Packaging.* As You Sow, p. 8. Retrieved from http://www.asyousow.org/ays_report/waste-and-opportunity -2015/
49   Greenpeace International (2011). *APP's Customers in the Toy Sector.* Retrieved from http://www.greenpeace.org/international/en/campaigns/forests/asia -pacific/app/toys/sector/
50   Godelnik, R. (2011, October 10). Mattel says yes to Greenpeace, no to rainforest destruction. *Triple Pundit.* Retrieved from http://www.triplepundit. com/2011/10/mattel-greenpeace-app/

potentially renewable, and compostable polymers designed to break down in commercial or home composting systems. Plastics from plants will continue to gain market share in response to demands for more sustainable packaging materials.

3.3.5 Municipalities

In most countries waste management is a local government responsibility, and over time this role has extended to include recycling of household packaging and paper. This has added to cost pressures because of the growing quantity of packaging waste requiring disposal and fluctuating prices for recyclable materials.

In the US the Northwest Product Stewardship Council stated in 2011 that "[local governments and their ratepayers are no longer able to invest the necessary financial resources to increase the diversion of materials from disposal to recycling".[51] Other stakeholders have argued that industry initiatives to fund recycling infrastructure, such as the Closed Loop Fund, are inadequate because of the substantial investments required to improve municipal recycling rates. Matt Prindiville, Associate Director of not-for-profit group UPSTREAM, claims that the US$100 million being invested by the fund is "not much money when you're talking about billions across the counties to run these recycling programs".[52]

While there is increasing momentum for EPR for packaging in the US, there are also concerns that EPR might undermine existing municipal programmes. This was identified as a potential barrier to EPR by Garth Hickle, Product Stewardship Team Leader with the Minnesota Pollution Control Agency:

> Unlike the situation for other products, around 80–85% of the US population already has access to kerbside recycling. You've also got a lot of investment and ownership from local government in the existing programs, so I'd say there's as much concern and hesitation from the municipal side as there is from the producer side on packaging. There are a lot of personal and historical connections to recycling programs, and there are concerns about ownership, job losses and redundant assets if producers take over responsibility for recycling. So there are lots of issues to be considered.[53]

51   Cited in MacKerron (2012), p. 12.
52   Laskow (2015).
53   Personal communication (interview) with G. Hickle, Product Stewardship Team Leader, Minnesota Pollution Control Agency, US, 5 February 2014.

UPSTREAM consulted with local government representatives in the US to identify their objectives for packaging EPR.[54] These included a shift in financing and (depending on local circumstances) management responsibilities, from a government–taxpayer basis to a producer–consumer basis. They also wanted to achieve an 80–90% recycling rate for most materials and improved packaging design for reuse, recycling or composting.

3.4 Packaging impacts

There is ample evidence to support stakeholder concerns about the environmental impacts of packaging, particularly around waste and litter. Emerging issues of concern include the impacts of plastic litter on marine ecosystems, the ecological and social impacts of plant-based plastics, and links between packaging and food waste.

3.4.1 Packaging waste management

In the 1970s (and in some cases the 1980s) beverages started to move out of refillable glass bottles and into single-use glass, plastic, metal or paperboard containers. This change, which was driven by a range of factors including the development of new packaging technologies and growth in self-serve retail stores,[55] had a significant impact on municipal waste:

> The end of the refillable triggered an onslaught of packaging production and increased consumption. It also created unprecedented level, and whole new types, of garbage. By the mid-1970s, packaging had already become the single largest category of municipal solid waste in the United States …[56]

Significantly higher recycling rates have been achieved since the 1970s, but packaging still makes up a substantial proportion of solid waste in most

---

54 UPSTREAM (2014). *Advancing Local Government's Interests through EPR for Packaging*. Rockland, ME. Retrieved from http://upstreampolicy.org/wp-content/uploads/2014/11/UpstreamEPRpaper2014FINAL3.pdf

55 Lewis, H. (2009). *Product Stewardship: Institutionalising Corporate Responsibility for Packaging in Australia* (Unpublished doctoral dissertation). Melbourne: School of Global Studies, Social Science and Planning, RMIT University.

56 Rogers, H. (2007). Message in a bottle: mass-scale trash as the outcome of our economic system. In J. Knechtel (Ed.), *Trash* (pp. 113-131). Cambridge, MA: The MIT Press, p. 114.

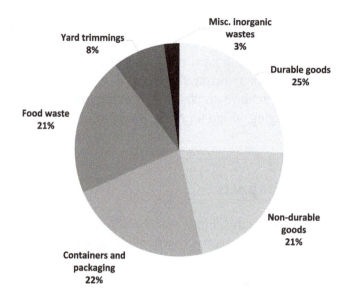

FIGURE 3.2   Composition of municipal solid waste disposed in the United States, 2013

Source: Based on US EPA (2015). *Advancing Sustainable Materials Management: 2013 Fact Sheet*. Washington, DC: United States Environmental Protection Agency, pp. 10-11. Retrieved from http://www.epa.gov/sites/production/files/2015-09/documents/2013_advncng_smm_fs.pdf. Waste discarded after composting and recycling. Excludes industrial, hazardous and construction waste

countries. In the US, for example, containers and packaging made up 30% of municipal waste generated and 22% of waste discarded by weight (Fig. 3.2). The cost of managing packaging waste disposal and recycling is a major driver for EPR in the US.

Implementation of the EU Directive on Packaging and Packaging Waste (DPPW) in the member states has significantly reduced packaging waste. The recycling and recovery targets in the Directive have largely been met, although there are some uncertainties about the quality of the data provided by some member states.[57] Between 1998 and 2011 the recycling rate for packaging increased from 47% to 64% in the older EU member states (EU-15), exceeding the target of 55%.[58]

The growing market for flexible and laminated plastics packaging is one of the biggest challenges for recycling. A typical example is the plastic

57   Bio Intelligence Service, Arcadis, and Institute for European Environmental Policy (2014). *Ex-post Evaluation of Certain Waste Stream Directives*. Report to the European Commission—DG Environment.

58   *Ibid.*, p. 303.

stand-up pouch, which is widely used for liquid detergents, beverages, soups and snack foods.

Increasing consumption of food and beverages away from home is another challenge, because the packaging associated with these products is less likely to be recycled than packaging consumed at home. This is one of the reasons why a powerful coalition of municipalities and environment groups in Australia is continuing to advocate for container deposit legislation in addition to kerbside recycling.[59]

3.4.2 Litter and marine debris

There is increasing evidence that plastic litter in the marine environment is causing environmental harm.[60] Initial concerns focused on injuries and death to wildlife from ingestion or entanglement, particularly seabirds, fish and turtles. More recently scientists have been studying the potential toxicity effects of marine plastics and micro-plastics as toxic substances are transferred into marine organisms and enter the food chain. These include chemicals that are added intentionally to products (for example flame retardants or plasticizers) as well as pollutants that are absorbed by plastics in the environment.

Most of the litter collected by Ocean Conservancy during its International Coastal Cleanup (involving 650,000 volunteers in 92 countries), is packaging (Fig. 3.3), particularly food wrappers, beverage bottles, caps and shopping bags.

There are many sources of marine litter, including waste disposal sites located along the coast or rivers; discharge from stormwater drains; deliberate or accidental littering of beaches and picnic areas; fishing industry activities; dumping at sea; and natural disasters.[61] The Ocean Conservancy study only measured litter that was accessible from land (e.g. on beaches) and is therefore not an accurate measure of total marine litter composition.

---

59   Boomerang Alliance (2014).
60   See Hardesty *et al.* (2014); UNEP (2009). *Marine Litter: A Global Challenge.* Nairobi: United Nations Environment Programme (UNEP). Retrieved from http://www.unep.org/pdf/unep_marine_litter-a_global_challenge.pdf; Stevenson, S. (2011). *Plastic Debris in the California Marine Ecosystem.* Los Angeles, US: California Ocean Science Trust; Pors, J. (2013). *Plastic Marine Litter: One Big Market Failure.* Amsterdam, the Netherlands: IMSA Amsterdam.
61   UNEP (2009).

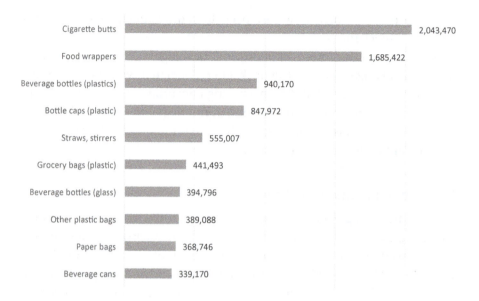

FIGURE 3.3   Top ten items collected from beaches, marine and freshwater environments, number of items, 2013

Source: Based on data from the International Coastal Cleanup in 92 countries in Ocean Conservancy (2014), p. 14

'Ghost fishing'—lost or discarded fishing lines, nets and pots—is also a major hazard for marine organisms).[62]

3.4.3 Resource consumption

Most packaging is made from commodity materials: paper and cardboard, plastics (mainly polyethylene (PE), polypropylene (PP) and polyethylene terephthalate (PET)), glass, steel and aluminium. With the exception of paper and cardboard, these are manufactured from non-renewable resources. The production of packaging materials also requires a significant amount of energy, most of which is fossil fuel-based.

Resource conservation strategies include design for efficiency (for example, lightweighting) and reuse or recycling at end of life. Recycling ensures that materials are diverted from landfill and used again for the same or a different purpose ("closed loop recycling" or "downcycling"). It does not,

62   UNEP (2015). Biodegradable Plastics & Marine Litter: Misconceptions, Concerns and Impacts on Marine Environments. Nairobi, Kenya: United Nations Environment Programme (UNEP) for the Global Programme of Action for the Protection of the Marine Environment from Land-based Activities (GPA).

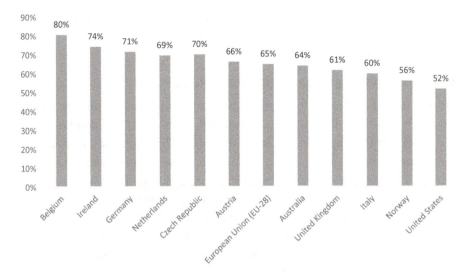

FIGURE 3.4   Recycling rates for packaging, selected countries, 2012

Sources: US EPA (2012). Municipal waste generation, recycling and disposal in the United States: facts and figures for 2012. Retrieved from http://www.epa.gov/osw/nonhaz/municipal/pubs/2012_msw_fs.pdf; Eurostat (2016); APC (2014). *Annual Report 2013–14. Australian Packaging Covenant* Sydney, Australia. Retrieved from http://www.packagingcovenant.org.au/data/Publications/APC_AR-2014_180x260mm-FA1.pdf

however, offer a complete solution. Despite significant progress in establishing recycling systems for packaging there are still significant amounts of non-renewable material being disposed to landfill each year. In the US only 51% of packaging was recycled in 2012, although some European countries have achieved recycling rates of up to 70–80% (Fig. 3.4).

Walter Stahel, Visiting Professor at the University of Surrey, UK, has pointed out that because of the short life-span of packaging materials there are great losses of materials at an aggregate level even when recycling levels are high. The implications for packaging were summarized in a report to the European Commission, which drew on his ideas:

> [I]f we assume that 100 tonnes of aluminium cans are put in the market at the beginning of the year and that the life span of a can is 3 weeks, with [a] recycling rate of 90%, at the end of the year only 17 tonnes will have remained in the circular economy …[63]

Another potential solution to the use of non-renewable resources for plastics packaging, in addition to recycling, is to shift to renewable plant-based

63   Bio Intelligence Service, Arcadis, and Institute for European Environmental Policy (2014), p. 108.

feedstocks such as wood, corn or sugarcane. This raises other sustainability challenges, which are explored in the next section.

3.4.4 Sustainability of packaging from plants

Around half of all packaging is manufactured from paper, which is associated with sustainability impacts including deforestation and displacement of indigenous communities.[64] The sustainability of wood fibre resources is becoming more of a focus for companies that use paper-based packaging, driven in part by pressure from environment groups such as Greenpeace.

At least half of the deforestation that has occurred over the past decade was for commercial agriculture.[65] The proportion for tropical forests was even higher. Deforestation is closely linked to export demand for commodities including pulp and paper. There are particularly concerns about the illegal conversion of tropical forests for agriculture (including timber plantations), which results in some of the worst impacts on the environment and local communities. Forest Trends estimates that between 16% and 49% of pulp and paper exports are sourced from illegal deforestation activities.[66]

Some plastics are also starting to be manufactured from plants, which raises similar questions about their environmental impacts. These "biopolymers" are made from crops such as corn, sugar or potatoes, and depending on their formulation are promoted as either renewable, compostable, or both. Some stakeholders have expressed concerns that biopolymers will increase competition for agricultural land, and could contribute to food shortages or rising prices. This does not appear to be a major problem, at least for the next decade.[67] Global production of bioplastics currently uses less than 1% of arable land, and the bioplastics industry is moving to alternative non-food feedstock materials such as wood and crop wastes.[68]

64   EUROPEN (2014).
65   Lawson, S. (2014). *Consumer Goods and Deforestation.* Washington, DC: Forest Trends. Retrieved from http://www.forest-trends.org/documents/files/doc_4718.pdf
66   *Ibid.*, p. 139.
67   O'Farrell, K., Millicer, H., Lewis, H., Hall, W., & Scheirs, J.(2014). *The Future Role of Bioplastics in Australian Consumer Goods Packaging.* Report to Woolworths Limited and Landcare Australia: Melbourne, Australia.
68   EuBP (2015). *Frequently Asked Questions on Bioplastics.* Berlin: European Bioplastics.

3.4.5 Avoided food waste

More evidence is emerging on the economic, social and environmental costs of food waste. Globally, around one-third of the food produced for human consumption each year, an estimated 1.3 billion tonnes, is lost or wasted globally each year.[69]

This issue is emerging as an important priority for governments at a national and international level for a number of reasons. Food and other organic materials break down in landfill and generate methane, a greenhouse gas about 25 times more potent than carbon dioxide.[70] From a social and ethical perspective, reducing food waste is one of the strategies that will help to improve future food security.[71] The United Nations estimates that around 1 billion people are already under-nourished[72] and world demand for food is expected to be around 77% higher in 2050 compared with 2007.[73]

Packaging plays a critically important role in protecting and extending the life of food products, which helps to minimize food loss and waste. Food loss is defined as food that is unintentionally spilled or spoilt in agricultural processes or the supply chain.[74] Some of this can be avoided by using better packaging, for example plastic crates instead of bags for distribution. Food "waste" is food that is fit for human consumption but thrown away (for example uneaten food in restaurants, or food that is past its "use by" date). There are many strategies that can be used to reduce food waste, including packaging fresh produce to extend its shelf-life and better labelling for

69   Gustavsson, J., Cederberg, C., & Sonesson, U. (2011). *Global Food Losses and Food Waste: Extent, Causes and Prevention.* Report by the Swedish Institute for Food and Biotechnology for the Food and Agriculture Organization of the United Nations: Rome, p. 4.

70   US EPA (2016). *Overview of Greenhouse Gases.* Retrieved from https://www3.epa.gov/climatechange/ghgemissions/gases/ch4.html

71   Lipinski, B., Hanson, C., Lomax, J., Kitinoja, L., Waite, R. & Searchinger, T. (2013). *Reducing Food Loss and Waste.* Washington, DC: World Resources Institute.

72   FAO (2010). *The State of Food Insecurity in the World 2010: Addressing Food Security in Protracted Crises.* Rome: Food and Agriculture Organization of the United Nations. Retrieved from http://www.fao.org/docrep/013/i1683e/i1683e.pdf

73   Linehan, V., Thorpe, S., Andrews, N., Yeon, K. & Beaini, F. (2012). *Food Demand to 2050: Opportunities for Australian Agriculture.* Presentation to *42nd ABARES Outlook Conference, 6–7 March.* Canberra: Australian Bureau of Agricultural and Resource Economics and Sciences.

74   Lipinski *et al.* (2013).

consumers.[75] More effective packaging is therefore one of the strategies that could contribute to food security in future, particularly in developing countries.[76]

More effective product packaging can also play an important role in reducing the environmental impacts associated with food waste. Life-cycle assessment (LCA) studies have demonstrated that the environmental impacts of a food product are generally greater than those of the packaging.[77] A UK study found that, on average for the products included in that study, the energy required to produce food packaging is only around 10% of the energy used to produce, distribute, store and prepare the food it contains.[78]

This challenges the popular belief that less packaging is always the best outcome. An optimized packaging system is tailored to meet the specific protection needs of the product; thus avoiding over-packaging that uses excessive amounts of material, and under-packaging that may result in both the product and its packaging being lost.

Sometimes more rather than less packaging is required to optimize the environmental performance of a product-packaging system, and there are still plenty of opportunities for optimization.[79] The Australian Institute of Packaging has suggested that "[p]ackaging's role in reducing food waste is the next challenge for packaging technologists, designers and engineers".[80]

3.5 Corporate strategy

Chapter 2 provided an overview of some of the policies and strategies that companies are using to understand and reduce the environmental and

75   Verghese, K., Lewis, H., Lockrey, S. & Williams, H. (2013). *The Role of Packaging in Reducing Food Waste in the Supply Chain of the Future*. Report prepared by RMIT University for CHEP Australia: Melbourne Australia. Retrieved from http://www. chep.com/resources/case_studies/how_packaging_can_reduce_food_waste/

76   Lipinski *et al.* (2013).

77   Verghese, K., & Carre, A. (2012). Applying life cycle assessment. In K. Verghese, H. Lewis, & L. Fitzpatrick (Eds.), *Packaging for Sustainability* (pp. 171-210). London: Springer.

78   INCPEN (2009). *Table for One: The Energy Cost to Feed One Person*, p. 4. Retrieved from http://www.incpen.org/docs/TableForOne.pdf

79   Verghese *et al.* (2013).

80   Australian Institute of Packaging (2016). *Save Food Packaging Awards*. Retrieved from http://aipack.com.au/2016-save-food-packaging-awards/

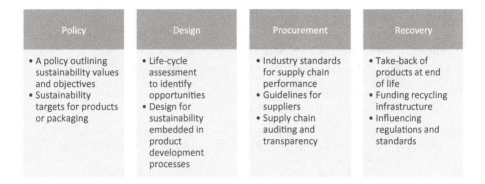

Policy	Design	Procurement	Recovery
• A policy outlining sustainability values and objectives • Sustainability targets for products or packaging	• Life-cycle assessment to identify opportunities • Design for sustainability embedded in product development processes	• Industry standards for supply chain performance • Guidelines for suppliers • Supply chain auditing and transparency	• Take-back of products at end of life • Funding recycling infrastructure • Influencing regulations and standards

FIGURE 3.5   Examples of corporate product stewardship actions

social aspects of their products, with a focus on marketing, design, procurement and recovery at end of life (Fig. 3.5). This section explores some of the actions being taken by corporate leaders in packaging.

3.5.1 Policy

Many well-known global brands in the packaging supply chain have sustainability goals for packaging that go well beyond compliance with regulations. These include commitments to reduce packaging, improve recyclability or reduce impacts in the supply chain (some examples are shown in Table 3.4). These are often documented in policies that identify their goals, design priorities and targets. Global policies and targets often need to be tailored for local circumstances, including the availability of recycling services.

In some cases companies have adopted stretch goals that are difficult to achieve but nevertheless help to drive innovation and continuous improvement. Starbucks, for example, committed to recycle all of the paper and plastic cups that customers dispose in store by 2015. While this has been challenging, progress is being made in collaboration with industry partners, municipalities and recyclers. To ensure that customers are able to recycle their packaging, either in-store or at home, Starbucks is working with a broad range of stakeholders to change local government policies and improve recycling systems.[81]

Many retailers are driving changes to packaging, particularly for private label products. In 2007 Marks & Spencer announced as part of its "Plan A"

81   MacKerron (2015); Starbucks (2013). *Starbucks Global Responsibility Report: Goals and Progress 2013*. Retrieved from http://globalassets.starbucks.com/assets/b48b38aed56e4fdd8dcdbbfad23e3242.pdf

TABLE 3.4   Examples of packaging targets

Company	Packaging goals and targets
Starbucks	• Serve 5% of beverages made in our stores in personal tumblers (cups) by 2015. • Implement front-of-store recycling in our company-operated stores by 2015. Source: Global Responsibility Report[1]
McDonald's Corporation	• 100% of fibre-based packaging from certified or recycled sources by 2020. • Optimize the weight and simplify the number of materials used in our packaging. • Work to use recoverable packaging with viable end-of-life options. Source: Corporate Social Responsibility & Sustainability Report 2012–2013[2]
Unilever	• Halve the waste associated with the disposal of our products (per consumer use) by 2020. • Reduce packaging. • Increase recycling and recovery rates. • Increase recycled content. • Tackle sachet waste. • Eliminate PVC. Source: Sustainable Living Plan 2013[3]
Nestlé	• Optimize the weight and volume of our packaging. • Lead the development and use of materials from sustainably managed renewable resources considering packaging and product performance requirements. • Support initiatives to recycle or recover energy from used packaging. • Use recycled materials where there is an environmental benefit and it is appropriate. Source: The Nestlé Policy on Environmental Sustainability[4]
Walmart	• Reduce packaging by 5% between 2008 and 2013 • Reduce global plastic shopping bag waste by an average 33% per store by 2013 compared with 2007 Source: 2013 Global Responsibility Report[5]
Dell	• Ensure 100% of product packaging is sourced from sustainable materials. Source: 2014 Corporate social responsibility report[6]

1   Starbucks (2013), pp. 14-17.
2   McDonald's (2014). *Our Journey Together for Good: McDonald's Corporate Social Responsibility & Sustainability Report 2012–13*, p. 39. Retrieved from http://www.aboutmcdonalds.com/mcd/sustainability.html
3   Unilever (2013). *Unilever Sustainable Living Plan 2013*. Retrieved from https://www.unilever.com/Images/slp_unilever-sustainable-living-plan-2013_tcm13-388693_tcm244-409814_en.pdf
4   Nestlé (2013). *The Nestlé Policy on Environmental Sustainability*, p. 2. Retrieved from http://www.nestle.com/asset-library/documents/library/documents/environmental_sustainability/nestl%c3%a9%20policy%20on%20environmental%20sustainability.pdf
5   Walmart (2014). *2013 Global Responsibility Report*. Bentonville, AR, US. Retrieved from http://corporate.walmart.com/global-responsibility/environment/global-responsibility-report
6   Dell (2014). *FY14 Corporate Responsibility Report: A Progress Report on Our 2020 Legacy of Good Plan*. Retrieved from http://i.dell.com/sites/doccontent/corporate/corp-comm/en/Documents/fy14-cr-report.pdf

environmental programme that it would cut its use of non-glass packaging by 25% by 2012. Other initiatives included plans to increase use of more sustainable raw materials for packaging such as recycled materials and Forest Stewardship Council certified boards.[82] In 2006, Walmart announced a 5% packaging reduction target to be achieved by 2013. An environmental scorecard is used to evaluate the sustainability performance of all suppliers and to encourage continuous improvement.[83]

3.5.2 Design

In many leading companies design for sustainability is integrated into product development processes.

At Nestlé, for example, all new products and those being renovated with new packaging must undergo an environmental sustainability assessment using EcodEX, Nestlé's LCA-based ecodesign tool. This evaluates the environmental performance of the packaged product, from agricultural production through to product manufacturing, packaging and end of life.[84] This recognizes that a holistic approach to assess the environmental performance of their products is required. The complete packaged product life-cycle (ingredients, production, packaging and consumer use) needs to be assessed taking into consideration multiple environmental impact categories.

Corporate drivers for integrating sustainability in design processes include ambitious corporate sustainability targets as well as government regulations in particular markets, such as the EU's "Essential requirements for packaging" and the Australian Packaging Covenant (APC). Design for sustainability, including efficiency and recyclability, is a core requirement for signatories to the APC. Many of the packaging initiatives undertaken by APC signatories have delivered financial and other business benefits as well as positive sustainability outcomes. Several examples, which are documented in a series of published case studies, are summarized in Table 3.5.

82   Marks & Spencer (2010). Your M&S: How We Do Business Report 2010. London: Marks and Spencer. Retrieved from http://annualreport2010.marksandspencer.com/downloads/M&S_HWDB_2010.pdf

83   Walmart (2008). *Sustainable Packaging Fact Sheet: Walmart is Taking the Lead on Sustainable Packaging.* Retrieved from http://nbis.org/nbisresources/packaging/walmart_packaging_factsheet.pdf

84   Nestlé (2014). *Nestlé in Society: Creating Shared Value and Meeting our Commitments 2014.* Retrieved from http://storage.nestle.com/nestle-society-full-2014/index.html#1/z

TABLE 3.5 **Examples of business outcomes from packaging sustainability case studies**

Company	Packaging sustainability initiative	Business benefits achieved or anticipated
Bristol-Myers Squibb Australia	Reusable cold chain packaging for medical and pharmaceutical products	Eliminated the need to purchase more than 15,000 single-use cool boxes and ice packs. Provided a value-add to customers, who avoided waste disposal costs.
Kathmandu	Redesign of the box for thermal clothing including use of FSC-certified fibre and a cut-out "window"	Packaging costs reduced overall owing to the cut-out window (less material) and less printing. The cut-out window improved sales by making the product more accessible to consumers wanting to feel its texture.
Kimberley-Clark Australia	Lightweighting Kleenex Cottonelle toilet paper packaging by reducing the plastic film gauge	13% reduction in film weight achieved by using a higher quality resin. This has production benefits because of the lower sealing temperature, which saves energy and improves productivity (machinery speed can be increased).
Nutrimetics	Redesign of plastic jars for skincare products to reduce material consumption (smaller size) and to make them recyclable (a shift to PET, which is highly recyclable, and a two-piece jar design allows different plastics to be separated prior to disposal)	Reduced packaging costs as the jars use at least 40% less material (depending on size). Improved customer satisfaction as the new design addresses concerns about perceived "excessive" packaging and non-recyclability.
D&D Technologies	Transition from retail clamshell packaging to stand-up pouches for pool safety locks	Met customer (retail) request for lower cost packaging, more space on pack to promote product benefits, improved packaging line efficiency, supports the shift to automated packing, less inventory.

Source: Lewis & Crittenden (2014)

PHOTO 3.1   Compostable plastic trays for Haigh's chocolates
Photo: Helen Lewis

Leading companies are driven by corporate values and policies as well as government policy. Haigh's Chocolates, for example, designs its packaging to be reusable, recyclable or compostable because environmental responsibility is seen as an integral component of its brand.[85] Feedback from customers indicates that they value and support Haigh's environmental initiatives. A recent innovation was the introduction of a biodegradable and water-dispersible plastic for its Ballotin box insert (Photo 3.1). Joint Managing Director Alistair Haigh said that the decision to incorporate biodegradable packaging had grown from the company's "overarching commitment to sustainability and environment".[86]

Under the EU Packaging Directive only packaging which complies with the "Essential Requirements" can be placed onto the market. These include reducing weight and volume to the minimum possible, reducing the impact of hazardous components and designing for recovery. A series of standards have been developed by CEN (the European Committee for Standardization) to support the Essential Requirements—these are voluntary but

85   Lewis, H. (2014). *Haigh's Chocolates: A Packaging Assessment Case Study*. Sydney: Australian Packaging Covenant. Retrieved from http://www. packagingcovenant.org.au/data/Case_study_Haighs.pdf

86   Plantic (2008). *Haigh's Chocolates Integrate Plantic Packaging*. Melbourne, Australia: Plantic Technologies. Retrieved from http://www.plantic.com.au/ Case%20Studies/Plantic_Haighs_CS(1).pdf

Photo 3.2   The Nestlé SMART Pack with marketing information on environmental benefits

Photo: Nestlé Australia Ltd

companies can use them to demonstrate compliance.[87] Like the APC, the CEN standards focus on the design process rather than specific outcomes. In contrast, the Chinese Excessive Packaging Law (2009) sets mandatory legal standards and controls for packaging.

Efficiency improvements are being pursued by most companies because they generally achieve both financial and environmental savings. Costco is a warehouse style retailer, whose corporate philosophy is to "Keep costs down and pass the savings on to our members".[88] One of the ways it does this is by optimizing packaging to reduce handling. Every product in Costco is delivered and displayed on pallets in a retail-ready format.

The use of lightweight packaging formats such as bags and pouches can lead to reductions in energy demand and greenhouse gas emissions compared with heavier and more conventional packaging formats provided that comparable protection is achieved. When Nestlé Oceania launched its Nescafé Gold coffee in a new laminated plastic pouch (Photo 3.2), it promoted the fact that non-renewable energy, water and greenhouse gas emissions were reduced by 73%, 66% and 75%, respectively, compared with a glass jar

87   EUROPEN (2005). *New Guide to CEN Packaging Standards.* Retrieved from http://www.europen-packaging.eu/component/publication/publication/10-press-releases/102-new-guide-to-cen-packaging-standards.html

88   PKN Packaging News (2014). *Less is More at Costco.* Sydney, Australia: Yaffa Publishing Group, p. 11.

over its life-cycle while providing equivalent protection for the product.[89] The Smart Pack was discontinued in 2013 and Nestle has since relaunched a compact pouch with additional environmental improvements.

In some cases improved efficiency is achieved through a redesign of the product *and* its packaging. Unilever, for example, launched smaller "compressed" deodorant sprays in 2013 for three of its brands—Sure, Dove and Vaseline—in the UK. Compared with the previous design, these use half the propellant, around 25% less packaging and a third less road transport. New technology for plastics packaging, which creates gas bubbles in the wall of the pack, is expected to save up to 27,000 tonnes of plastic and deliver cost savings of up to €50 million when applied across the full portfolio of Unilever products.[90]

Design for recycling remains a high priority for many companies, despite the potential life-cycle benefits of flexible plastic packaging, which is not widely recycled. This reflects the focus on recycling by government regulators and the strong association between recyclability and sustainability in the minds of many consumers (see the discussion on consumer perceptions in Section 3.3.1). Foodstuffs, a large retailer in New Zealand, redesigned its meat tray to improve its recyclability after negative coverage in the media (Case study 3.7.1).

Unilever is repositioning its packaging strategy to achieve more ambitious goals:

> We want to move to a circular economy, enabling more packaging
> to either remain in loops or have the best possible opportunity to be
> recycled … "Circular economy" means designing products so that
> resources are used in a cyclical way. Materials can be regenerated and
> constantly flow round a "closed loop" system, rather than being used
> once and then discarded.[91]

From a practical perspective Unilever's intention is to support a circular economy through strategies such as modular packaging, design for

89   RMIT (2015). *Life Cycle Assessment of Nestlé NESCAFE Gold Packaging*. Retrieved from http://www.rmit.edu.au/about/our-education/academic-schools/ architecture-and-design/research/research-centres-and-groups/centre-for-design-and-society/research-areas/sustainable-products-and-packaging/ projects/life-cycle-assessment-of-nestl-nescaf-gold-coffe

90   Unilever (2013), pp. 6-7.

91   Unilever (2016). *Moving to a Circular Economy*. Retrieved from https://www. unilever.com/sustainable-living/what-matters-to-you/recycling-and-moving -to-a-circular-economy.html

disassembly and reassembly, wider use of refills, recycling and using post-consumer recycled waste.[92]

3.5.3 Procurement

Most product manufacturers and retailers do not manufacture their own packaging, and therefore rely on their suppliers to help them achieve their corporate sustainability goals or targets for packaging. McDonald's, for example, works in partnership with suppliers to develop innovative and more sustainable packaging solutions.

There are over 35,000 McDonald's fast food restaurants operating in more than 100 countries and serving around 70 million customers each day. The company acknowledges that suppliers, employees and franchisees (like the three legs of a stool) are all essential to the achievement of its business strategy:

> Since McDonald's does not actually produce ingredients used in our menu items, our suppliers are a critical leg of our three-legged stool. We fully expect our suppliers to share our values and commitments and have implemented numerous programs to encourage this.[93]

Sustainability is an integral part of the way that McDonald's measures the performance of suppliers. All new packaging is evaluated using its "Eco-Filter" tool, which gives a score based on six weighted criteria: packaging weight, recycled content, renewable materials, material health, greenhouse gas emissions and end-of-life recovery options. A minimum Eco-Filter score is one of the requirements in McDonald's global packaging standards, along with other criteria including operational performance, consumer performance, regulatory compliance, design and brand image/graphics.[94]

Other large retailers are helping to drive packaging sustainability through their procurement processes. Walmart launched an online packaging scorecard in 2008 to gather information on suppliers' packaging and to rank it using nine weighted environmental indicators. Walmart's goal of a 5% reduction in packaging by 2013 was achieved through a range of initiatives including eliminating unnecessary packaging and reducing the mass of

---

92   *Ibid.*
93   McDonald's (2014), p. 11.
94   McDonald's Australia (2013). *Australian Packaging Covenant Action Plan 2013–2015.* Sydney Australia. Retrieved from https://mcdonalds.com.au/sites/mcdonalds.com.au/files/action_plan_2013_to_2015_final.pdf

remaining packaging materials.[95] The packaging scorecard has now been integrated into Walmart's Sustainability Index, which the company uses to engage suppliers in projects to improve the sustainability of their products. The index is being integrated into the procurement process, allowing buyers to "evaluate supplier performance against the biggest issues and opportunities across the life-cycle of their products". By the end of 2012 the index had been applied to 190 categories, or 30% of Walmart US sales.[96]

Many consumer goods manufacturers and retailers are using procurement policies and guidelines to improve the sustainability of paper-based packaging, for example by specifying packaging certified to recognized international standards. These include standards developed by the Forest Stewardship Council (FSC), which aim to promote environmentally appropriate, socially beneficial and economically viable management of the world's forests.[97] Many packaging companies and end users now specify that their packaging is "FSC certified" and use the FSC logo on the label.

In October 2011 toy manufacturer Mattel responded to the Greenpeace campaign (see "Environment groups" above) by launching new sustainable sourcing policies. These included maximizing post-consumer recycled content where possible; avoiding virgin fibre from "controversial sources"; and maximizing the percentage of fibre certified by a credible third party. Mattel announced that by 2015, 85% of its paper packaging would be composed of recycled material or sustainable fibre.[98] According to one media commentator, "[t]his was not just a huge win for Greenpeace, but also a huge reminder to APP and other companies: rainforest destruction is bad for business".[99]

3.5.4 Reuse and recycling

The recovery of packaging at the end of its life for either reuse or recycling is one of the key objectives of product stewardship. Companies are taking action in a variety of different ways to support packaging recovery, depending on their corporate priorities as well as local regulations and recycling services. Options may include reuse or refill systems, financial support for

---

95   Walmart (2014).
96   *Ibid.*, p. 63.
97   Forest Stewardship Council (2014). *Our Vision and Mission*. Retrieved from https://ic.fsc.org/en/about-fsc/vision-mission
98   Mattel (2011, October 11). *Mattel Announces Sustainable Sourcing Initiative*. Retrieved from http://investor.shareholder.com/mattel/releasedetail.cfm?releaseid=611230
99   Godelnik (2011).

recycling infrastructure, a company take-back programme, or participation in a collective industry compliance programme.

Corporate strategies need to adapt to local circumstances, including government policies, cultural norms around reuse or recycling, and available recycling services. To meet their sustainability goals in this area companies may need to collaborate with a range of stakeholders to achieve change. Unilever documents this challenge in its Waste and Packaging Strategy:

> The infrastructure for dealing with post-consumer waste varies hugely between countries. To meet our targets, recycling rates in some of our markets must double or even treble. We share a responsibility with our consumers, and with other players in the supply chain, to minimise packaging waste as far as possible, so we are seeking opportunities to contribute ideas, expertise and resources to shaping initiatives and policies to have the best chance of long-term success ... Unilever will evaluate individual initiatives and policies on their own merits, including their appropriateness to a country's context.[100]

3.5.4.1 Reuse or refill systems

Refill systems for beverage bottles have declined in most developed countries, with some exceptions. In Canada refillable bottles continue to be used for beer, driven by provincial regulations, economics and cultural preferences.[101] Many fast food restaurants provide a refill option for hot beverages, but take-up rates tend to be low. Starbucks aimed to serve 5% of its beverages in "personal tumblers" (refillable cups) by 2015, but in 2013 had achieved only 1.8%.[102]

Some companies have trialled in-store refill systems for liquid household products. In 2010 Asda supermarkets in the UK ran a trial that offered consumers the opportunity to save money by refilling private label fabric softeners in a plastic pouch that could be reused ten times in store. When the trial was announced, Julian Walker-Palin, Asda's head of corporate policy for sustainability and ethics told *Greener Packaging* magazine that the system provided benefits across the supply chain: "Manufacturers don't have to pack bottles, more product can be fitted on to distribution trucks and

100 Unilever (2015). *Our Waste & Packaging Strategy*. Retrieved from https://www.unilever.com/sustainable-living/the-sustainable-living-plan/reducing-environmental-impact/waste-and-packaging/index.html

101 GRRN (n.d.). *Canada's Experience with Refillable Beverage Containers*. Retrieved from http://refillables.grrn.org/content/canadas-experience-refillable-beverage-containers

102 Starbucks (2013).

consumers use less packaging".[103] The trial was not successful, however, and Asda decided not to continue with the service. Sales of the fabric conditioners used in the trial did not meet projections, and only a limited number of consumers refilled the pouches more than twice.[104]

Refill systems are largely confined to niche markets including health food stores. Restore Products, for example, has installed refill stations in natural product stores in the US for its own brand of plant-based household cleaning products.[105] Belgian company Ecover provides refill stations in hundreds of health food shops in the UK but claims that it would not be feasible to offer the same service in supermarkets.[106]

Almost all of the growth in reusable packaging has been for business-to-business applications. A common example is the reusable, "retail-ready" fresh produce crates being introduced by retailers for fresh produce (Photo 3.3). Data from the two compliance organizations in Belgium (Fost Plus for household packaging and Val-l-Pac for non-household packaging) shows that reusable packaging put onto the market by Fost Plus and Val-l-Pac members increased by 3.7% between 2011 and 2012, and all of this growth was in industrial and commercial applications.[107] Over the previous ten years the quantity of reusable household beverage packaging in Belgium had remained stable while industrial and commercial use steadily increased.

3.5.4.2 Financial support for recycling

Companies that have a commitment to improve recycling rates for their packaging, such as Unilever, Nestlé and Starbucks, realize that they can't achieve this on their own. If the infrastructure for recycling their packaging is non-existent or inadequate, they often work with external organizations to find a solution.

103 Mohan, A.M. (2009, July 19). UK's Asda supermarkets to trial refillable packaging. Greener Package. Retrieved from http://www.greenerpackage.com/reusability/uk%E2%80%99s_asda_trial_refillable_packaging?webSyncID=8b1435e9-8063-8653-7e03-5e8199db366d&sessionGUID=e3107942-42d3-3b2a-0011-3c96c7a4e7d2

104 Mesure, S. (2011, January 30). Shoppers' green fatigue hits refill revolution. *Independent*. Retrieved from http://www.independent.co.uk/environment/green-living/shoppers-green-fatigue-hits-refill-revolution-2198462.html

105 Imhoff, D. (2004). *Paper or Plastic: Searching for Solutions to an Overpackaged World*. San Francisco: Sierra Club Books.

106 Mesure (2011).

107 IVCIE (2013). *Activity Report 2013*. Brussels, Belgium: Interregionale Verpakkingscommissie, p. 28.

Photo 3.3   Reusable retail-ready crates for fresh produce

Photo: Helen Lewis

While taking action within its own stores to recover used packaging, Starbucks found that some issues required collaboration with its competitors, municipalities and paper mills to improve the recyclability of paper-based packaging.[108] In Brazil, Unilever works with other members of the global Consumer Goods Forum and a local NGO, CEMPRE, to support recycling through retail drop-off points and cooperatives that sort used packaging materials for recycling. In 2016 the company supported 141 recycling stations and 45 cooperatives that generate income for workers and their families. In Indonesia Unilever is piloting a new technology to convert plastic sachet waste into an industrial fuel.[109]

Another example of financial support for recycling is the Closed Loop Fund in the US, which is supported by Procter & Gamble, Johnson & Johnson, Walmart, Coca-Cola, PepsiCo, Keurig Green Mountain, Goldman Sachs and Unilever. The Closed Loop Fund was established in 2014 by consumer goods manufacturers and retailers to increase the recycling rate for packaging and food waste. Low interest loans are provided to municipalities, and below-market interest rate loans to the private sector, to improve the infrastructure for collection, sorting, reprocessing and manufacture into new products.[110]

One of the objectives for industry partners is to improve access to recycled materials. CEO and co-founder of the Closed Loop Fund, Ron Gonen, has argued that support for kerbside recycling also helps to achieve several "bottom line benefits" for corporations.[111] These include:

- Reduced operating costs through increased supply of recycled materials and reduced price volatility

- Meeting consumer demand for products that can be recycled

- Proactively working with state and local governments on legislation

- Providing shareholders and consumers with clear metrics on sustainable practices and greenhouse gas goals.[112]

108 MacKerron, C. (2015); Starbucks (2013).
109 Unilever (2016).
110 Closed Loop Fund (n.d.). *About the Closed Loop Fund*. Retrieved from http://www.closedloopfund.com/page/about
111 Gonen, R. (2015). *Closed Loop Fund Presentation* to *Increasing Packaging Recycling in the US*. Webinar: Product Stewardship Institute.
112 *Ibid.*

An example cited by Gonen is Walmart, which supported the Closed Loop Fund after finding that suppliers couldn't meet its request for more recycled material in products because of inadequate supply.[113]

3.5.4.3 Voluntary industry take-back programmes

Companies are often prepared to support voluntary take-back programmes for packaging, albeit for different reasons.

The REDcycle programme in Australia (Case study 3.7.2) collects "soft plastics" such as shopping bags, cling wrap and biscuit wrappers for recycling. The need for a recycling solution for these plastics, which are generally not accepted in kerbside collections, had been identified by the Australian Food and Grocery Council in its packaging sustainability strategy.[114] Some of the Council's members formed a partnership with RED Group to fund a collection programme through supermarkets ("REDcycle"). Founder and Director Liz Kasell describes the programme as "... a less conventional and more collaborative approach to a significant and over-looked waste stream".[115]

Companies that joined in the REDcycle programme were not responding to a regulatory threat. Most were driven by their corporate sustainability targets or Australian Packaging Covenant commitments.[116]

In contrast, the threat of regulation was the catalyst for both PETCO in South Africa and the Glass Packaging Forum in New Zealand. PET resin manufacturers, converters, bottlers and importers in South Africa formed a company (PETCO) in 2004 to improve waste management and recycling of PET packaging. PETCO's activities, which include subsidies for collection and recycling, are funded by a voluntary levy paid by converters on PET resin purchased and grants from brand owners, resin producers and retailers.[117]

An important driver for the PET industry in South Africa was a desire to avoid regulation, following the introduction of minimum weights and a

---

113 *Ibid.*
114 AFGC (2012). *Future of Packaging White Paper.* Canberra, Australia: Australian Food & Grocery Council. Retrieved from http://www.helenlewisresearch.com. au/wp-content/uploads/2012/12/AFGC-White-Paper-7Mar2012.pdf
115 Personal communication (interview) with L. Kasell, Director of Development, The RED Group, 14 August 2014.
116 Lewis & Crittenden (2014).
117 PETCO (2016). Who we are. Retrieved from http://petco.co.za/who-we-are/

mandatory levy on plastic shopping bags in 2003.[118] Instead they negotiated a voluntary memorandum of understanding with the Department of Environmental Affairs, which gave them flexibility to determine how they would achieve mutually agreed targets.

Similarly, Case study 3.7.3 describes how the beverage industry in New Zealand responded when the market for recycled glass collapsed in 2005, and the central government threatened to "intervene". Glass manufacturers and users worked together to establish an industry stewardship programme that provided short-term subsidies for collectors and invested in more sustainable collection and recycling systems.

Another voluntary model is TerraCycle's "post-back" collection service for hard-to-recycle plastic packaging and other waste streams. Based on the philosophy that "there is no such thing as waste", TerraCycle works with brand owners and manufacturers to find new ways to reuse or recycle packaging that is not accepted in mainstream programmes. TerraCycle's solution is an alternative business model that founder Tom Szaky calls "sponsored waste".[119] The company's Global Vice President for Business Development and Client Services, Michael Waas, explains the model:

> We focus on recycling non-recyclable wastes. We do that by working with the manufacturers, [who] ... subsidise the recycling of their waste. What we've learned is that every waste stream in the world is technically recyclable. The reason why some things are considered non-recyclable is that ... collection and recycling costs more than the recovered material is worth. We work with companies who subsidise the collection and recycling costs and allow TerraCycle to collect non-recyclable waste. We specialise in turning that recovered waste into something usable, usually a recycled material that can then be sold to a manufacturing partner.[120]

TerraCycle has expanded from its US base to become a global operation. By 2015 the company was working with over 100 brand owners in 21 countries, including the USA, Canada, Japan, Israel, Australia, New Zealand and many countries in Western Europe. National programmes (called

118 Nashman, A. (2009). Extended producer responsibility for packaging waste in South Africa: Current approaches and lessons learned. *Resource Conservation and Recycling*, 54(3), 155-162.

119 Szaky, T. (2011, April 20). How many business models can one company have? *New York Times*. Retrieved from http://boss.blogs.nytimes.com/2011/04/20/how-many-business-models-can-one-company-have/

120 Personal communication (interview) with M. Waas, Global Vice President, Business Development and Client Services, 8 April, 2015.

"Brigades") are established to collect materials that were previously not recycled. Some programmes have a cost, but most offer free shipping and a charity donation for each item of rubbish collected.

As You Sow criticized the TerraCycle programme as nothing but a "stop-gap" measure, but it can also be seen (using an alternative metaphor) as an important stepping stone on the pathway to more established recycling systems.[121] For example, one of TerraCycle's programmes, for Activia polypropylene (PP) yoghurt tubs in the UK, was wound back in 2014 as municipal recycling programmes for PP became available to most of the population.[122] Like the Australian REDcycle programme, TerraCycle plays a valuable role in developing innovative end markets for recycled materials; raising awareness of recycling among consumers and manufacturers; and encouraging manufacturers to get more involved in recycling their own products.

3.5.4.4 Compliance with EPR laws

In countries with established EPR laws, most companies join a producer responsibility organization to meet their take-back obligations for household packaging. In Europe there are at least 80 PROs operating just for packaging.[123] Within this context companies can maximize the benefits of product stewardship by "finding the best form of collective compliance".[124]

The type of producer responsibility ranges from financial only (payment of a fee) through to full organizational responsibility. In Taiwan, for example, companies simply pay a fee to the government to fund recycling. In contrast, most producers in Europe must join a PRO that contributes to the costs of collection and recycling on their behalf. In Belgium municipalities are responsible for collection and sorting of household packaging, with their costs reimbursed by the PRO, Fost Plus. Under this arrangement producers have partial organizational responsibility, whereas in Austria and Germany they have full responsibility.[125]

Almost all of the EPR laws for packaging in the EU allow for individual producer responsibility, i.e. companies can take back and recycle their own

---

121   MacKerron (2015).
122   M. Waas, personal communication.
123   Bio Intelligence Service (2014). *Development of Guidance on Extended Producer Responsibility (EPR)*. Report to European Commission—DG Environment.
124   Personal communication (interview) with D. Perchard, Managing Director, Perchards Ltd., 2 October 2013.
125   Bio Intelligence Service (2014).

TABLE 3.6 Comparison of EPR schemes for packaging in selected countries in the EU, 2014

Member state	Number of collective PROs	Costs covered by producers	Producer fees (€/tonne of packaging recovered)
Austria	6	100% of collection and net treatment costs for separately collected packaging, plus some other costs.	172
Belgium	2	100% of collection and net treatment costs for separately collected packaging, plus some other costs.	119
Czech Republic	1	As above.	91
France	1	75% of "optimized" collection and net treatment costs for separately collected household packaging, plus other costs.	153
Netherlands	1	100% of collection and net treatment costs for separately collected packaging, plus some other costs.	52
UK	22	An estimated 10% of collection and net treatment costs for separately collected household packaging.	10

Source: Based on Bio Intelligence Service (2014), pp. 43-71

packaging.[126] This is more common for business-to-business rather than household packaging. In Belgium, for example, 194 companies were registered as individual compliers for industrial and commercial packaging in 2013.[127]

Producers' compliance costs also vary widely. Analysis of six case studies in the EU (Table 3.6) estimated that fees paid per tonne of packaging recovered ranged from €10/t in the UK to €172/t in Austria.[128] Costs are dependent on a number of factors, including the extent to which financial responsibility is shared with local government. According to the EU study, producers in the UK pay a lower fee because they are only covering an estimated 10% of collection and recycling costs. Unlike many European schemes, the UK system was not intended to cover full costs.

126 *Ibid.*
127 IVCIE (2014). *Activity Report 2014*. Commission Interregionale de l'emballage: Brussels, Belgium, p. 21. Retrieved from http://www.ivcie.be/admin/upload/page/file/564.pdf
128 Bio Intelligence Service (2014), p. 71.

Cost-sharing arrangements can be contentious when they are considered unfair or inefficient. In response to pressure from stakeholders, the Japanese Packaging and Container Law was amended in 2006 to, among other changes, shift more of the costs onto producers.[129] The law had previously been criticized by citizens groups and municipalities for not fully incorporating EPR principles and providing very weak incentives for packaging reduction.[130] The European Commission's circular economy package proposes that producers pay the true end-of-life costs of products to encourage design for reuse or recycling.[131]

In Ontario, producers must pay for half of the net costs of collecting and recycling packaging through the Blue Box kerbside recycling programme, which is run by municipalities. This has been renegotiated to keep producer costs down:

> Because of producers' protests over what they attribute to be government waste and inefficiency, producers only have to pay half of what the entire system would cost if "operating under best practices", and downward adjustments are made to municipalities costs if their practices do not have certain best-practice elements.[132]

3.6 Conclusions

The examples and case studies presented in this chapter highlight the diversity of approaches to packaging stewardship within firms. Leading companies in different sectors, including food, beverage, retail and consumer electronics, have sustainability policies that specifically address packaging. Many of these companies have integrated their sustainability goals in product development and procurement processes, and are working in partnership with industry peers and supply chain partners to address broader industry challenges.

129   Lewis, H., & Akenji, L. (2012). *A Stakeholder Framework for Product Stewardship: Packaging Policy Case Studies from Australia and Japan*. Hayama, Japan: Institute for Global Environmental Strategies.
130   *Ibid.*
131   European Commission (2015). *Closing the Loop—An EU Action Plan for the Circular Economy 2015*. Brussels, Belgium.
132   SAIC (2012), pp. 4-9.

Government regulations have played an important role in promoting corporate responsibility for packaging, particularly at end of life. EPR regulations in Europe have helped to institutionalize the principle of producer responsibility within firms, and their influence has extended to other jurisdictions around the world.

Regulations are not the only driver. Many of the actions outlined in this chapter were taken in response to cost pressures (e.g. shifts to more efficient packaging), the expectations of customers, or pressure from environment groups on issues such as waste and deforestation. Regulatory compliance is important, but high profile brands such as Mattel, Starbucks, McDonald's and Nestlé are equally focused on their reputation and the need to operate in alignment with community values and expectations. Companies know for example, that "rainforest destruction is bad for business".[133] The examples and case studies cited in this chapter provide evidence that companies will take action voluntarily when there is a business case to do so.

This opens up a range of policy options for governments, depending on the strength of other drivers and the commitment of industry groups to voluntary action. Voluntary agreements with government, under threat of more onerous regulation, have arguably been successful for packaging in Australia and New Zealand. Industry groups in Canada and the US are advocating EPR regulations that provide companies with greater flexibility and self-determination than European models. The advantages of voluntary initiatives where there is strong industry support for action and the need to work with regulators to achieve back-up regulations where this is lacking (i.e. where there are large numbers of free-riders) are explored further in Chapter 6.

3.7 Case studies

Case study 3.7.1 Design for recycling at Foodstuffs New Zealand

3.7.1.1 Summary

Foodstuffs New Zealand is the country's largest grocery retailer and distributor, with 763 sites. It comprises three separate business entities, including two cooperatives (one in the North Island and one in the South Island) of independent stores. There is also a federation body, Foodstuffs (NZ) Limited

---

133 Godelnik (2011).

("Foodstuffs"), which manages the supply of own-brand products and provides support on corporate issues such as sustainability. Retail brands include New World and PAK'nSAVE supermarkets and Four Square convenience stores.

In 2013 the company developed a new corporate approach to sustainability that includes a commitment to recyclable packaging for its own-brand products. Two successful redesign projects, for seafood boxes and meat trays, demonstrate the benefits of a collaborative approach to product stewardship involving consumers, packaging suppliers and local councils. The shared value outcomes include a reduction in waste to landfill, improved consumer satisfaction and cost savings.

3.7.1.2 Drivers for product stewardship

In 2012 Foodstuffs received "awards" for worst packaging in a public poll called the Unpackit NZ Packaging Award, organized by community group Wanaka Wastebusters. The awards were for two of Foodstuffs' own-label products:

- Fresh vegetables on a polystyrene tray with plastic overwrap (first prize)

- Multi-meat packs that contained four individually wrapped pieces of meat on a polystyrene tray and then wrapped in plastic (third prize).[134]

The reason given by the organizers for these awards was that foamed polystyrene trays were not easily recycled in New Zealand (NZ). At the time of the announcement, Foodstuffs reported that the company had already started to implement a sustainability programme and was looking at ways to reduce its use of polystyrene trays.[135]

In 2013 Foodstuffs received additional nominations, including one for a half-watermelon on a foam tray. According to Sustainability Manager Mike Sammons, the negative media publicity that Foodstuffs received as a result of the awards provided further impetus for a packaging redesign.[136]

---

134 Caliendo, H. (2012, June 11). And the worst packaging award for 2012 goes to ... *Plastics Today*. Retrieved from http://www.plasticstoday.com/blogs/And-the-worst-packaging-award-for-2012-goes-to-0604201201

135 *Ibid.*

136 Personal communication (interview) with M. Sammons, Sustainability Manager, Foodstuffs, 2 March 2015.

In that same year Foodstuffs decided to develop a new, corporate approach to sustainability. Prior to this sustainability issues were managed by individual stores. There were pockets of good practice but no overall policy or strategy. Mike Sammons was employed as the first sustainability manager and started to develop strategies on key issues including waste, energy and packaging. This included a commitment by Foodstuffs to shift to 100% recyclable packaging for own-brand products.

3.7.1.3 Stewardship strategies

Two design projects illustrate the company's approach to packaging sustainability and recyclability. Both projects involved extensive consultation to understand the fate of packaging at end of life and collaboration with suppliers to find a better solution.

Recyclable cardboard seafood boxes

A waste audit in stores revealed the high costs of managing used expanded polystyrene (EPS) seafood boxes. These costs, estimated to be around NZ$1.30 per box, included storage space at back-of-store, time spent breaking up boxes for disposal and waste collection costs.

The search for a new solution started with a reassessment of packaging requirements. EPS had been used for a long time because it kept the product cool during transport. Consultation with supply chain partners revealed that seafood was transported in refrigerated vehicles, which meant that packaging did not require high levels of insulation.

Foodstuffs approached packaging suppliers with a specification for cardboard seafood packaging that was manufactured from recycled material, was 100% recyclable and had slightly better insulation than a conventional cardboard box. Prototypes were developed and then tested to ensure that cool temperatures could be maintained throughout the supply chain. Following these tests a new seafood box was rolled out for all Foodstuffs seafood in the North Island, and is being considered by independent suppliers.

According to Mike Sammons, the solution emerged from a fresh look at the problem:

> It's a cardboard box, just slightly thicker—it's not rocket science. It just took someone to go back of store, and to say, "do you know how much this is costing to dispose of? Do you know how much these cardboard boxes cost to buy?"… The stores just thought "this is something we have to do, cram it into the bin", until a few of the stores said "this is ridiculous, we must be able to come up with something better than this".

Recyclable plastic meat trays

Meat is traditionally packed on a black, foamed polystyrene tray, which is not recyclable in New Zealand. It also has a separate soaker pad. Plastic recyclers generally don't accept foamed polystyrene, and meat juices create additional handling issues because of the potential for them to contain pathogens. According to Mike Sammons, Foodstuffs use around 100 million meat trays each year, and all of the polystyrene trays go to landfill.[137] The cost to consumers is around 6–8 cents a tray because municipalities are shifting to "pay-as-you-throw" pricing models for waste disposal.

Mike Sammons began by speaking to local councils and recyclers to find out which materials were recycled at kerbside and what their preference would be for meat trays. After that a decision was made to use polyethylene terephthalate (PET), and preferably recycled PET (rPET). He notes that this approach appears to be unusual:

> The interesting thing about the process is that it became apparent that packaging manufacturers never spoke to Councils; retailers never spoke to councils … Councils didn't really speak to recyclers about what could or couldn't be recycled. The chain was broken, no one spoke to each other. Auckland City Council said to me "you're the first retailer who's ever come to speak to us about packaging, and about recycling".[138]

The company invited proposals from packaging companies for a new PET or rPET meat tray without a soaker pad but with the ability to handle meat juices. After two years of development the tender was awarded in early 2015 to a local NZ company, Alto Packaging, for its innovative and recyclable tray with 50% rPET (Photo 3.4).

The design project was supported by consumer research on packaging. A survey through the New World Facebook page received 8,500 responses, with the overwhelming majority (80%) supporting a shift away from polystyrene meat trays. Over 60% also said that packaging could influence their choice of supermarket. According to Sammons, "that gave me the impetus to go to initial trials".

The new meat trays were successfully trialled in selected stores in 2015 and rolled out nationally in 2016.

---

137 *Ibid.*
138 *Ibid.*

PHOTO 3.4   Mike Sammons, Sustainability Manager, with the recyclable PET meat tray

Photo: Foodstuffs New Zealand

3.7.1.4 Shared value outcomes

The most important environmental benefit is the significant reduction in waste to landfill. EPS and foamed polystyrene are not widely recycled in NZ, with most going to landfill. The new seafood box can be recycled by retail stores with other cardboard packaging, while consumers are able to add the meat tray to their kerbside recycling bin. Foodstuffs has estimated that "New World and PAK'nSAVE customers can avoid sending the equivalent of 14 Olympic size swimming pools full of polystyrene to landfill each year".[139]

The seafood box is less expensive to buy, and instead of paying NZ$1.30 per box for disposal the stores receive a rebate from their waste contractor. Freight costs for seafood have fallen 16% per year because the packaging takes up less space. The overall saving is "hundreds of thousands of dollars".[140]

139 Foodstuffs New Zealand (2015). *New World and PAK'nSAVE Butcheries Announce Move to Banish Polystyrene Trays.* Wellington, NZ.

140 M. Sammons, personal communication.

The new meat tray costs the same as the previous version but is expected to generate additional benefits for Foodstuffs including increased loyalty from customers. So far customer feedback has been "extremely positive", with 90% rating the packaging as better than the tradition polystyrene tray, 8% rating it the same and 2% preferring the old foam tray.[141] The new packaging has also attracted praise from Wanaka Wastebusters, creator of the Unpackit NZ Packaging Awards. Its spokeswoman called the Foodstuffs meat packaging "groundbreaking".[142]

The shift to recyclable meat trays will also save disposal costs, which are borne by ratepayers rather than consumers. Councils in NZ are increasingly moving to the "polluter pays" principle through "pay by weight" charging for waste disposal. Foodstuffs estimated the cost of disposal to be around 5–8 cents a tray, so in the longer term the initiative will save their customers money.

Case study 3.7.2 REDcycle soft plastics recycling

> [Our program] is founded in the understanding that we can't solve problems in isolation—that's where collaboration comes in. The model depends on everyone involved in the life cycle of a product also being engaged in its recovery. We're dealing with a very low value mixed material, which is why landfill was previously the only option. We had to develop a model that looked at the product in a completely different way (Liz Kasell, Founder and Director, RED Group).[143]

3.7.2.1 Summary

RED Group, an Australian based consulting and recycling company, has developed an innovative stewardship programme for "soft plastics" through supermarkets in partnership with packaging manufacturers, brand owners, retailers and recyclers. Soft plastics include checkout bags and flexible packaging used for biscuits, pasta, rice, breakfast cereals and other food products.

The programme, called REDcycle, is innovative because it collects a mixed plastics waste stream that has very little commercial value; it provides a solution for packaging that was not being collected through municipal

---

141 Personal communication (email) with M. Sammons, 13 October 2015.

142 Fulton, T. (2015, September 23). Foodstuffs trials recyclable plastic meat tray. *Stuff.co.nz*. Retrieved from http://www.stuff.co.nz/business/money/72256398/foodstuffs-trials-recyclable-plastic-meat-trays

143 L. Kasell, personal communication.

collections; and it is entirely funded by industry partners on a voluntary basis.

3.7.2.2 Drivers for product stewardship

The project began as an initiative by RED Group to collect and recycle soft plastics through schools. It was the brainchild of Founder and Director Liz Kasell, who explained how the idea came to her:

> It started with a really innocent question ... why is my hard plastic being picked up at kerbside for recycling, yet I'm seeing how much soft plastic is being generated in every single part of what I do ... and none of it is being picked up in my kerbside bin. That's plastic too. Why?
>
> ... I expected this to be a quite small project that was really run through schools. I expected the model to only suit schools because I wanted to combine it with an educational program ...[144]

The "quite small" schools-based project evolved into a national collection and recycling programme, in part because it addressed a problem that had also been identified by the food and beverage industry. The Australian Food & Grocery Council (AFGC) developed a packaging white paper in order "to support a more strategic and proactive role for the industry in packaging sustainability".[145] The white paper identified the recovery of soft plastics as one of its priorities for product stewardship, and AFGC subsequently worked with RED Group to find a national solution for soft plastics.

There was a more direct business case for retailers and manufacturers. For Coles Supermarkets it was about the value they could provide to customers. When Kasell first approached the retailer to seek support for the project she met with representatives from waste, sustainability, innovation and marketing before finding a strong internal champion in the customer care group:

> This is something Coles felt they were doing for their customers. It was really easy to "sell" to senior management as an opportunity for customers to do the right thing ... that a lot of Australians out there were starting to care how much plastic was going in their waste bin. "Let's take responsibility for what we're putting out into the market, and give our customers a way to bring it back".[146]

---

144 *Ibid.*
145 AFGC (2012), p. 4.
146 L. Kasell, personal communication.

After the company agreed to become a partner in the programme, the marketing team was very supportive. The programme provided a positive story that the team could promote to the media about the company's commitment to the environment and to assisting its customers to recycle tonnes of packaging that was previously destined for landfill.

The motivation for product manufacturers who agreed to fund the national roll-out was similar. Nicole Hall, Senior Communications Manager for Kellogg Australia New Zealand, explained why the company was keen to join the programme:

> RED Group provided us with a solution to a problem that we hadn't yet been able to solve, which was providing consumers with a recycling options for our cereal liners. In our Covenant action plan we had committed to looking for a solution. RED Group also brought to the table a very well-structured proposal on how commercial partners could work with their organization. It was a compelling solution that helped us make progress against our corporate commitments.[147]

For companies such as Kellogg it was also a way of meeting a strategic environmental objective. Kellogg's five-year action plan for the Australian Packaging Covenant had included a commitment to investigate recycling options for cereal liner bags.[148] REDcycle provided the company with a ready-made solution.

3.7.2.3 Stewardship strategies

The project began as a small pilot in the Australian state of Victoria. With seed funding from the Victorian State Government, RED Group started collecting used checkout bags and polypropylene "green bags" through primary schools.

This evolved into a partnership with Coles to collect all soft plastics in its supermarkets (Photo 3.5). A trial in Melbourne in 2011 was followed by a national roll-out in 2012. The collected plastics were manufactured into recycled plastic products such as bench seats that Coles then donated to local primary schools across the country. Initially the service was only offered in 100 stores in metropolitan Melbourne, but after a successful trial it was rolled out to all 480 Coles stores nationally. A grant from the Australian

---

147 Lewis & Crittenden (2014), p. 3.

148 Kellogg (Aust) Pty Ltd (2010). *Australian Packaging Covenant Action Plan 2011–2015*. Sydney. Retrieved from http://www.packagingcovenant.org.au/data/ActionPlans/Kellogg%20%28Aust%29%20Pty%20Ltd_AP.pdf

PHOTO 3.5 REDcycle collection bin in a Coles supermarket

Photo: RED Group

Packaging Covenant (the co-regulated product stewardship programme for packaging) assisted with infrastructure costs.

Since then, the programme has continued to expand with the support of packaging manufacturers and food and grocery brand owners. Liz Kasell initially approached the AFGC, who strongly endorsed the programme and helped to set up meetings with its members. Her initial target was the "top ten" brand owners whose products made up a large percentage of recovered plastic packaging, and all of the companies signed up to provide ongoing financial support. One of the keys to their support was an appreciation that this was something that their customers were willing to support:

> The brand owners were surprised … they thought their plastic pack-
> aging had been going to landfill. The program was only in Melbourne
> at that stage. The fact that someone had been sitting there in Mel-
> bourne pulling bags apart and analysing packaging types, returned by
> customers … Not only recovered, *returned* by customers. From a stew-
> ardship perspective that's really key. That really resonated with brand
> owners … [that their] customers were willing to go to the effort of tak-
> ing all this packaging, saving it and taking it back to Coles for recy-
> cling. I said to the brand owners, your customers are willing to do this,
> what are you prepared to do? Are you willing to meet them halfway?
> The halfway point is supporting this program so we can expand it and
> offer it to more customers across the country. That was really it.[149]

In 2014 the programme started to roll out to Woolworths supermarkets, bringing the total to 500 drop-off points. The collected plastics are sorted by RED Group, then sent to a local recycling business, Replas, to be turned into plastic bench seats, bollards, lumber replacement and other moulded plastic products. Participating brand owners are able to place the REDcycle logo (Fig. 3.6) on their packaging with advice on how to recycle.

In 2014 the funding partners (stewards) included Amcor Flexibles, Arnott's, Birds Eye, Mondelēz, Coles, George Weston Foods, Goodman Fielder, Kellogg's, Kimberly-Clark, SunRice, Unilever and Woolworths.

3.7.2.4 Shared value outcomes

The amount of soft packaging recycled each year through REDcycle is relatively small compared with the amount going to landfill, but it continues to grow. The programme's website states that "[m]ore than 150 million pieces of plastic—enough to circle Australia twice—have been saved from landfill by the REDcycle programme since the programme was launched nationally

149 L. Kasell, personal communication.

This packaging is recyclable in Australia through
the REDcycle Program. To find your nearest
drop off location, visit www.redcycle.net.au.

FIGURE 3.6   REDcycle logo on packaging

in 2012".[150] In 2015 the number of collected pieces had increased to more than 200 million.

The programme provides brand owners with a way of supporting the recovery of their plastics bags and wrappers. This in turn allows them to deliver on their corporate sustainability and their Australian Packaging Covenant commitments. Kasell explains it this way:

> Many of the brand owners had a range of products that were packaged in various materials—cardboard, glass, hard plastics—so they were able to provide a kerbside solution for a number of products in their range, but soft plastics was this major gap. They had no solution other than [advice on their packaging], "don't litter". That really was a huge gap for many of them, especially for companies like Arnott's, where the majority of what they have is in soft plastic. They had customers calling up every now and then saying "we love our Tim Tams but we hate putting our wrappers in the bin". We came to them with [a solution that] … was already working.[151]

Retailers also benefit because they can provide a service to environmentally aware consumers and can demonstrate that they are achieving environmental and social outcomes. On its corporate responsibility website Coles states that:

---

150 RED Group (2015). *REDcycle News*. Retrieved from http://redcycle.net.au/redcycle/redcycle-news
151 L. Kasell, personal communication.

PHOTO 3.6   A bench made from recycled plastics at the entrance to Coles Supermarket, Fairy Meadow, NSW

Photo: Helen Lewis

> Coles now provides soft plastics recycling program in over 470 stores across Australia and in June 2013 our customers are recycling an average of 4 tonnes of soft plastic packaging material each week. Through our partnership with the RED Group and Replas we have been able to recycle this material into garden seats to schools and kindergartens.[152]

The programme has a high profile at the entrance to Coles' newer stores (Photo 3.6).

152 Coles Supermarkets Australia (n.d.). *Recycling and Waste Reduction.* Retrieved from   https://www.coles.com.au/corporate-responsibility/responsible -sourcing-and-sustainability/waste

Case study 3.7.3 Glass Packaging Forum

> A voluntary glass packaging product stewardship scheme is the best
> way to protect the interests of members in the face of continued calls
> on government for mandatory product stewardship schemes or the
> introduction of container deposit legislation enabled through the leg-
> islation (Glass Packaging Forum).[153]

3.7.3.1 Summary

The Glass Packaging Forum in New Zealand promotes the environmental
benefits of glass packaging and manages the government-accredited Glass
Packaging Stewardship Program. Established in 2006, the Forum provides
grants for recycling and litter infrastructure and educational activities.

The environmental outcomes include a 69% recycling rate for container
glass in 2015 and an increase in the amount of glass diverted to high value
"closed loop" applications. A direct benefit for the packaging supply chain
is the avoidance of a mandatory container deposit scheme or take-back
regulations.

3.7.3.2 Drivers for product stewardship

In New Zealand product stewardship for packaging has been promoted
through voluntary agreements rather than regulation. There have been two
"accords" between the packaging supply chain (brand owners, retailers and
manufacturers), the central government and local governments, with the
second accord signed in August 2005. Industry signatories agreed to work
towards more sustainable packaging outcomes and certain material recovery rates (55% for glass by 2008). Industry plans were coordinated by the
Packaging Council of New Zealand.

According to John Webber, General Manager of the Glass Packaging
Forum and previously the CEO of the Packaging Council, by November 2005
glass recycling was a "shambles":

> For the first time in New Zealand's history the supply of recycled glass
> supply exceeded what the glass makers could use. As a result, particu-
> larly in certain outlying areas, some glass ended up being stockpiled.
> The glass maker dropped its price for colours it didn't want to buy.
>
> I received a phone call from the office of the then Minister, Mar-
> ion Hobbs, a Labour Minister. I was advised that in her view industry
> had dropped the ball between August and November, and that pres-
> sure from local government would require the central government to

153 Glass Packaging Forum (2015). *Product Stewardship Scheme*. Retrieved from
www.glassforum.org.nz/product-stewardship-new/

> intervene. Without knowing what that intervention would be and how
> long it would take, I rang Lion, DB Breweries and Coca-Cola. [I was
> told] ring the Ministers office and tell her staff that the major play-
> ers in the glass packaged goods industry would address the problem.
> Please give us time.[154]

A group was formed within the Packaging Council called the Glass Users
Group, to develop a coordinated response. Millions of dollars were raised
from members to subsidize local collectors and freight of the unwanted
glass to Australia for recycling. This cleared the stockpiles but subsidies
were not considered to be a sustainable solution.

A new organization was then formed outside the Packaging Council,
called the Glass Packaging Forum. A levy system was introduced to fund
recycling and other activities, with companies charged a fee per tonne of
glass that they manufactured or used in the New Zealand market place.
These companies include the major glass packaging manufacturers, brand
owners and retailers.

3.7.3.3 Stewardship strategies

After the initial stockpiles had been cleared the group decided that subsi-
dizing collections was not acceptable in the long run. Webber notes that:

> We'd solved the short term problem [but] would need to find another
> way. The other way was to look for alternative uses for glass, particu-
> larly in provincial areas.[155]

Grants were provided to municipalities and community groups for projects that would collect more glass in a "furnace ready" form, i.e. colour-
sorted and ready to be recycled back into packaging (see Photo 3.7 for an
example).

At the time municipalities were starting to move away from separate
collection containers for glass at kerbside, which allowed the bottles to be
colour-sorted in the truck. The new "single-stream" bins reduced the quality of the collected glass, with mixed colours and more breakage, making it
less attractive to the glass manufacturer.

To address this new challenge, the Forum also invested in research and
development to open up new markets for crushed glass, such as top dress-
ing for golf courses, mulch for vineyards, as a filtration medium for waste-
water treatment and in road making and construction.

---

154 Personal communication (interview) with J. Webber, 23 October 2014.
155 *Ibid.*

PHOTO 3.7   Collection point for colour-sorted glass containers

Photo: Glass Packaging Forum

Two of the Glass Packaging Forum's programmes have now been accredited by the government under the Waste Minimization Act:

- The Glass Packaging Scheme, which will fund initiatives that aim to increase the recycling rate to 78% by 2017

- The Public Place Recycling & Litter Abatement Scheme, which aims to increase the availability of recycling bins in public places and reduce litter volumes by 10% by 2020

In 2014 a new organization was established called the Packaging Forum Inc., which addresses the environmental impacts of a wider range of packaging materials. The Glass Packaging Forum is aligned with this group.

3.7.3.4 Shared value outcomes

Over the four years to 2012–13 the environmental benefits include:

- Over 50,000 tonnes of glass recycled through projects or funding from the scheme

- An increase in the percentage of glass recycled as a percentage of consumption from 66% to 69%

- An increase in the quantity of glass recycled into higher value or "closed loop" applications.[156]

A clear benefit for the industry is that voluntary initiatives have (so far) avoided the need for regulations such as a mandatory deposit on beverage containers. The industry's strategy to avoid regulation began with the Packaging Accord and subsidies for freight, and later evolved into accredited programmes to address glass recycling and litter more broadly. According to Webber:

> … [we] realized that if we were going to mitigate against the possibility of [deposits] being introduced, one of the things we could do was meet the government's request that industry consider formal accredited product stewardship schemes.[157]

The transition to the Packaging Forum was driven by the need to develop more effective product stewardship programmes for other materials, such as plastics and metals. The industry is up-front about its preference for voluntary stewardship. According to the Packaging Forum's promotional brochure:

> New voluntary schemes will provide industry with better protection against calls for legislation to be enacted and will demonstrate to New Zealanders that industry is committed to delivering whole of life solutions to packaging waste.[158]

156 Glass Packaging Forum (n.d.). *Key Performance Indicators.* Retrieved from www.glassforum.org.nz/downloads/ps_kpis.pdf

157 J. Webber, personal communication.

158 The Packaging Forum (2014). *A New Packaging Organisation: Focused on Community Outcomes.* Auckland, New Zealand: Packaging Forum.

4
Electrical and electronic equipment

4.1 Introduction

Waste electrical and electronic equipment (WEEE or "e-waste") has become an important focus for product stewardship policy and practice in recent years. E-waste has been defined as "all types of electrical and electronic equipment (EEE) and its parts that have been discarded by their owner as waste without the intention of re-use".[1]

The quantity of e-waste is increasing rapidly. This is due to a range of factors, including unprecedented growth in mobile and internet-connected devices, the fast pace of new product development and shorter product life-spans.[2] This is problematic for several reasons. EEE contains hazardous materials such as lead, cadmium and mercury, as well as valuable metals such as copper and gold. As corporate and government policy starts to focus on a circular economy (discussed in Section 7.2.1), strategies that reduce hazardous components and facilitate reuse or recycling are becoming mainstream. They are also increasingly being seen as a business opportunity:

---

1   Step Initiative (2014). *White Paper: One Global Definition of E-waste.* Solving the e-waste problem (Step). Bonn, Germany: Step Initiative, pp. 4-5. Retrieved from http://www.step-initiative.org/files/step/_documents/StEP_WP_One%20 Global%20Definition%20of%20E-waste_20140603_amended.pdf

2   Allen, J. (2015, November 3). Our connected, mobile, recycled and green future. *Triple Pundit.* Retrieved from http://www.triplepundit.com/special/ circular-economy-and-green-electronics/our-connected-mobile-recycled -and-green-future/

Drivers		Strategies		Benefits
• Social legitimacy, linked to the expectations of stakeholders • Evidence of product impacts • Business priorities and targets	→	• Corporate policy, goals & targets • Strategies for design, procurement, recovery	→	• Sustainability outcomes • The business benefits for individual firms (cost savings, market access, reputation etc.)

FIGURE 4.1   Framework for product stewardship

> The topic of green electronics is no longer a purely environmental discussion. As these products continue to touch every corner of the globe, an increased focus on their sustainability presents new opportunities for technological, environmental and financial progress.[3]

This chapter uses the framework developed in Chapter 1 (see Fig. 4.1) to understand product stewardship for EEE. A systematic, structured approach to the life-cycle management of products enables companies to maximize the benefits for the business and for stakeholders. This requires a strong evidence base, so the chapter begins with background information on product and market trends, including a fast rate of growth in consumption and rapid technological change. This is followed by a general overview of the drivers for producer responsibility including stakeholder expectations and evidence of environmental and social impacts.

Leading companies in the sector are responding to these drivers with a range of policy, design, procurement and product recovery strategies. These are discussed in Section 4.5, drawing on examples and studies from across the globe. The concluding section draws together some of the lessons for other product stewardship policies and programmes.

More detailed case studies are provided in Section 4.7. These describe the drivers, strategies and benefits of four industry initiatives:

- **Close the Loop Ltd** collect and recycle used ink and toner cartridges for original equipment manufacturers (OEMs) in the US and Australia. With a culture of innovation and collaboration, Close the Loop demonstrates how a carefully designed take-back programme can generate multiple benefits for participating businesses, including access to "closed loop" recycled materials and business intelligence data.

---

3   Allen (2015).

- **Fisher & Paykel** is a global appliance manufacturer based in New Zealand. Since 1993 the company has voluntarily provided a free take-back and recycling service for end-of-life appliances. This has achieved significant environmental benefits, and from a business perspective has helped to build brand loyalty and differentiate the company in a competitive market.

- **TechCollect** is an industry funded, national recycling programme for waste computers, computer accessories and TVs in Australia. It was established by many of the world's largest technology firms to meet their obligations under national extended producer responsibility (EPR) regulations. Its members place a high priority on environmental compliance and safety in the recovery chain and work closely with regulators on policy development.

- **MobileMuster** collect and recycle used mobile phones and phone batteries with funding from handset manufacturers and carriers. In 2014 MobileMuster became the first voluntary programme accredited by the Australian Government under the Product Stewardship Act.

4.2 Market trends

The EEE sector covers a diverse and complex range of products (see Table 4.1). Two trends with important implications for the life-cycle management of products are discussed below: the fast rate of technological change and growing demand for consumer electronics.

4.2.1 New technologies

The market for consumer electronics is changing rapidly as new products are developed and existing products converge into more flexible, multi-purpose devices. One of the implications for the management of products at end of life is that the mix of products coming onto the market today is likely to be very different from the mix of products coming to the end of their life. Some of the most significant technical trends in recent years have been:

- The switch from cathode ray tube (CRT) screens to flat panel displays for computers and TVs

TABLE 4.1 Electrical and electronic equipment

Product category	Examples
Large equipment	Refrigerators and freezers, washing machines, dishwashers, clothes dryers, electric cookers, electric heating appliances, large printers, photocopiers, photovoltaic panels
Small equipment	Vacuum cleaners, sewing machines, irons, toasters, coffee machines, hair dryers, clocks, watches, microwaves, video cameras, electrical and electronic toys, small medical devices, power tools
Small information technology (IT) and telecommunications equipment	Personal computers, tablets, fax machines, calculators, telephones (fixed and mobile), answering machines, GPS, modems, connected watches
Screens and monitors	Televisions, computer monitors, laptops, notebooks, tablets
Lamps	Straight fluorescent lamps, compact fluorescent lamps, high intensity discharge lamps, low pressure sodium lamps
Temperature exchange equipment	Refrigerators, freezers, air conditioners, heat pumps

Source: Based on Baldé, C.P., Wang, F., Kuehr, R. & Huisman, J. (2015). *The Global E-waste Monitor: 2014*. Bonn, Germany: United Nations University, IAS-SCYCLE

- The phase out of chlorofluorocarbons (CFCs) from refrigerators

- A shift away from nickel cadmium (NiCd) batteries to lithium ion

- The removal of polychlorinated biphenyls (PCBs) from capacitors[4]

The switch from CRTs to flat screen displays has been particularly problematic for recycling. The supply of used CRTs has grown exponentially as take-back and recycling regulations have been introduced around the world. Supply exceeds demand, however, because of the limited number of companies that can safely recover leaded glass from CRTs. This has resulted in large stockpiles of TVs and computer displays in countries such as the US.[5] The recycling infrastructure for flat panel displays is also limited.

4.2.2 Increasing demand for electronic equipment

Ownership of consumer electronics continues to grow. When Accenture surveyed consumers in 11 countries in 2012, they found that consumers in

4   Huisman, J., Federico, M., Kuehr, R., Maurer, C., Ogilvie, S., Poll, J., … Stevels, A. (2007). *2008 Review of Directive 2002/96 on Waste Electrical and Electronic Equipment (WEEE)*. Bonn, Germany: United Nations University.

5   McMillan, R. (2014, March 24). America needs a bunker to store its mountain of toxic TVs. *WIRED*. Retrieved from http://www.wired.com/2014/03/crts/

every country anticipated spending more on consumer electronics in 2013 than they had in the previous year.[6] Expenditure in 2012 was highest in the emerging economies such as China and Brazil as they continue to "catch up" to consumption patterns in more developed economies.

Mobile phones are one of the fastest growing consumer products, with rapid growth in markets such as China, India, Brazil and Russia.[7] The number of active mobile phones in the world was estimated to be 7.4 billion in 2014, which would mean there were more phones than people.[8]

A recent trend is the growth in "smart phones", tablets and other mobile technologies. Ownership of smart phones grew from 26% in 2009 to 58% in 2012.[9] Consumers are now focused on fewer, multi-function devices such as smart phones that function as phones, cameras, computers and much more. Between 2011 and 2012, ownership of tablets doubled while ownership of single-function devices such as digital cameras, DVD players and portable music players remained static or declined.[10] The growth in tablets and smart phones will present particular problems for recycling schemes at end of life because of their complex structure, large number of component materials, and batteries that are not easily accessible and removable.

While leading manufacturers and brand owners are taking steps to reduce the environmental impacts of their products, the problem is one of scale:

> Ironically, one of the most significant sustainability challenges for mobile devices isn't the finished product, but the voracious rate of device consumption ... While the worldwide population grows 1.2 percent annually, the number of mobile devices multiplies five times faster. This unprecedented consumption comes with undeniable environmental costs, from an escalation in e-waste to the rapid depletion of resources.[11]

6   Accenture (2013). *It's Anyone's Game in the Consumer Electronics Playing Field*, p. 25. Retrieved from https://www.accenture.com/us-en/~/media/Accenture/Conversion-Assets/DotCom/Documents/Global/PDF/Technology_6/Accenture-Consumer-Electronics-Products-and-Services-Usage-Report.pdf

7   Nokia (2005). *Integrated Product Policy Pilot Project Stage 1 Final Report: Life Cycle Environmental Issues of Mobile Phones*. Espoo, Finland: Nokia Corporation.

8   Pramis, J. (2013, February 28). Number of mobile phones to exceed world population by 2014. *Digital Trends*.

9   Accenture (2013), p. 7.

10   *Ibid.*

11   Allen (2015).

4.3 Stakeholder expectations

The list of stakeholders for EEEs is similar to those for packaging, but their issues of concern are different. This is because electrical and electronic products, unlike packaging, consume significant amounts of energy, water and other materials during use. Many are made with toxic materials that, if not managed carefully, can be hazardous to people and the natural environment after disposal.

A summary of concerns for a number of stakeholders is provided in Table 4.2. Some of the most important—consumers, producers, government regulators, environment groups and municipalities—are discussed in more detail below.

4.3.1 Consumers

Consumers have a critically important role to play in recycling programmes for e-waste. The ultimate success of these programmes depends on the willingness of consumers to take them to a drop-off location or arrange for collection, which is why the concept of "shared responsibility" is often extended to include consumers. Carmel Dollisson, manager of one of Australia's regulated e-waste schemes, TechCollect (Case study 4.7.3), notes that, while product stewardship is ultimately about companies "doing the right thing", they can't do it on their own: "Everyone must be accountable for the product once it's sold and living in someone's home. Consumers need to take some responsibility".[12]

Consumer engagement is critical to the success of any recycling programme, but recycling programmes for TVs and computers can be particularly difficult or inconvenient for consumers. The products are often large and heavy, and may need to be taken to a specially designated drop-off location. Some consumers choose to leave their unwanted products on the street, or to dump them illegally, presumably because recycling is too difficult or inconvenient, or because they don't know how to recycle them. Surveys by industry and advocacy groups suggest that the majority of consumers don't know their options when a product reaches the end of its useful life.[13]

---

12   Personal communication (interview) with C. Dollisson, General Manager, Australia New Zealand Recycling Platform, 6 August 2014.

13   Pike Research (2009). *Electronics Recycling and E-waste Issues: Executive Summary*. Boulder, CO, p. 5. Retrieved from http://www.navigantresearch.com/wp-content/uploads/2009/02/EWASTE-09-Executive-Summary.pdf

TABLE 4.2   Stakeholder interests in electrical and electronic products

Stakeholder	Interests
Consumers	• Availability of a convenient recycling service • Incentives for recycling
Product manufacturers	• Corporate reputation and sustainability goals • EPR regulations that provide a "level playing field" • Cost of compliance with regulations • Responsible recycling standards and transparency in recovery chains
Retailers	• Corporate reputation and sustainability goals • Meeting compliance obligations under some EPR regulations (e.g. many US regulations)
Government agencies	• Quantity of e-waste • Conservation of non-renewable resources (linked to the goal of a "circular economy") • Design for recycling • Toxic components—impacts in manufacturing, disposal and recycling • Government procurement of energy efficient products
Environment groups	• Toxic components—impacts in manufacturing, disposal and recycling • Quantity of waste
Municipalities	• Local government involvement in planning and implementation • Reduced costs of waste management to ratepayers • Maintaining or improving the level of recycling service

Mobile phones are smaller and easy for consumers to transport to drop-off points, which are often conveniently located in retail stores and other public places. One of the most significant challenges for recycling programmes is the reluctance of many consumers to recycle their old phones. The Australian Mobile Telecommunications Association (AMTA) monitors consumer attitudes and behaviour closely to inform its MobileMuster recycling programme (Case study 4.7.4). In 2013–14 AMTA found that 37% of consumers had two or more handsets at home, and estimated that there were 23 million handsets in storage at home or at work.[14]

Storage of e-waste at home, which is often referred to as "hoarding", influences the quantity of e-waste available for collection. An understanding of consumer use and disposal behaviour is therefore important in setting benchmarks and monitoring collection rates. Following stakeholder criticism of low recycling rates for mobile phones, AMTA undertook extensive research to identify opportunities for improvement:

14   AMTA (2014). *MobileMuster's 2013–14 Annual Report*. Sydney: Australian Mobile Telecommunications Association, p. 6.

> [AMTA] did quantitative market research to see where all the phones were going, what was happening to them. Everyone was saying they were going to landfill. In fact they were sitting in cupboards and drawers.[15]

Financial incentives are sometimes used to encourage reuse or recycling. Apple for example, allows customers in several countries to bring in older devices in exchange for a credit for a newer model.[16]

4.3.1.1 Organizational consumers

Large consumers of EEE such as government agencies are using their procurement policies to drive improved environmental performance. These often refer to voluntary standards or initiatives. The voluntary US ENERGY STAR standards, for example, were introduced in 1992 with "a small group of pioneering partners". In 1993 President Bill Clinton signed Executive Order 12845, which required federal agencies to purchase ENERGY STAR products when buying new office equipment. By the following year more than 2000 ENERGY STAR qualified products were available and all of the largest manufacturers were participating in the programme.[17]

Many government agencies in the US refer to the Electronic Product Environmental Assessment Tool (EPEAT) in their procurement documents.[18] EPEAT combines criteria for design, production, energy use and recycling with independent verification of manufacturer claims. The criteria, which are classified as either "required" or "optional", are used to rate each product as achieving the gold, silver or bronze standard.

EPEAT has been influential in driving support for producer responsibility initiatives such as the Close the Loop recovery programme for used printer cartridges (Case study 4.7.1). The company's ability to recover 100% of the materials from cartridges has also allowed its customers to meet additional procurement criteria within EPEAT:

15 Personal communication (interview) with R. Read, previously Manager Recycling, Australian Mobile Telecommunications Association (until February 2016), 1 November 2013.
16 Apple (2015). *Environmental Responsibility Report: 2015 Progress Report, Covering FY2014*. Retrieved from https://www.apple.com/environment/pdf/Apple_Environmental_Responsibility_Report_2015.pdf.
17 US EPA (2012). *20 years of ENERGY STAR*. Retrieved from https://www.energystar.gov/index.cfm?c=about.20_years
18 Green Electronics Council (2015). *EPEAT*. Retrieved from http://www.epeat.net

A big driver today is procurement guidelines. If you want to supply possibly the biggest purchaser of printers and copiers in the world—the US Government—you need EPEAT certification; bronze, silver or gold. We help our customers to get gold certification in America and other parts of the world. We're the only company that we're aware of that can help companies to meet two of the voluntary criteria in the EPEAT guidelines, which are reuse of toner powder and use of post-consumer recycled plastics. Most recyclers send toner to a waste to energy facility, whereas we can use it as a modified polymer in asphalt. That's a good business builder for us.[19]

4.3.2 Producers

The market for new and used EEE is overwhelmingly global, and most large producers are multinational. An outcome of this is that corporate environmental initiatives also tend to be global. Apple, for example, has committed to accept any used Apple product for "responsible recycling" in every country in which it operates. Like many of its industry peers, Apple rigorously enforces its high sustainability standards:

The vast majority of our recycling is handled in region, so we can make sure our recycled materials are not being dumped unsafely in developing countries—a common practice in our industry ... We currently work with 140 partners around the globe whose facilities are rigorously evaluated annually on health and safety, environmental compliance, material tracking, social responsibility, and other Apple mandates.[20]

Most of the global brands have environmental policies and strategies to minimize life-cycle impacts through design for sustainability and recovery at end of life. Their priorities tend to mirror those of regulators and non-government organizations, i.e. elimination or reduction of toxic components, and safe and environmentally responsible reuse or recycling. Producers have helped to disseminate good recycling practices around the globe through the development and implementation of environmental and safety standards (see Section 4.5.3 "Procurement").

Many leading manufacturers support regulation of e-waste recycling to minimize the free-rider problem. Dell, for example, has developed a set of detailed principles for product recovery legislation, which are published

19   Personal communication (interview) with S. Morriss, Founder and Director, Close the Loop, 4 May 2014.
20   Apple (2015), p. 21.

on its website.[21] The company has also partnered with the United Nations Industrial Development Organization (UNIDO) to facilitate the development of appropriate e-waste regulations and policies in developing countries.[22]

When it comes to regulation, producers want "a simple, stable and cost-efficient implementation which ensures that all actors are playing on a level playing field".[23] In Europe many producers have expressed a preference for regulations that allow for competition between producer responsibility organizations (PROs) because this drives prices down.[24] In the US, producers attempted to develop a national regulatory framework because they wanted to avoid having to deal with potentially 50 different e-waste laws.[25] This initiative failed when producers, retailers and state government agencies failed to agree on a financing mechanism.

4.3.3 Government regulators

Companies are required to meet an increasing number of product-related regulations (a brief overview is provided in Table 4.3). These include:

- Restrictions on the use of hazardous substances

- Laws that require producers to take back their products at end of life

- Laws that impose a financial fee on producers to fund recycling (advance disposal fee)

There are also laws in many jurisdictions that impose minimum energy efficiency standards and labelling requirements. These include the

21 Dell (2014). *Dell's Policy Statement on Electronics Recycling.* Retrieved from http://www.dell.com/learn/us/en/uscorp1/corp-comm/individual-producer-policy
22 Trahant, G. (2014, October 1). United Nations and Dell form partnership for electronic waste solutions. *SocialEarth.* Retrieved from http://socialearth.org/united-nations-dell-form-partnership-electronic-waste-solutions
23 Kunz, N., Atasu, A., Mayers, K. & van Wassenhove, L. (2014). *Extended Producer Responsibility: Stakeholder Concerns and Future Developments.* INSEAD Social Innovation Centre with support from European Recycling Platform, p. 17. Fontainebleau: INSEAD.
24 *Ibid.*
25 Renckens, S. (2008). Yes, we will! Voluntarism in US e-waste governance. *RECEIL,* 17(3), 286-299.

TABLE 4.3 Examples of product-related laws and policies for electrical and electronic equipment

Type of regulation or policy	Detail	Purpose	Examples
Take-back requirement or advance disposal fee paid by producers	Producers are physically or financially responsible for recovery of products at end of life.	To promote design of recyclable products by internalizing disposal/recycling costs; to shift the costs of recycling from taxpayers to producers and consumers; to increase levels of recycling.	• Asia: China (Ordinance on the Administration of the Recovery and Treatment of Waste Electrical and Electronic Products), Taiwan, India (E-waste (Management and Handling) Rules, 2011), South Korea, Japan • Europe: EU member states (Directive 2012/19/EU on Waste Electrical and Electronic Equipment) • US: 23 states • Canada: 9 out of 14 provinces • Oceania: Australia
Consumer responsibility for recycling	Consumers must pay a fee to support recycling, either in the purchase price or at disposal	To shift the costs of recycling from taxpayers to producers and consumers; to increase levels of recycling.	• Asia: Japan (the Home Appliances Recycling Law extends to consumers) • US: California
Design requirements	Regulations require design for recycling (e.g. ease of disassembly, removal of batteries etc.) or restrict hazardous components: particularly lead, mercury, cadmium, hexavalent chromium, and certain flame retardants and plasticizers	To reduce toxic pollution caused by disposal of e-waste at end of life (landfill or incineration).	• Asia: China (Measures for Administration of the Pollution Control of Electronic Information Products) • Europe: EU member states (WEEE Directive and Directive 2011/65/EU on the Restriction of the Use of Certain Hazardous Substances) • US: some states restrict the use of hazardous components in line with the EU RoHS Directive
Reporting on conflict minerals	Producers must report on the use of minerals from conflict or high risk areas	To prevent the extraction and processing of minerals contributing to human rights abuses and the financing of conflict.	• US: Dodd-Frank Wall Street Reform and Consumer Protection Act 2010

European Union's Energy Label, which was established in 1995 and is mandatory for all white goods and other household appliances.

The increasing volume of e-waste going to landfill, the increasing costs associated with their waste management, and the presence of toxic substances have been the major drivers for regulation in the European Union, North America and other developed countries such as Japan and Australia. The scope of these regulations varies; ranging from TVs and computers (Australia) to almost all electrical and electronic products (the European Union (EU) and British Columbia). Programmes that collect a wider range of products have a number of potential benefits, including increased efficiencies in recycling and material recovery processes that may reduce costs per unit recycled.[26]

The Japanese Government was the first to mandate producer responsibility for appliances, with the Home Appliance Recycling Law introduced in 1998. Manufacturers are obligated to finance recycling of their own products, although costs are partially covered by a recycling fee paid by consumers (in California e-waste recycling is entirely funded by consumers through a recycling fee collected by retailers at time of purchase).

The EU followed Japan with its Directive on Waste Electrical and Electronic Equipment (the WEEE Directive), which was introduced in 2002 and updated in 2012. The Directive requires that member states: encourage the design and production of EEE to facilitate recycling; ensure that producers or third parties acting on their behalf set up systems to treat WEEE using best available technologies; ensure that producers meet certain minimum recovery targets, e.g. 80% for large household appliances; and ensure that producers pay for collection, treatment, recovery and environmentally sound, responsible disposal of e-waste from households.

The revision of the WEEE Directive in 2012 broadened its scope to include all electrical and electronic products. It also changed the collection target from 4 kg per capita to 45% of products sold in the previous 3 years by 2016, increasing to 65% by 2019, and the introduction of recycling and treatment standards. Design for recycling will also be encouraged through changes to the EU Ecodesign Directive that were announced as part of the circular economy package. Proposals include mandatory product design and

26   The Economist Intelligence Unit (2015). *Global E-waste Systems: Insights for Australia from Other Developed Countries*. Report for the Australia New Zealand Recycling Platform: Melbourne.

marking requirements to make it easier and safer to dismantle, reuse and recycle electronic displays (e.g. flat computer or television screens).[27]

Electrical and electronic products contain a number of substances of concern to regulators. The EU's Directive on the Restriction of the Use of Certain Hazardous Substances in Electrical and Electronic Equipment (the RoHS Directive) was introduced in 2002. Member states must ensure that new electrical and electronic equipment put on the market does not contain lead, mercury, cadmium or hexavalent chromium, and certain flame retardants and phthalate plasticizers in particular applications.

These two EU Directives have influenced the approach taken in other jurisdictions, including China. The "transplant" of EPR regulations to China was partially driven by media exposure of the pollution caused by imported electronic scrap in southern rural areas of China, and the role of regulations in promoting structural change towards a circular economy.[28]

China introduced the Measures for Administration of the Pollution Control of Electronic Information Products ("China RoHS") in 2006. This was followed by the Ordinance on the Administration of the Recovery and Treatment of Waste Electrical and Electronic Products ("China WEEE") in 2009. Manufacturers and importers pay a fee to a government-managed fund that subsidizes the recovery and recycling of e-waste. Recycling enterprises must be licensed by the relevant municipal government and meet environmental, health and safety standards.[29]

Prior to this the European Directives were already starting to have an impact on Chinese producers:

> The diffusion of design change for recycling in products spread quickly with the promulgation of two EU Directives on e-waste in 2003. In particular the … [RoHS Directive] … launched a global campaign to eliminate several environmentally sensitive substances … from electronic products. It brought a shock to electronics producers in China … green manufacturing suddenly became a hot issue within the industry as the requirements of the two EU Directives quickly spread through the global supply chain.[30]

27   European Commission (2015). *Closing the Loop: An EU Action Plan for the Circular Economy 2015*. Brussels, Belgium: EC, p. 4.
28   Tong, X., & Yan, L. (2013). From legal transplants to sustainable transition. *Journal of Industrial Ecology*, 17(2), 199-212.
29   Design Chain Associates (2009). *Regulations on Recovery Processing of Waste Electrical and Electronic Products* (translation). Retrieved from http://www. chinarohs.com/chinaweee-decree551.pdf
30   Tong & Yan (2013), p. 204.

Governments around the world have also responded to global problems by developing international conventions that countries implement through national laws. There are three important international conventions applying to EEE:

- The Montreal Protocol on Substances that Deplete the Ozone Layer ("Montreal Protocol") has largely phased out the use of ozone-depleting substances including chlorofluorocarbons (CFCs) used as refrigerants and as the blowing agent in foams

- The Basel Convention on the Control of Transboundary Movements of Hazardous Wastes and Their Disposal ("Basel Convention") aims to reduce the movement of hazardous waste from developed to developing countries

- The Minamata Convention on Mercury aims to reduce the use of mercury in products and to reduce mercury-containing waste

4.3.4 Environment groups

Non-government environment groups have applied pressure on producers and regulators to reduce the toxicity and waste associated with e-waste. Greenpeace, for example, began its "Toxic Tech" campaign in 2005 to encourage electronics manufacturers to eliminate toxic substances and take back their products for recycling. Reports by Greenpeace International[31] and the Basel Action Network[32] have helped to focus attention

---

31   See Brigden, K., Labunska, I.D. Santillo, D. & Allsopp, M. (2005). *Recycling of Electronic Wastes in China & India: Workplace & Environmental Contamination*. Amsterdam, The Netherlands: Greenpeace International. Retrieved from http://www.greenpeace.org/international/PageFiles/25134/recycling-of-electronic-waste.pdf; Brigden, K., Labunska, I., Santillo, D. & Johnston, P. (2008). *Chemical Contamination at E-waste Recycling and Disposal Sites in Accra and Korforidua, Ghana*. Amsterdam, The Netherlands: Greenpeace International. Retrieved from http://www.greenpeace.org/international/Global/international/planet-2/report/2008/9/chemical-contamination-at-e-wa.pdf; Cobbing, M. (2008). *Toxic Tech, Not in Our Backyard: Uncovering the Hidden Flows of E-waste*. Amsterdam, The Netherlands: Greenpeace International. Retrieved from http://www.greenpeace.org/international/Global/international/planet-2/report/2008/2/not-in-our-backyard.pdf

32   BAN, & SVTC (2002). *Exporting Harm: The High Tech Trashing of Asia*. Seattle, WA: Basel Action Network and San Jose, CA: Silicon Valley Toxics Coalition. Retrieved from http://ban.org/E-waste/technotrashfinalcomp.pdf

on the negative impacts of e-waste exports (see Section 4.4.5 "Recycling in developing countries").

Greenpeace publishes a semi-regular *Guide to Greener Electronics*, which ranks mobile phone and computer manufacturers on their progress in eliminating harmful substances and in taking responsibility for their products at end of life. In 2014 Greenpeace nominated Indian electronics manufacturer Wipro as the "greenest" company in its international survey with a score of 7.1 out of 10.[33]

4.3.5 Municipalities

Local governments are dealing with increasing volumes of e-waste at their disposal facilities. Many participate in formal recycling programmes established by state governments or by industry, or fund their own programmes. The increasing costs associated with e-waste disposal, as well as the costs of storing and recycling hazardous products such as TVs and computer screens, have prompted local governments in many countries to call for increased producer responsibility for waste management to reduce costs to ratepayers.

Local councils in New Zealand (NZ) have been engaged in discussions with the central government and industry over many years on the best way to manage e-waste. The latest report commissioned by the government concluded that there was insufficient data for the minister to declare e-waste a priority under the Waste Minimisation Act and to consider regulation.[34] This attracted criticism from municipalities, with one councillor arguing that it was "hugely frustrating for Councils to discover there is still no clear pathway to e-waste product stewardship":

> Councils came together in July 2013 and unanimously passed a remit at the LGNZ [Local Government New Zealand] Conference calling on the Minister to declare e-waste a priority product and a timetable for the development of regulations; two years on, we are no further ahead.

33   Greenpeace International (2012). *Guide to Greener Electronics*. Retrieved from http://www.greenpeace.org/international/en/campaigns/detox/electronics/Guide-to-Greener-Electronics/Previous-editions/How-the-companies-line-up-18/

34   SLR Consulting, & MS2 (2015). *E-waste Product Stewardship: Framework for New Zealand*. Report to the Ministry for the Environment: Wellington, NZ. Retrieved from http://www.globalpsc.net/wp-content/uploads/2015/08/eWasteNZ_Final_Report_0615_EN.pdf

One of the reasons this remit was unanimously passed was because all
local government agencies are currently paying a high price to manage e-waste responsibly.[35]

4.4 Product impacts

4.4.1 Hazardous substances

E-waste contains a number of hazardous components, many of which are
toxic in the natural environment and pose a threat to human health if not
managed appropriately (some examples are listed in Table 4.4). This has
been one of the primary drivers behind EPR regulations.

Inappropriate disposal or recycling can generate three levels of toxic
emissions; all of which need to be considered:

- **Primary emissions**. Hazardous substances contained in e-waste,
  such as lead, mercury or polychlorinated biphenyls (PCBs)

- **Secondary emissions**. Hazardous by-products of e-waste substances arising from improper treatment (e.g. dioxins or furans
  formed by incineration or inappropriate melting of plastics with
  halogenated flame retardants)

- **Tertiary emissions**. Hazardous substances used in recycling (e.g.
  cyanide or other leaching agents) and released because of inappropriate handling and treatment[36]

Policies such as the EU's RoHS Directive 2012/19/EU are only able to
influence primary emissions, and to a certain extent, secondary emissions.
This is because "even the 'cleanest/greenest' products cannot prevent tertiary emissions if inappropriate recycling technologies are used".[37]

Many regulations and standards require the removal of hazardous components before shredding or further processing. The Responsible Recycling
(R2) standard, for example, specifies that certain "focus materials" must be

---

35   Shelton, L. (2015, September 10). Wellington group concerned at "do nothing"
     report on electronic waste. *Wellington Scoop*. Retrieved from http://wellington.
     scoop.co.nz/?p=81615

36   Schluep, M., Hagelueken, C., Kuehr, R., Magalini, F., Maure, C., Meskers, C., …
     Wang, F. (2009). *Recycling: From E-waste to Resources*. Nairobi: United Nations
     Environment Programme and United Nations University.

37   *Ibid.*, p. 12.

TABLE 4.4 Examples of hazardous components in e-waste

Product or component	Potentially hazardous component
Circuit boards, lamps, switches, wiring	Mercury, antimony, arsenic, barium, beryllium, cadmium, chromium, lead, selenium, PCBs
CRTs	Lead, cadmium
Cold cathode fluorescent lamps (CCFLs) in liquid crystal display (LCD) screens	Mercury, barium oxide, strontium oxide
Batteries	Some contain lead, cadmium, mercury and/or corrosive electrolyte
Plastic housings for computers, TVs etc.	Flame retardants e.g. polybrominated biphenyls (PBBs)
Refrigerators and freezers	Ozone-depleting substances in older appliances, e.g. CFCs and hydrochlorofluorocarbons (HCFCs), also have a high global warming impact

removed prior to shredding or materials recovery because of their toxicity, workplace health and safety risk, public health risk or environmental effects.[38] These are:

- PCBs
- Mercury
- CRT glass
- Batteries
- Printed circuit boards, except for those that do not contain lead solder and have undergone processing to remove mercury and batteries

Under R2, CRTs, batteries and circuit boards don't need to be removed prior to shredding if processing occurs in facilities that meet all applicable regulatory requirements to receive the focus materials and that use technology designed to safely and effectively manage them.

The E-Stewards standard has a more extensive list of components that need to be removed, including toner and ink cartridges.[39]

---

38 R2 Solutions (2013). *The Responsible Recycling ("R2") Standard for Electronics Recyclers.* Boulder, CO: R2 Solutions.

39 Basel Action Network (2013). *Review Version: Performance Requirements Excerpted from the E-Stewards Standard for Responsible Recycling and Reuse of Electronic Equipment.* Seattle, WA: Basel Action Network. Retrieved from

TABLE 4.5   Global quantities of e-waste generated

Year	E-waste generated (Mt)	Population (billion)	E-waste generated (kg/person)
2010	33.8	6.8	5.0
2011	35.8	6.9	5.2
2012	37.8	6.9	5.4
2013	39.8	7.0	5.7
2014	41.8	7.1	5.9
2015	43.8	7.2	6.1
2016	45.7	7.3	6.3
2017	47.8	7.4	6.5
2018	49.8	7.4	6.7

Note: The data for 2015–2018 are forecasts

Source: Baldé et al. (2015), p. 24

The refrigerants in cooling and freezing devices are ozone depleting and contribute to global warming. The EU's Ozone Depleting Substances Regulation requires all ozone-depleting substances to be removed from refrigeration equipment as both the coolant and the insulating foam can contain ozone-depleting substances.[40] Similar laws were introduced in many other jurisdictions in accordance with the Montreal Protocol.

4.4.2 Waste management

Regulators have also been influenced by growing quantities of e-waste. The total amount of e-waste generated globally is estimated to have increased by 24% between 2010 and 2014 (Table 4.5). The United Nations University has estimated that 41.8 million metric tonnes (Mt) of e-waste were generated globally in 2014, and this is expected to grow to around 50 Mt in 2018.[41] The largest categories of waste are small equipment (12.8 Mt) and large equipment (11.8 Mt) (see Fig. 4.2).

http://e-stewards.org/wp-content/uploads/2014/09/eStewards_Standard_Review_Version.pdf
40   Huisman et al. (2007).
41   Baldé et al. (2015), p. 24.

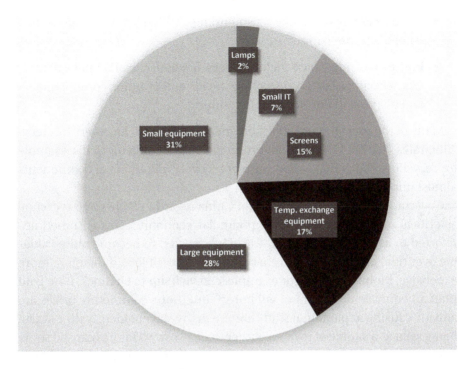

FIGURE 4.2   E-waste generated globally by category, percentage of total, 2014

Source: Derived from Baldé *et al.* (2015), p. 24

4.4.3 Resource conservation

Electrical and electronic products are a major consumer of precious and speciality metals and an important contributor to world demand for these materials.[42] Booming demand for the metals is linked to the functionality of products and the specific metal properties needed to achieve these. For example, electronics contribute almost 80% of the world's demand for indium (transparent conductive layers in LCD glass), over 80% for ruthenium (magnetic properties in hard disks) and 50% for antimony (flame retardants).[43]

"State of the art" recycling generally involves the following steps:

• Removal of toxic components and materials

---

42   Schluep *et al.* (2009).
43   *Ibid.*, p. 8.

- Pre-processing—manual dismantling, mechanical separation (shredding, breaking, sorting)

- End-processing—base metal refinery, precious metal refinery, plastics recycling, battery recycling, treatment of other components and disposal of non-recyclable residues[44]

Many of the precious and speciality metals in e-waste have very low recycling rates (see Table 4.6). Some products are very difficult to disassemble for recycling, which makes the reuse or recovery of individual components almost impossible.

Governments in Europe, Japan and China regard EPR laws and recycling as critical to the achievement of a "circular economy". This is sometimes referred to as "urban mining". E-waste is expected to become more valuable over time as some minerals become less accessible and therefore more expensive. Mobile phones, for example, can yield up to 60 times more gold than an equivalent amount of gold ore.[45] In Europe commodity prices are already causing a "paradigm shift" among many stakeholders, with e-waste being seen as a source of revenue rather than a cost.[46] This has caused some concerns among PROs due to "leakage" of products through unofficial recycling channels that make it more challenging for them to meet their compliance targets.

4.4.4 Energy and greenhouse gas emissions

Life-cycle assessment (LCA) studies often show that most of the environmental impacts associated with electrical and electronic products occur during the use phase. One study found that for large household appliances such as dishwashers, washing machines, dryers and refrigerators, the use phase accounts for at least 90% of the total environmental burden.[47] This is linked to consumption of energy, water and consumables (e.g. washing powder) over the life of the product. Recycling a washing machine at the end of its life instead of sending it to landfill is beneficial, but the saving is

---

44   Baldé *et al.* (2015).
45   AMTA (2014), p. 15.
46   Kunz *et al.* (2014).
47   Otto, R., Ruminy, A., & Mrotzek, H. (2006). Assessment of the environmental impact of household appliances. *Appliance*, 63(4), 32-35.

TABLE 4.6   Metals commonly used in EEE, percentage of global production and global recycling rates

Type of metal	Metal	Demand for EEE as a percentage of production (2006)*	Global recycling rate (2011)**
Ferrous	Manganese (Mn)	–	> 50%
	Iron (Fe)	–	> 50%
	Nickel (Ni)	–	> 50%
Non-ferrous	Zinc (Zn)	–	> 50%
	Lead (Pb)	–	> 50%
	Aluminium (Al)	–	> 50%
	Copper (Cu)	30%	> 50%
	Tin (Sn)	33%	> 50%
Precious	Silver (Ag)	30%	> 50%
	Gold (Au)	12%	> 50%
	Palladium (Pd)	14%	> 50%
	Platinum (Pt)	6%	> 50%
Speciality	Cadmium (Cd)	–	10–25%
	Cobalt (Co)	19%	> 50%
	Mercury (Hg)	–	1–10%
	Lithium (Li)	–	< 1%
	Lanthanum (La)	–	< 1%
	Cerium (Ce)	–	< 1%
	Praseodymium (Pr)	–	< 1%
	Neodymium (Nd)	–	< 1%
	Indium (In)	79%	< 1%
	Antimony (Sb)	50%	1–10%
	Ruthenium (Ru)	84%	10–25%
	Bismuth (Bi)	16%	< 1%
	Selenium (Se)	17%	< 1%

Sources: * Schluep *et al.* (2009) p. 9. ** UNEP International Resource Panel (2011). *Recycling Rates of Metals, A Status Report*. Nairobi: United Nations Environment Programme.

very small compared with the impacts and potential savings that can be achieved during the use phase.[48]

4.4.5 Recycling in developing countries

E-waste recycling can have a number of environmental, health and safety impacts if it is not undertaken in a controlled way. The risks include:

- Contact with toxic substances such as mercury or lead

- Risks of fire and explosions associated with used batteries

- Water pollution if chemicals used in processing are not recovered and treated appropriately

The risks associated with e-waste collection, transport, handling and processing are global, but there are particular concerns in developing economies that have a large and poorly regulated "informal" recycling sector. The informal sector involves a large number of micro enterprises, often family groups, who dismantle e-waste and sometimes recover valuable components, using manual and unregulated processes.

The damage caused by recycling in Africa and Asia has been well documented by groups such as Greenpeace and the Basel Action Network.[49] More recently Adam Minter has documented some of the environmental, health and safety impacts in Guiyu, "China's biggest and most notorious e-waste recycling zone".[50] Printed circuit boards, for example, are generally shredded, but only after the precious metals have been removed by hand. The boards are first heated over a hot stove to melt the lead solder. Workers who do this often have very little personal protection beyond a face mask and goggles, and the resulting fumes pollute the local environment. The gold is then removed using highly corrosive acids, by workers without safety equipment, and used acid is often dumped in local waterways.[51]

---

48 Koerner, M., & Turk, R. (2010). *Life Cycle Assessment of Clothes Washing Options for City West Water's Residential Customers: Communications Report.* Report prepared by ARUP for City West Water: Melbourne, p. 5. Retrieved from http://www.epa.vic.gov.au/our-work/programs/sustainability-covenants/ past-sustainability-covenants/~/media/Files/bus/sustainability_covenants/ docs/Life-Cycle-Assessment-of-Clothes-Washing-Options-Communications -Report.pdf

49 See, for example, BAN, & SVTC (2002).

50 Minter, A. (2013). *Junkyard Planet.* New York: Bloomsbury Press.

51 *Ibid.*

The Chinese Government has started to regulate the e-waste recycling industry in Guiyu and elsewhere in the country. Their national e-waste law requires enterprises that recycle e-waste to be licensed by the relevant municipal government and meet environmental, health and safety standards.

The Indian Government is also trying to formalize and control the informal recycling sector through new regulations, including enactment of EPR requirements. According to Raghupathy *et al.* the sector comprises a large number of tiny, unorganized units that provide jobs for thousands of people and support formal waste management agencies such as municipalities.[52] They generally only get involved in dismantling, but some also extract valuable metals using crude processes that impose high risks on workers and the environment. "Formal" recyclers are now starting to enter the market, as a result of growing awareness and increased attention from policy-makers. These businesses are likely to operate with higher environmental management standards and utilize more advanced recovery technologies. However, they have trouble competing with informal collectors, who operate door-to-door and can offer higher prices than more formal recyclers. Formal recyclers have higher overhead costs to comply with environmental, health and safety regulations.[53]

Poor recycling practices have also become a major issue for governments, producers and NGOs in developed countries that export e-waste to Africa and Asian countries. There is disagreement between some stakeholders, however, over the most appropriate responses.[54] The European Electronics Recycling Association (EERA) opposes the export of e-waste to non-OECD countries and countries that have not signed the Basel Convention. EERA argues that e-waste should only be exported if the receiving operation complies with European standards. In contrast, the US Institute of Scrap Recycling Industries (ISRI) is not opposed to exports to non-OECD countries or non-signatories to the Basel Convention (the US is not a signatory) as long as certain conditions are met. The ISRI supports voluntary standards such as R2.[55] R2 and other voluntary industry standards that aim to improve recycling practices are summarized in Table 4.9.

52   Raghupathy, L., Kruger, C., Chaturvedi, A., Arora, R., & Henzler, M. (2010). E-waste recycling in India: bridging the formal-informal gap. *Recycling International*, May 2010, 80-83.

53   *Ibid.*

54   Reintjes, M. (2013). Inferior exports are killing innovation, claims Zonneveld. *Recycling International*, November 2013, 35.

55   *Ibid.*

4.4.6 Conflict minerals

Many leading electronics manufacturers are taking action to identify and avoid the use of minerals from sources that contribute to human rights abuses or conflict. This has been driven by increased awareness of impacts in the Democratic Republic of Congo and adjoining countries, as well as government initiatives.[56] The minerals of concern include tin, tantalum, tungsten and gold; all of which are used in the consumer electronics industry.

4.5 Corporate strategy

4.5.1 Policy

Most global electronics and appliance manufacturers have a strong commitment to corporate social responsibility and specific goals for product stewardship. At Canon, for example, responsibility for the life-cycle impacts of products is integrated into every aspect of the business (Table 4.7). This is driven by the company's commitment to corporate social responsibility (CSR) and its responsiveness to stakeholder needs and expectations. Since 1996 the company has had a goal of becoming "… a truly excellent global company that is admired and respected by people around the world".[57] Canon's environmental vision takes a full life-cycle approach:

> Canon's vision for a sustainable society is one that promotes both enriched lifestyles and the global environment. We have established "Action for Green" as our environmental vision for achieving this goal. Under this vision, we are working closely with our customers and business partners to reduce environmental impact, focusing on the entire product life cycle.[58]

The life-cycle environmental impacts of Canon products are measured by calculating carbon dioxide (CO_2) emissions over their total life-cycle. The quantity of used parts and recycled materials, as well as end-of-life treatment, feed into this calculation. The performance of each Canon company

---

56 For example: OECD (2013). *OECD Due Diligence Guidance for Responsible Supply Chains of Minerals from Conflict-Affected and High-Risk Areas.* Paris: OECD Publishing. Retrieved from http://www.oecd.org/daf/inv/mne/GuidanceEdition2.pdf

57 Canon (2015). *Canon Sustainability Report 2015.* Tokyo: Canon, p. 5.

58 *Ibid.*, p. 26.

TABLE 4.7   Canon's approach to corporate social responsibility and product stewardship

Corporate philosophy	Kyosei: "Living and working together for the common good"
CSR policy	Includes a commitment to "contributing to the realization of a better society as a good corporate citizen" and to achieving growth through "sound and fair business activities".
Stakeholder engagement	An annual stakeholder survey helps to identify CSR issues for Canon.
CSR management	CSR activities are developed under the leadership of senior management.
CSR issues	These include "global environmental conservation", with four priorities: • Response to resource depletion • Measures against environmental pollution • Response to climate change • Conservation of biodiversity. Other product-related issues are addressed under "customer care" (product safety) and "fair operating practices" (response to conflict minerals).
Canon Group Environmental Charter	Outlines environmental assurance activities, which include two specifically related to products: 2. "Assess the environmental impact of entire product lifecycles and explore ways to minimize environmental burden" 5. "In procuring and purchasing necessary resources, give priority to materials, parts and products with lower environmental burden".
2015–2017 product-related goal	Canon measures "lifecycle carbon dioxide emission improvement index per product" and has a target of 3% improvement compared with the previous year.
Environmental performance evaluation system	The Global Environment Center evaluates the environmental performance of product operations, manufacturing and sales companies using criteria linked to the environmental goals. Environmental evaluations account for 10% of overall consolidated performance.
Environmental action plan for 2015	Includes several product-related goals: • Promoting environmentally conscious design—implement smaller, lighter weight products; promote designs with product lifecycles in mind … • Reducing CO_2 emissions during use—combine increased functionality and image resolution with lower energy consumption … • Strengthening the promotion of product recycling—expand collection and recycle systems for products throughout the Canon Group; encourage remanufacturing, parts reuse and recycling; create advanced materials recycling technologies.

Source: Based on Canon (2015)

is evaluated annually against a range of criteria including financial, management and operational measures. Environmental performance, including measures related to reduction of greenhouse gas emissions, product recycling, environmental communications and chemicals management, accounts for about 8% of the overall score.

Canon is not alone in setting ambitious goals and targets, particularly in the information technology (IT) sector. Dell's ambitious 2020 Legacy of Good Plan includes commitments to "reduce the energy intensity of our product portfolio by 80% and to use only packaging that is 100% compostable or recyclable".[59]

Indian electronics manufacturer Wipro has a vision that "business must get involved in social issues because it is the right thing to do, and not because of compliance pressures".[60] Through a rigorous evaluation and consultation process the company has identified "product and service stewardship" as one of the ten most material issues to Wipro and its stakeholders. One of its goals in 2012–13 was to ensure that by 2014 95% of waste from its IT operations in India was being recycled.[61] In 2012 Greenpeace International awarded Wipro the highest score in its *Guide to Greener Electronics.*[62]

4.5.2 Design

Over the past few decades most leading manufacturers have taken steps to reduce the environmental impacts of their products, particularly during the use stage of the life-cycle. Since the 1980s there has been a strong focus on the energy efficiency of household appliances, driven by energy efficiency and mandatory labelling standards. Data from BSH Hausgeräte, the largest manufacturer of household appliances in Europe (Bosch and Siemens brands) indicates that energy consumption fell by around 70% for refrigerators and 30% for dishwashers and washing machines between 1990 and 2005.[63]

Water efficiency has also improved. The BSH Hausgeräte study reported that water consumption of a front-loader washing machine has fallen from

59   Dell (2012). *2020 Legacy of Good Plan.* Retrieved from http://i.dell.com/sites/doccontent/corporate/corp-comm/en/Documents/2020-plan.pdf
60   Wipro (2013). *The Butterfly's Journey: WIPRO Sustainability Report 2012–13.* Bangalore, India: Wipro, p. 28. Retrieved from http://wipro.org/resource/Wipro-sustainability-report-2012-13.pdf
61   *Ibid.*
62   Greenpeace International (2012).
63   Otto *et al.* (2006).

30 L/kg in 1970 to 7.2 L/kg in 2006, a saving of around 75%. The authors argue, however that "… no major decrease seems possible in the future … [due to] … the physical necessities of washing".[64] Changes in consumer behaviour probably offer the best opportunities to further improve efficiencies, for example reducing the frequency of washing, avoiding dryers, turning appliances off at the wall and using the "cold water" setting.[65]

While many household appliances may be reaching peak efficiency, technological developments are still driving improvements in the ICT sector. Apple, for example, states that "… we look at three ways to reduce a product's energy consumption: more efficient power supplies to bring electricity from the wall to the device, more efficient hardware, and smarter power management software".[66]

Within the IT sector the trend away from desktop computers to laptops, tablets and smart phones has facilitated significant efficiency and environmental improvements. The environmental impacts of a computer tend to increase with weight, particularly for greenhouse gas emissions.[67] Laptops and notebooks, for example, have lower emissions than desktop computers. This is demonstrated in Figure 4.3 for several Apple products: the iPhone has the lowest impact, followed by the tablet, notebook and desktop computer.

The European WEEE and RoHS Directives, and similar regulations in China and elsewhere, have driven a shift away from toxic substances to more environmentally acceptable alternatives. Some of Apple's achievements in phasing out some of the worst offenders, including lead and mercury, are illustrated in Table 4.8.

Design to improve recovery at the end of a product's life—through reuse, remanufacturing or recycling—is a common strategy used by leading companies to reduce the environmental footprint of their products. Appliance manufacturers such as Fisher & Paykel (Case study 4.7.2) have labelled their plastic components by polymer type to facilitate sorting and recycling of individual materials. Fuji Xerox Australia designs printers and other office

64   *Ibid.*, p. 3.
65   Koerner & Turk (2010).
66   Apple (2015), p. 9.
67   Teehan, P., & Kandikar, M. (2013). Comparing embodied greenhouse gas emissions of modern computing and electronics products. *Environmental Science & Technology*, 2013(47), 3997-4003; Apple (2014). *Measuring Performance, One Product At a Time*. Retrieved from https://www.apple.com/lae/environment/reports/

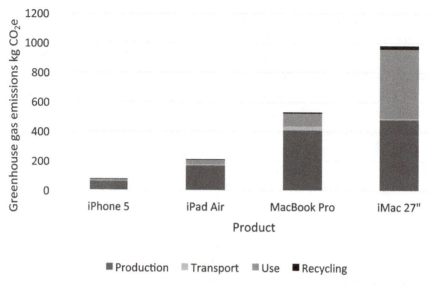

FIGURE 4.3 Life-cycle greenhouse gas emissions for selected Apple products, 2013

Source: Derived from Apple (2014)

TABLE 4.8 Reduction of toxic substances at Apple

Substance of concern	Action taken
Beryllium	Found in the copper alloys used to make connectors and springs. iPhone 6, iPad Air 2 and MacBook were designed without the use of beryllium.
Mercury	Found in fluorescent lamps that used to backlight Mac displays. It was eliminated from Apple displays in 2009.
Lead	Formerly used in display glass and solder. It was phased out completely in 2006.
Arsenic	Traditionally used for clarity in glass. Apple display glass has been arsenic-free since 2008.
Polyvinyl chloride (PVC)	Widely used by other companies in computers, cables and power cords. Apple began phasing out PVC in 1995.
Brominated flame retardants (BFRs)	These toxic compounds are added to plastic enclosures, circuit boards and connectors. They were eliminated from Apple products in 2008.
Phthalates	Used to soften plastics in cables and power cords. Apple eliminated them from cables and power cords in 2013.

Source: Based on Apple (2015), p. 24

equipment for durability, repair and remanufacturing.[68] In contrast, note-books and tablets are becoming smaller and more difficult to recycle. The MacBook Air, for example, has been described as "a machine built to be shredded, not repaired, upgraded, and reused".[69]

Many companies are aiming to "close the loop" by incorporating material from recycled products into the manufacture of new products. Lexmark's 2013 CSR report outlines its commitment to closed-loop recycling for toner cartridges:

> Lexmark continues our innovative closed-loop toner cartridge recy-cling operations. Through the award-winning Lexmark Cartridge Collection Program, our engineers can reclaim a feed stream of high-impact polystyrene plastic. After returning this material to near-new quality, the plastic is used to manufacture new toner cartridges. Lexmark is an industry leader in reclaimed plastic with 10 percent average postconsumer plastic content across all toner cartridges. Our goal is to increase the postconsumer plastic content of our toner cartridges to 25 percent by 2016.[70]

This highlights one of the important business benefits of a product take-back programme. OEMs can keep control of a valuable source of raw mate-rials by supporting a product take-back programme and designing their products to optimize the value of materials at end of life.

Many leading EEE manufacturers go "beyond compliance" by integrating design for environment (DFE) procedures in business systems that apply in all of the countries in which they operate, regardless of whether or not design requirements are mandated by law. Bosch, for example, has a DFE "Norm" (standard) that must be followed by all of its business divisions and regional subsidiaries, and a "Checklist for sustainable product development at Bosch".[71]

68 Fuji Xerox Australia (2014). *Taking the Lead for Growth: Fuji Xerox Australia Sustainability Report 2014*. Macquarie Park, Australia.

69 Minter (2013), p. 256.

70 Lexmark (2014). *Lexmark Global Citizenship: Our Products—Materials*, p. 46. Retrieved from http://csr.lexmark.com/materials.html

71 Lewis, H. (2014). *Robert Bosch (Australia): A Packaging Assessment Case Study*. Sydney: Australian Packaging Covenant. Retrieved from http://www.packagingcovenant.org.au/data/Case_study_R.Bosch.pdf

4.5.3 Procurement

To identify the "material issues" that it would focus on for its sustainability report in 2014, Fuji Xerox Australia surveyed its internal and external stakeholders. Through this process the company identified six priorities including "procuring responsibly".[72]

Supply chain management is an essential to ensure that a company's environmental and social goals are being met. "Responsible procurement" is driven by stakeholder interests as well as corporate sustainability policies. This may include:

- The development of technical standards or guidelines that suppliers have to meet, for example for restricted substances

- A process for supplier reporting and evaluation against the company's standards

- A process for supplier engagement and education to improve their performance over time.

Wipro is at an early stage of what it calls its "ethical supply chain" programme. The company undertook a risk assessment of its supplier base in 2012 and in the following year held its first meeting with suppliers to outline Wipro's ethical supply chain policies and procedures. The next steps for the company are to prioritize risk areas and select suppliers for detailed engagement to improve environmental and social performance. New procedures will be developed, and over time the company expects to include sustainability considerations in procurement decisions.[73]

Dell has a more established supply chain management programme. Suppliers are expected to adhere to the company's social and environmental responsibility (SER) standards and to use these to influence their own suppliers. The company has made a commitment to 100% transparency of key issues within the supply chain, and to working with suppliers to mitigate risk in those areas.[74] Dell does not have the same reporting requirements as a public company but still wants to be open and accountable:

> Our goal of demonstrating 100% transparency does not change with Dell's privatization and if anything only increases in its urgency. Not only is transparency important to us, but it is also important to our customers, who are demanding increasingly greater detail about a

72   Fuji Xerox Australia (2014).
73   Wipro (2013).
74   Dell (2012), p. 9.

variety of issues, including conflict minerals and labor issues. Though Dell may not have reporting requirements now as a private company, many of our customers do, so we must operate in an open and transparent manner.[75]

Dell's supply chain management programme involves:

- SER standards that include criteria for carbon, water, waste, worker health and safety, and human rights and dignity

- Audits of supplier performance and working with them to improve compliance

- Workshops and webinars with Tier 1 suppliers to share SER best practices

- Publishing aggregated supplier audit results[76]

Due diligence and transparency within the electrical and electronic products sector is supported by a number of voluntary standards and certification programmes. For example, the Conflict-Free Sourcing Initiative, which was set up by some of the larger electronics companies in 2008, provides resources and tools to guide sourcing and reporting of conflict minerals.[77]

4.5.4 Reuse and recycling

Electrical and electronic products often cascade through a hierarchy of secondary uses throughout their lifetime. When a consumer decides to buy a new computer or household appliance, for example, they might give away or sell their old product to someone else. When the product eventually "dies" and is no longer worth repairing, it may end up at an e-waste recycler where materials are separated for reprocessing. Valuable components may be separated and sold for another use, such as the "smart drive" in a Fisher

75 Dell (2014). *FY14 Corporate Responsibility Report: A Progress Report on our 2020 Legacy of Good Plan*, p. 25. Retrieved from http://www.dell.com/learn/us/en/uscorp1/dell-fy13-cr-report?c=us&l=en&s=corp&cs=uscorp1

76 Dell (2012).

77 For example: Conflict Free Sourcing Initiative (2013). *Reasonable Practices to Identify Sources of Conflict Minerals: Practical Guidance for Downstream Companies*. Electronic Industry Citizenship Coalition and the Global e-Sustainability Initiative. Retrieved from http://www.conflictfreesourcing.org/media/docs/news/CFSI_DD_ReasonablePracticesforDownstreamCompanies_Aug2013.pdf

& Paykel dishwasher (Case study 4.7.2), before the remaining materials are reprocessed and sold to other manufacturers.

Most end-of-life product management strategies focus on recycling, either through individual or collective take-back programmes (discussed below), but some industry leaders combine remanufacturing with recycling to achieve superior environmental and commercial outcomes. Fuji Xerox Australia was a pioneer in remanufacturing with the establishment of its Eco Manufacturing Centre in Sydney in 2000, although the company had started remanufacturing parts in 1993. Before that time, used or damaged parts had been sent to landfill, which was costly and environmentally wasteful. The company is primarily a service provider, leasing printers and other office equipment with its own leasing finance company. This means that "it is in the firm's interest to develop robust machines and to recover worn and damaged components from the firm's customers for remanufacture".[78] At the Eco Manufacturing Centre, used or failed components from Australia and the Asia-Pacific region are tested, re-engineered and reassembled into "new" products. This process has many benefits. Apart from lower costs, it enables the company to examine the technical causes for failure and opportunities to extend the life of the product and improve performance. It also generates environmental benefits by reducing demand for raw materials and reducing waste to landfill.[79]

4.5.4.1 Recycling

All electrical and electronic products are potentially recyclable, but collection rates and recycling efficiency vary significantly depending on the value of the component materials. Recovery of printed circuit boards for example, is driven by the value of the copper, gold, silver and lead elements. In contrast, LCD panels have limited value because of the difficulties involved in recovery of the material components. According to Huisman *et al.* there are limited technologies for recovering LCDs and little economic evidence to justify recovery of the liquid crystals that can contain up to 500 different liquid crystal components (most processes focus on recovery of the glass components only).[80]

---

78 Benn, S., Dunphy, D., & Angus-Leppan, T. (2011). Fuji Xerox Australia Eco-manufacturing Centre. In S. Benn, D. Dunphy, & B. Perrott (Eds.), *Cases in Corporate Sustainabiity and Change* (pp. 28-41). Prahran, Australia: Tilde University Press, p. 32.

79 *Ibid.*

80 Huisman *et al.* (2007).

4.5.4.2 Voluntary industry recycling programmes

Producers can support recycling in several ways, for example by taking back and recycling their own products, by contracting a third party to recycle the company's products on their behalf, or by joining a collective industry recycling programme.

While EPR laws for e-waste are now becoming more widespread, many corporate recycling programmes were introduced voluntarily to meet CSR or sustainability policies. Canon launched its toner cartridge recycling programme in 1990 in the United States, Germany and Japan, and in 2015 celebrated 25 years of successful recycling. Canon's sustainability report notes that it was based on the philosophy of *kyosei*, which is Canon's guiding corporate philosophy of "living and working together for the common good", and in recognition that they have a responsibility to "pursue ideal recycling for resource circulation".[81]

Cartridge recycling was also introduced to protect the company's reputation after some customers became concerned about waste:

> Canon was one of the first companies to implement [cartridge recycling]. They were the first to have a toner cartridge system for MFDs [multi-function devices]. That was around 22 years ago. Before that you used to pour the toner in, and it was done by technicians. And then Canon realised that customers could do it, so there was a cost saving, but there was a waste of toner cartridges and bottles. So they set up the first recycling program for toner cartridges in the world … It was about customer perceptions of waste.[82]

Today the company collects used toner cartridges in 24 countries and regions and processes them at four sites close to major consumer markets. One of these is a new automated cartridge recycling facility at Canon Ecology Industry Inc., the company's recycling hub in Japan.

Canon has a global commitment to recycle used cartridges, despite the fact that in many markets it is not a regulatory requirement. In Australia, for example, Canon supports the voluntary "Cartridges 4 Planet Ark" (C4PA) programme, managed by Close the Loop, which collects and recycles used ink and toner cartridges with financial support from the OEMs (see Case study 4.7.1). In 2007 Close the Loop extended its activities to the US, where it provides the recycling and data capture "back end" for Staples' cartridge collection programme. A third factory opened in Belgium in 2014.

---

81   Canon (2015), p. 15.
82   Personal communication (interview) with J. Leslie, Manager Sustainability, Canon Australia, 13 November 2013.

When Steve Morriss originally set up Close the Loop, he convinced global equipment manufacturers to provide financial support by identifying multiple business benefits. While environmental outcomes including zero waste to landfill were very important to these companies, Morriss was also able to address a significant business problem. This was the desire by OEMs to manage their own empty cartridges in order to minimize reputational risks and warranty claims associated with third party cartridge refillers. Over time the recycling programme generated additional value for OEM partners through the business intelligence it was able to provide (Case study 4.7.1).

Most voluntary recycling programmes are driven by corporate sustainability or CSR policies rather than any direct benefit to the business. Fisher & Paykel's appliance recycling programme was influenced by a corporate culture that values waste minimization and environmental responsibility (Case study 4.7.2). Apple has a global commitment to recycling all its products, stating that "[e]very Apple Retail Store in the world will now take back Apple products for free and recycle them responsibly. We believe we must be accountable for every Apple product at every stage of use".[83]

Companies like Canon and Apple operate "beyond compliance" around the world to meet their own high sustainability standards. Dell has also positioned itself as a global leader on e-waste recycling policy and practice:

> Dell is committed to providing efficient and easy product recovery options directly to customers to facilitate responsible product retirement with or without mandates. We accept responsibility for continually improving the environmental design aspects of our products and their end-of-life management. We have consistently been an IT industry leader in disposal convenience for consumers and overall volume of collections. This includes jurisdictions without recycling laws as well as those with laws that require collection by producers but do not set targets. Dell encourages this same level of responsibility and investment from other IT producers and indeed, all producers of all electrical products.[84]

Global brands such as Dell place a high priority on protecting their corporate reputation, and do not want to be associated with unsafe or environmentally damaging e-waste recovery processes in developing countries. There is no doubt that the export of e-waste to developing countries, and the associated negative publicity, is a risk to reputation.[85] In 2009 Dell

83   Apple (2015), p. 3.
84   Dell (2014). *Dell's Policy Statement on Electronics Recycling*.
85   Reintjes (2013).

was the first IT company to state publicly that it would prohibit the export of non-working parts and end-of-life equipment to certain developing countries.[86]

A number of standards have been developed to improve environmental, health and safety performance in the recycling chain and to provide a more "level playing field" for recyclers. There are many common elements, including:

- An environmental, health and safety management system

- Environment, health and safety practices

- Compliance with all legal requirements

- Ensuring that downstream recyclers meet similar standards

- Data destruction

However, there are importance differences relating to scope, definitions of hazardous waste and limitations on export (Table 4.9).

Development of the R2 Standard was a three-year, multi-stakeholder process led by the US EPA. According to one of its primary drafters, John Lingelbach, some recyclers were concerned that they were being undercut by companies who were using the term "recycling" quite loosely.[87] They were not meeting the same levels of recovery, or minimum environmental, health and safety standards. Customers wanted greater assurance that recyclers were managing used electronics responsibly. The standard was published in 2008 and became an accredited programme in 2010. There are now over 500 certified e-waste recycling facilities in 21 countries.[88]

Other standards have since been launched in the US and Europe. The Basel Action Network (BAN) in the US was originally involved in multi-stakeholder dialogue to develop R2, but walked away because it "could not in good conscience agree with the group and vote to field test a draft of the standard that would violate laws in importing countries, as well as allow

---

86   Clancy, H. (2013, May 12). Dell steps up e-waste recycliing with African hub. *Forbes*. Retrieved from http://www.forbes.com/sites/heatherclancy/2013/12/05/dell-steps-up-e-waste-recycling-with-african-hub/

87   Lingelbach, J. (2014). The Responsible Recycling Standard. In *R2 Standards and Solutions for CRT Glass and Plastics Recycling*. Sydney: TES-AMM.

88   Sustainable Electronics Recycling International (2015). *About SERI*. Retrieved from https://sustainableelectronics.org/about

TABLE 4.9　Voluntary e-waste recycling standards

Standard	Owner	Recovery options	Hazardous wastes	Limitations on export
The responsible recycling ("R2") standard for electronics recyclers www.r2solutions.org	R2 Solutions	Hierarchy of reuse, followed by materials recovery, then energy recovery or disposal.	Requires careful management of "focus materials": PCBs, mercury, CRT glass, batteries, circuit boards.	
The e-Stewards standard for responsible recycling and reuse of electronic equipment www.e-stewards.org	Basel Action Network (BAN)	Hierarchy of direct reuse or working equipment, followed by refurbishment & repair, then materials recovery, and finally disposal.	Does not allow disposal of hazardous electronic waste in landfill. Broad definition including asbestos; most batteries; CRTs and CRT glass; circuit boards and lamps containing certain substances; mercury; PCBs, radioactive waste, selenium & arsenic. Also identifies "problematic components or materials" that may require special controls, e.g. alkaline batteries; inks and toner; plastics with halogenated materials or brominated flame retardants.	Bans exports from OECD to non-OECD countries and non-signatories to the Basel Convention.
WEEELABEX normative documents (3): collection, logistics, treatment http://www.weee-forum.org/weeelabex-0	WEEE Forum	Refers to the waste hierarchy in the Waste Framework Directive 2008/98/EC: prevention, reuse, recycling, other recovery e.g. energy recovery, disposal.	Hazardous waste requirements are based on the EU WEEE Directive 2002/96/EC and other European regulations. Provides detailed guidance on "de-pollution" (removal of components before recycling) and treatment of CRTs, flat panel displays, lamps, temperature exchange equipment, household appliances with CFCs, HCFCs and hydrofluorocarbons (HFCs).	Bans cross-boundary shipments to operators whose operations don't comply with WEEELABEX and WEEE Directive or an equivalent set of requirements. Export of uncleaned CRT glass (with fluorescent coatings) is prohibited.

toxic substances in solid waste disposal facilities".[89] BAN is a not-for-profit organization "working globally to prevent the illegal and unjust trafficking of hazardous waste, based on the *Basel Convention*".[90] BAN led the development of another standard called "e-Stewards", which has a more expansive definition of hazardous waste and stricter export restrictions.

The European equivalent is WEEELABEX, which was developed through a four-year multi-stakeholder process.

4.5.4.3 Compliance with EPR laws

Under most EPR laws producers can meet their compliance obligations by either implementing their own recycling programme ("individual producer responsibility"), or by joining a collective producer responsibility organization (PRO). In most countries there are a number of competitive PROs for e-waste (Table 4.10), often with one dominant PRO that has a large market share.[91]

In the EU most PROs were set up in the 2000s following the adoption of the WEEE Directive in 2002. Most collect WEEE from municipal collection sites or retailers but the full extent of financial responsibility varies. While most local authorities collect WEEE free of charge at their waste management centres, they either bear the collection costs themselves (e.g. Denmark and Sweden) or receive compensation from the PROs (e.g. Finland and France).[92]

Cost is an important consideration for producers when choosing a compliance organization. A case study on the European Recycling Platform (ERP) argued that PROs specifically set up by producers to meet their compliance obligations are at a natural disadvantage compared with waste management companies that already operate waste management services.[93] However, many choose to join an industry-led scheme such as the ERP to ensure that the PRO acts in their long-term interests to optimize processes and costs.[94]

89   Basel Action Network (2013). *The e-Stewards Story*. Retrieved from http://e-stewards.org/about-us/the-e-stewards-story/
90   Basel Action Network (2013). *Review Version: Performance Requirements Excerpted from the E-Stewards Standard for Responsible Recycling and Reuse of Electronic Equipment*, p. 1.
91   Bio Intelligence Service (2014). *Development of Guidance on Extended Producer Responsibility (EPR)*. Report to European Commission—DG Environment.
92   *Ibid.*
93   Mayers, K., & Butler, S. (2013). Producer responsibility organisations: development and operations. *Journal of Industrial Ecology*, 17(2), 277-289.
94   *Ibid.*

TABLE 4.10   Comparison of producer responsibility schemes for e-waste in selected countries in the EU, 2014

Member state	Number of collective PROs	Costs covered by producers	Producer fees €/ tonne of product collected
Denmark	4	HH: 100% transport and net treatment costs C&I: 100% collection and treatment costs	Not available
Finland	3	100% collection, transport & net treatment costs	Not available
France	4	100% collection, transport & net treatment costs	HH: €384/t
Ireland	2	100% transport & net treatment costs	HH: €160/t
Latvia	5	100% collection, transport & net treatment costs	Not available
Sweden	2	100% collection, transport & net treatment costs	Not available
United Kingdom	39	100% net, transport & treatment costs	Not available

HH = household, C&I = commercial and industrial

Source: Bio Intelligence Service (2014), pp. 61-73

When a number of Australian producers established their own PRO, ANZRP, to meet new recycling regulations for TVs and computers (Case study 4.7.3), its founding members drew on the experiences of other PROs including the ERP. Unlike the other approved services (called "Arrangements") under the regulations, which include DHL Supply Chain and several e-waste recycling companies, ANZRP's sole purpose is to recycle e-waste on behalf of its members. The organization claims that being "industry run" is one of its strengths as a product stewardship model.[95]

The WEEE Directive (article 12) requires that each producer is responsible for financing at least the collection, treatment, recovery and environmentally sound disposal of WEEE from private households that have been deposited at collection facilities. It also requires that each producer shall be responsible for financing these activities "relating to the waste from his

95   ANZRP (2014). *TechCollect Annual Report 2013–14*. Melbourne: Australia New Zealand Recycling Platform, p. 2.

4 ELECTRICAL AND ELECTRONIC EQUIPMENT

own products".[96] This principle is potentially powerful because it provides a direct incentive for producers to design products that are easier to recycle. In practice most PROs allocate costs to producers on a collective basis, so there is little financial incentive for individual companies to improve recyclability.[97]

In Europe fees paid by producers vary between member states and product types.[98] In Denmark, for example, fees are aligned with the collection and treatment costs of each type of e-waste. In France fees depend on some environmental criteria including recyclability, lifetime and the presence of hazardous substances. In some jurisdictions, such as China and Taiwan, producers are only responsible for financing recycling programmes that are managed by government agencies.

Compliance with local e-waste laws sometimes requires additional investment by producers in the development of supporting policy frameworks and infrastructure. Dell has been very proactive in Kenya, for example, where it has built a regional e-waste handling facility with local partners to recycle products using safe and environmentally sustainable processes.

4.6 Conclusions

Producer responsibility for electrical and electronic equipment is more likely to be driven by regulation than other sectors such as packaging because of the more immediate environmental risks associated with toxic or ozone-depleting substances. It is also more likely to be linked to supply chain pressure, with leading companies establishing company or industry-wide standards on issues such as toxic substances, conflict minerals and recycling standards.

The environmental and social impacts of these products are very different from those associated with packaging, highlighting the need for different responses. Toxicity issues are much more prominent and justify a greater role for government regulation. The consumption of energy, water and other consumables during the use of these products means that companies must consider and promote more sustainable practices by consumers.

---

96   European Commission (2012). *Directive 2012/19/EU on Waste Electrical and Electronic Equipment (WEEE)*. Brussels, Belgium.
97   Mayers & Butler (2013).
98   Bio Intelligence Service (2014).

Most recycling programmes also require a commitment from consumers to take their used product to a recycling drop-off point, or to pay for recycling. The principle of "shared responsibility" is therefore particularly important for EEE, both during use and at end of life.

The companies featured in this chapter, such as Apple, Canon, Dell and Fisher & Paykel, are just some of the companies that play a leadership role in the life-cycle management of electrical and electronic products. They have strategic goals and practical programmes that aim to minimize the environmental and social impacts of their products at every step, from raw materials extraction through to the end of their life.

Many of the leading companies in this sector have also taken a proactive approach to regulation, working together in many cases to design appropriate regulatory frameworks. They acknowledge stakeholder concerns about the risks and impacts of toxic substances in landfill or during recycling, and have taken action to address them.

E-waste laws are supported by a number of voluntary industry standards that promote best practices in the reuse and recycling of products at end of life. This has been important in addressing regulatory gaps, particularly in developing countries, where global brands face reputational risks associated with environmentally damaging or socially unacceptable practices. The fact that these standards, such as WEEELABEX and R2, are administered by private entities rather than government "opens doors for producers and PROs to take more responsibility".[99]

4.7 Case studies

Case study 4.7.1 Printer cartridge recycling at Close the Loop®

> You force any company into anything and they're going to be prickly; they're going to do the minimal contribution. Voluntary programs focus on the upside for the company (Steve Morriss, Founder and Director, Close the Loop).[100]

99   Kunz *et al.* (2014).
100 Personal communication with S. Morriss, 2014.

PHOTO 4.1   Printer cartridges ready for recycling

Photo: Close the Loop

4.7.1.1 Summary

Close the Loop Ltd was established in Australia to collect and recycle used ink and toner cartridges for OEMs. The programme was extended to the United States in 2007.

Close the Loop's goal of "zero waste to landfill" has been achieved through a focus on innovation and R&D, which has enabled it to divert all of the materials in a used cartridge to value-added markets. This gives the company a competitive edge because some programmes don't recover mixed plastics and/or toner. Close the Loop demonstrates how a carefully designed take-back programme can generate multiple benefits for participating businesses, including access to "closed loop" recycled materials and business intelligence data.

4.7.1.2 Drivers for product stewardship

Steve Morriss conceived the idea for Close the Loop in 1999. At the time he owned a small business supplying genuine and remanufactured inkjet and toner cartridges, primarily to schools and universities, but business pressures led to a significant change in direction:

> We started to get price pressure from the big multinationals like Corporate Express. In order to keep the business, I knew that I had to come up with something other than price, because as a small family-owned business there was no way we were going to be able to compete on price. So I offered a rather bold move, to take back and recycle everything we supplied.[101]

This provided the company with a unique selling proposition that enabled it to keep its two biggest university accounts. "From that point onwards I knew that there was a certain customer who valued environmental best practice over price. That was a very important realization" says Morriss.

The next challenge was to find a sustainable financial model. Morriss's first approach was to other cartridge remanufacturers, who agreed it was a "great idea" but they weren't prepared to fund it. "Then I had to think, who WOULD pay for this, and the obvious ones were the printer and copier manufacturers".

> The main driver [for them] at that time was to be able to manage their own empty cartridges. They were receiving a large number of warranty claims because some third party cartridge refillers were putting any old toner in the cartridge, and then it would gum up on the fuser assemblies and cause all sorts of printer problems. Of course the owner of the printer would ring the agent of HP or Canon or Lexmark, even though it wasn't a HP or Canon or Lexmark cartridge that caused the damage. So it was very understandable to me that the OEMs had a huge driver there. They wanted to control their own empties.[102]

The other motivating factor for OEMs at the beginning of the programme was the European Union's WEEE Directive, which would require producers to take physical and/or financial responsibility for their products at end of life.

4.7.1.3 Stewardship strategies

Close the Loop became a stand-alone business in early 2001, providing a voluntary, multi-vendor, producer responsibility collection and recycling programme for toner and inkjet cartridges. Morriss originally had trouble convincing the OEMs that he could deliver on the recycling service, but "the tide turned" when he invited environmental organization Planet Ark to be

101 *Ibid.*
102 *Ibid.*

his marketing partner. Planet Ark's involvement gave the programme credibility and a higher profile with both consumers and OEMs.

The multi-vendor recycling programme in Australia, branded "Cartridges 4 Planet Ark (C4PA)" is supported by a large group of OEMs including Brother, Canon, Epson, HP, Konica Minolta, Kyocera, Oce and Panasonic. These companies collectively represent around 60% of sales in Australia. Each OEM pays for recycling of its own products and shares the reverse logistics costs. Cartridge collection boxes are provided free of charge to offices, and consumers can drop off their used cartridges at participating retail stores. There are now 45,000 collection points in offices and retail stores in Australia and 120,000 in the US.

Close the Loop also collects and recycles cartridges for individual OEMs such as Fuji Xerox, Lexmark, Toshiba and Sharp, who collect cartridges through their own collection networks. In the United States the company provides "back end" support (recycling, data capture and reporting) for business supplies retailer, Staples.

At the two processing facilities (Australia and the US) cartridges are sorted and certain types returned to the OEM for their own remanufacturing programmes. The rest are shredded to separate raw materials for reuse. Through a strong focus on research and innovation Close the Loop has been able to develop new markets for recycled plastics and toner from used cartridges, which means that 100% of all cartridges and toner bottles are recycled. Plastics including high impact polystyrene (HIPS) and acrylonitrile butadiene styrene (ABS) are recycled back into high quality post-consumer resins, which are supplied back to equipment manufacturers for use in making new printers, copiers or cartridges. Mixed or residual plastics are recovered as eWood©, a timber replacement product for landscaping and construction (Photo 4.2). Recovered toner powder is refined and turned into an additive called modified toner polymer (MTP), which is added to asphalt to improve its performance. The company's website states that "Close the Loop is NOT *a waste management* business. We are a *zero waste materials recovery* business".[103]

103 Close the Loop (2015). *Materials Recovery.* Retrieved from http://www. closetheloop.com.au/materials-recovery/closing-the-loop/

PHOTO 4.2   eWood© retaining wall

Photo: Close the Loop

4.7.1.4 Shared value outcomes

Cartridge recycling programmes help OEMs to meet their CSR or sustainability goals by reducing product waste at end of life. Close the Loop's website states that:

> Each day across our two facilities (Australia and USA) we keep over 48.6 tonnes of material out of landfill. We recover irreplaceable resources that are used to make a new generation of products whilst achieving tonnes of carbon savings every day.[104]

The carbon claim is supported by a life-cycle assessment undertaken for Lexmark, which found that recycling toner cartridges rather than disposing of them to landfill reduced greenhouse gas emissions by between 43 and 55%, depending on the model.[105]

---

104 *Ibid.*

105 Lexmark (2013). *Corporate Social Responsibility Report 2012*, p. 51. Retrieved from http://csr.lexmark.com/pdfs/2012_lexmark_csr.pdf

While these outcomes are important to OEMs, their support for the programme is also driven by more direct business benefits including access to business intelligence data. Close the Loop records the flow of ink or toner to the device. Close the Loop scans every cartridge that enters its facilities and uses this data to prepare business intelligence reports for each customer. This includes:

- The number of "grey market", counterfeit or "clone" products entering the market under a company's brand name

- Where their cartridges are being collected, which enables OEMs to map the location of their devices across the country

- The number of pages printed by each cartridge

- Which end users are replacing cartridges too early (i.e. wasting toner)

The cartridge recycling programme also enables OEMs to meet a higher performance standard within EPEAT®, a rating system developed by the US-based Green Electronics Council:

> A big driver today is procurement guidelines. If you want to supply [what is] possibly the biggest purchaser of printers and copiers in the world—the US Government—you need EPEAT certification; either bronze, silver or gold. We're the only company in the world that can help meet two voluntary criteria of EPEAT guidelines. One of these involves reuse of toner powder—reusing 75% of the toner powder—which our products MTP and TonerPave® help us do. Toner powder, other than Close the Loop, in our understanding goes to waste to energy. It's a good business builder for us.
>
> The other element of EPEAT we can help with is return of post-consumer recycled plastics ... If you want to reach a gold standard you have to have at least 25% recycled plastics content in your product.[106]

A proportion of the plastics recovered by Close the Loop is returned to OEMs for manufacturing printer and copier parts. This can help companies to maintain control of their raw materials while meeting environmental performance targets. In 2013 Lexmark reported that its toner cartridge product line contained an average of 10% post-consumer recycled plastics, and it was aiming to increase this to 25% by 2016.[107] Close the Loop supplies post-consumer resin from cartridge recycling to Lexmark and other customers.

106 Personal communication with S. Morriss, 2014.
107 Lexmark (2013), p. 49.

Morriss describes the processing and refining of plastics as "a huge growth area" for the business. The company can also provide advice on design improvements that would improve the value of recovered materials. Close the Loop worked with one large OEM to reduce the number of different types of plastic in a cartridge, and to ensure that similar plastics (particularly HIPS and ABS) were easy to identify and separate.

Case study 4.7.2 Appliance recycling at Fisher & Paykel

> New Zealand's clean, green reputation has formed part of our philosophy for decades. Today we strive to emphasise sustainability in everything we do, from comprehensive recycling programs in New Zealand and abroad, to continual energy and water consumption reduction efforts both in manufacturing and new product design.[108]
>
> Fisher & Paykel's work on recovering and recycling end-of-life whiteware represents a pioneering approach to product stewardship and producer responsibility in the Southern Hemisphere, if not globally[109]

4.7.2.1 Summary

Fisher & Paykel manufactures white goods including washing machines, dishwashers and refrigerators. Established as a private company in New Zealand in 1934, the company has grown into a global company operating in 50 countries and manufacturing in Mexico, Italy, Thailand, China and NZ. Fisher & Paykel was bought by Haier Group in 2012.

Since 1993 Fisher & Paykel has provided a free take-back and recycling service for end-of-life appliances. This has achieved significant environmental benefits, which include less waste to landfill and recovery of metals and plastics. From a business perspective it has helped to build brand loyalty with retailers and to differentiate the company in a competitive market.

108 Fisher & Paykel (n.d.). *Sustainability*. Retrieved from http://www.fisherpaykel. com/au/company/sustainability/

109 Gertsakis, J., & Wilkinson, S. (2006). *Whiteware Sector Product Stewardship Study*. Fitzroy, Victoria: Product Ecology and Responsible Resource Recovery Ltd for the Ministry for the Environment, p. 23. Retrieved from https://www. mfe.govt.nz/sites/default/files/product-stewardship-whiteware-may06.pdf

4.7.2.2 Drivers for product stewardship

According to the manager of recycling, George Gray, the company's commitment to recycling dates back to the early 1990s.[110] At that time marketing managers who attended international trade fairs for home appliances noticed that more European manufacturers were starting to design their products for energy efficiency, disassembly and recyclability. One of these managers was Gary Paykel (son of the co-founder), who started to promote environmental initiatives, including recycling, throughout the organization.

There was already a culture of waste minimization and cleaner production within the organization, driven by engineering director Graeme Currie. Lindsey Roke has worked for the company for over 40 years, and he remembers Currie as an environmentalist "before the term was invented". For example, he avoided the use of scarce materials wherever possible and switched to powder coating because it was less polluting. "Recycling fitted the culture without it being a major event, provided it didn't cost huge amounts of money".[111]

Today the recycling programme is integral to Fisher & Paykel's commitment to sustainability, which includes measures to reduce environmental impacts through attention to design, cleaner production and the recovery of products at end of life.

4.7.2.3 Stewardship strategies

In 1993 Fisher & Paykel started taking back their own appliances to find out what would be involved in recycling, and to use this knowledge to improve recyclability of new products. This pilot evolved into a national recycling initiative. Fisher & Paykel now take back any used appliance for recycling, regardless of the brand, following feedback from retailers that they preferred a solution for all used appliances.

A recycling facility was built next door to the manufacturing plant in Auckland. Every designer at Fisher & Paykel is given an induction tour of the facility soon after joining the company so that they understand the implications of their design decisions on the ability to repair and recycle a product. George Gray explains the importance of this approach:

> I do tours for all the new people coming into Fisher & Paykel with regards to recycling. The one thing I talk to them about that they don't

---

110 Personal communication with G. Gray, Recycling Manager Fisher & Paykel, 20 October 2014.

111 Interview with L. Roke, Technical Advisor, Fisher & Paykel, 20 October 2014.

always contemplate is that if you design something to take it apart, it's not only at the end of its life, it's in the middle of its life as well. Because the recycling operation is right next door to the repair workshop. I see time and time again, things are too hard to take apart. So design for disassembly is really quite important.[112]

The recycling operation provides a direct information feedback loop to the research and development group.[113] Plastic components, for example, are all labelled by polymer type so that they can be visually identified and sorted prior to recycling to maximize their value.

Collection of used appliances is undertaken in several different ways:

- In Auckland appliances are delivered directly to customers by Fisher & Paykel, which enables the company to backload the unwanted appliance directly to the recycling plant.

- Used appliances are accepted by retail partners throughout New Zealand when a new Fisher & Paykel appliance is purchased. In the North Island appliances are back-loaded to Auckland by Fisher & Paykel after delivering new stock, while in the South Island appliances are collected by its recycling partner, SIMS Pacific Metals.

- Customers can drop their used appliances for free at locations in Auckland, Wellington and Christchurch.

Working but unwanted fridges and freezers ten years or older are collected through a programme called "Take-back", which Fisher & Paykel runs in partnership with the Energy Efficiency and Conservation Authority (EECA). The primary aim of that programme is to reduce energy consumption by removing inefficient appliances from active use.

All of the collected appliances are delivered to Fisher & Paykel's recycling facility, where they are partially disassembled to separate different materials for recycling. Refrigerators are safely de-gassed and the synthetic refrigerants recovered for destruction, and the plastic components and compressor removed for recycling. The motors from SmartDrive™ washing machines are removed intact and sent to a company called EcoInnovation, which uses them to make low cost, domestic-scale hydro electricity generators [68] now sold in many parts of the world.[114]

112 Personal communication with G. Gray, 2014.
113 Gertsakis & Wilkinson (2006).
114 Wilkinson, S. (2014, March 6). 20 years of recycling at Fisher & Paykel. *ResourceRecovery.biz*. Retrieved from http://www.resourcerecovery.biz/

PHOTO 4.3   Plastics from used appliances

Photo: Simon Wilkinson

Wherever feasible the plastics are removed, sorted according to polymer types and sold to plastics recyclers in New Zealand or overseas. There are at least two dozen polymer types used in Fisher & Paykel products, and most of these have a market if they can be supplied to recyclers in a relatively clean and consistent state.

After the main plastic components have been removed the refrigerator cabinets and other appliances are then collected by Sims Pacific Metals, who shred them to extract the various metals for recycling. The rate of material recovery is around 77% for refrigerators, 85% from dishwashers, and up to 95% for cooking appliances due to their higher metal content.

The type and quantity of material removed by Fisher & Paykel prior to shredding changes from time to time. The recycling manager has to constantly balance the amount of disassembly that is undertaken prior to shredding with the value of the recovered materials. This helps to ensure that the programme remains commercially viable. For example, if something has a high nickel content and the price of nickel is high, it will be removed by Fisher & Paykel prior to shredding. If the price drops it might be left in the

opinion/20-years-recycling-fisher-paykel

PHOTO 4.4   The warehouse at Fisher & Paykel's recycling facility
Photo: Simon Wilkinson

product. At times the operation is profitable, but in 2014 lower steel prices made it more challenging from a commercial perspective.[115]

Packaging is also collected for reuse or recycling where freight distances make this viable.[116] Cardboard shipping cartons in good condition are reused for shipping new products that are manufactured in Auckland or sold to a second-hand dealer for reuse, while those in poorer condition are sold as scrap cardboard to be pulped for remanufacture. Some boxes are reused internally by the Fisher & Paykel spare parts division. Expanded polystyrene (EPS) is also recycled wherever possible.

4.7.2.4 Shared value outcomes

Around 25,000 appliances are recycled by Fisher & Paykel every year, which means that more than half a million appliances or 30,000 tonnes of material have been diverted from landfill over a 20-year period.[117]

In the absence of a voluntary take-back programme many of these appliances would have been collected by local councils and then shredded to

---

115   Personal communication with G. Gray, 2014.
116   Gertsakis & Wilkinson (2006).
117   Wilkinson (2014).

recover the metal content only. However, the removal of plastics and other materials by Fisher & Paykel prior to shredding has both environmental and commercial benefits. It reduces the amount of unrecyclable "floc", made up of plastics, wood, glass and rubber, which is disposed to landfill after shredding.[118] Without a waste-to-energy infrastructure in New Zealand, this mixed, residual material is very difficult to recycle. The plastics that are removed at Fisher & Paykel's recycling plant before shredding are diverted from landfill and also have a commercial value. Polystyrene and ABS, for example, are granulated and re-pelletized by a local recycler and sold to manufacturers for use in products such as plastic chairs.[119]

The financial costs and benefits of the programme fluctuate over time depending on commodity prices. According to George Gray the primary business benefit is through marketing:

> Marketing is always pushing the recycling program. They are trying to sell our products to dealers in a highly competitive market where the products are all very similar. There is an added benefit in saying "we have a recycling plant and can take back all of your used appliances and deal with them in an environmentally responsible manner". The other companies can't say that.[120]

Through its proactive voluntary programme Fisher & Paykel has, so far, avoided the potential costs of a regulated scheme. The company is able to maintain control of programme costs, for example by using its direct relationship with retailers and the existing logistics network to maximize transport efficiencies, at least in the North Island.

There are risks associated with the voluntary initiative, however, including the potential for free-riders to take advantage of the programme and the volatility of prices for recycled materials.[121] Despite these risks Lindsey Roke is unsure about the benefits of a regulated scheme:

> I'm a bit sceptical that we could do it without putting so much overhead onto it that we'd sink the profitability ... My general philosophy is that you should only regulate things that are not commercially viable to recycle.[122]

118 *Ibid.*
119 *Ibid.*
120 Personal communication with G. Gray, 2014.
121 Gertsakis & Wilkinson (2006).
122 Interview with L. Roke, 2014.

Case study 4.7.3 TechCollect e-waste recycling

> ANZRP is in great shape but we can't afford to rest on our laurels in
> an intensely competitive and constantly shifting environment (Mark
> Mackay, Chairman ANZRP).[123]

4.7.3.1 Summary

TechCollect is an industry funded, free to the community and small business, national recycling programme for computers, computer accessories
and televisions (e-waste). It was established by the Australia New Zealand
Recycling Platform (ANZRP) with funding from many of the world's largest
technology firms.

ANZRP is one of the four approved producer responsibility organizations
("Arrangements") operating under the Federal Government's National Television and Computer Recycling Scheme, and the only not-for-profit association. Government regulations were introduced after intense lobbying
from many of the technology brand owners who wanted legislation to stop
free-riders. ANZRP continues to work with regulators to improve the operation of the scheme.

4.7.3.2 Drivers for product stewardship

The origins of the programme date back to the early 2000s, when several
industry associations representing OEMs for TV and computers worked on
small-scale, voluntary take-back programmes in collaboration with state
government agencies.

Many of the larger consumer electronics manufacturers were driven by
global CSR policies and the fact that they were already funding recycling
programmes in Europe and Japan. According to John Gertsakis, who was
working as a consultant to the TV industry at the time, manufacturers were
asking, "when are we going to do something in Australia?"[124]

Government pressure was another driver. The New South Wales state
government had listed computers and TVs among other "wastes of concern" that were under consideration for mandatory producer responsibility schemes and the Australian Government had funded several studies on
recycling e-waste.[125]

---

123 ANZRP (2014), p. 3.
124 Interview with J. Gertsakis, 14 May 2014.
125 DECC (2007). *Public Consultation Report: NSW Extended Producer Repsonsibil-
ity Priority Statement*. Sydney: Department of Environment & Climate Change.

PHOTO 4.5   A TechCollect collection event for TVs and computers

Photo: ANZRP

The two distinct industry sectors, representing computer manufacturers and TV manufacturers, had different views on the need for regulation. The TV industry had already undertaken a recycling pilot in Melbourne, which demonstrated that a take-back programme was technically feasible.[126] However, they were absolutely convinced that regulation would be required to address free-riders:

> [They said]… we'll do it but only if everyone shares the cost, because they could see that Chinese manufacturers were growing in power and market share … They [felt there] was no way they could have funded [recycling] on a voluntary basis without those other players taking advantage …[127]

Computer manufacturers had also established a pilot project called Byte-back with Sustainability Victoria (a state government agency). The project was designed to test various models to determine the most effective

Retrieved from http://www.epa.nsw.gov.au/resources/waste/080322-epr-statement07.pdf

126   Gertsakis, J., & Lewis, H. (2003). *Beyond the Dead TV*. Melbourne: EcoRecycle Victoria.

127   Interview with J. Gertsakis, 14 May 2014.

take-back methods. Under the scheme, participating OEMs paid for their own brands and Victorian taxpayers paid for the rest, which was about 50% of the waste collected.

Janet Leslie, Sustainability Manager for Canon Australia, was heavily involved in Byteback and national policy negotiations:

> The Byteback programme proved the point that voluntary schemes were not effective due to the large number of free riders. There had to be a regulatory safety net to make a national scheme equitable.[128]

Eventually all of the key industry associations agreed that national regulation was essential. The associations and their members worked intensively with government officials and politicians to design appropriate measures.

The Australian Government introduced framework legislation, the Product Stewardship Act (2011), closely followed by the Product Stewardship (Televisions and Computers) Regulations. Under the regulations companies that manufacture or import TVs or computers ("liable parties") must take responsibility for recycling products at end of life by joining and supporting a government-approved service. In 2014 there were five approved services, including ANZRP through its public-facing TechCollect programme.

4.7.3.3 Stewardship strategies

ANZRP was established as a not-for-profit association by many of the leading computer and television brands. After approval from the government in March 2012 ANZRP started setting up permanent and temporary collection sites under the "TechCollect" brand.

In the process of establishing the operation its founding members drew on lessons from other PROs including the European Recycling Platform. Unlike other approved services (called "Arrangements") under the regulations, including waste management service providers, ANZRP's sole purpose is to recycle e-waste on behalf of its members. The organization claims that being "industry run" is one of its strengths as a product stewardship model:

> Our industry for industry model, with some of the biggest global technology brands on our Board—again unique among scheme arrangements—ensures that we balance our [not-for-profit] status with strong commercial acumen and pragmatism.[129]

128 Personal communication (email) with J. Leslie, Manager Sustainability, Canon Oceania, 10 March 2016.
129 ANZRP (2014), p. 2.

The programme is funded by major brands representing more than 43% of all liable parties by product volume.[130] Costs are shared between all members based on their relative share of the market by import volumes. Management of the programme delivery was originally out-sourced to a third party service provider, but in 2013 this was moved in-house to reduce costs.

Under the regulations industry is required to recycle a progressively higher proportion of total waste TVs and computers; rising from 30% in 2012–13 to 80% in 2021–22. ANZRP is required to collect a minimum quantity of product, which is calculated based on the market share of its members.

E-waste is collected nationally through a combination of permanent sites and special events operated in partnership with municipalities. These are primarily at council transfer stations and waste management depots. In 2013–14 the programme added a business-to-business service, where e-waste is collected directly from individual businesses.

After collection the TVs and computers are recycled by one of TechCollect's recycling partners, who include E-Cycle, PGM, Sims, TES-AMM and Total Green Recycling. Recyclers are audited by independent specialist auditors to ensure that they meet environmental and safety standards, something that CEO Carmel Dollisson says is "vital to protecting our members' reputations and applies to everything we do …".[131] An Australian Standard (5377: 2013) has been developed in collaboration with other industry stakeholders and the federal government, and a certification process is under development. In addition to compliance with the standard, ANZRP requires its recycling partners to demonstrate that they have the capability to invest in technology and processes to improve recycling in Australia.

Recycling partners must also ensure that at least 90% of the material in TVs and computers is recovered, which is the mandated material recovery target. The scheme as a whole experienced a setback in 2013–14 when over-collection and limited markets for glass from CRTs resulted in a 6,000 tonne stockpile. This problem was resolved through a combination of government funding and approval of export permits for CRT glass. TechCollect's recycling partners successfully recycled all of their CRT glass.

An active marketing programme has been used to promote TechCollect services to consumers, something that Dollisson says "sets us apart from our competitors".[132] The organization has also worked closely with stakeholders

---

130 *Ibid.*, p. 6.
131 *Ibid.*, p. 5.
132 *Ibid.*, p. 5.

to drive e-waste education and awareness. One of the ongoing challenges for ANZRP and the other approved service providers, is the need to manage the supply of e-waste to avoid under-collection (and non-compliance with targets) as well as significant over-collection (and excess costs).

The Chairman of ANZRP, Mark Mackay, comments that the organization is now developing a long-term plan that strives for continuous improvement:

> ANZRP is in great shape but we can't afford to rest on our laurels in an intensely competitive and constantly shifting environment. We're now turning our attention to developing and implementing a long-term plan to drive our business towards 2020.[133]

This plan will focus on member retention and acquisition, meeting members' liability, driving down costs and recycling responsibly.

4.7.3.4 Shared value outcomes

In 2013–14 an estimated 131,600 tonnes of TVs and computers reached the end of their life. The recycling target for all liable parties was 33% or 43,430 tonnes, and the amount achieved was 52,736 tonnes.[134] Prior to the commencement of the scheme it was estimated that the recycling rate was only 10%, with the remainder either stockpiled or disposed to landfill. TechCollect recycled 27,894 tonnes of product, exceeding its target by almost 2,000 tonnes.[135]

Carmel Dollisson believes that TechCollect offers two important benefits to industry participants: regulatory compliance and assurance that companies can achieve by working with an environmentally responsible programme to meet their commitments.

> We are fortunate that a number of our members are leaders and drove the legislation and joined willingly. There is another group of companies for whom this is merely a compliance program. [Our members] … say it's important to me or my brand or an element of our consumer base that we do the environmental "right thing". So they are choosing us because they know we are providing a responsible recycling outcome.[136]

ANZRP provides its members and local government partners with data that they can use to promote the programme's achievements to their own

---

133 *Ibid.*, p. 3.
134 Department of the Environment (2015). *National Television and Computer Recycling Scheme: Outcomes 2013–14*. Canberra: Department of the Environment, p. 3.
135 *Ibid.*, p. 8.
136 Personal communication with C. Dollisson, 2014.

PHOTO 4.6   Components recovered from e-waste

Photo: ANZRP

stakeholders. This is communicated through regular newsletters as well as individualized reports to each organization.

Of concern to many stakeholders, however, was the fact that the early targets (30% in year one and 33% in year two) became an effective "cap" on industry-funded recycling. This was a problem for local councils in particular, who wanted service providers such as ANZRP to take all of their collected e-waste:

> With this scheme it was always stated that the scheme in year one would do 30%, and state and local government had to do the balance. That concept was lost ... to the point that state governments didn't have the budget. They assumed the new federal scheme would pick up 100%. We were in the middle of the digital switch, so we had TVs coming out of the woodwork on every street corner. The scheme was only geared to take 30% of the volume, so there was lots of frustration and misunderstanding that had to be dealt with by the co-regulatory arrangements. Lots of people were saying "you can't have our stuff unless you take 100%".[137]

137 *Ibid.*

The federal government responded to the concerns of local government and other stakeholders, including social enterprises involved in e-waste recycling, by increasing the recycling target to 50% in 2015–16 (compared with the original target of 37%). The Minister for the Environment claimed that this would "boost recycling and protect jobs". At the same time he reminded stakeholders that the Australian scheme is based on shared responsibility rather than full industry responsibility:

> This scheme is the centrepiece of a national approach to e-waste, where responsibility is shared between industry, under the scheme, and state, territory and local governments. It is important though that state, territory and local governments continue to manage e-waste that remain outside the national scheme's targets.[138]

Case study 4.7.4 MobileMuster phone and battery recycling

> In the world of product stewardship MobileMuster is a unique program. Unlike many schemes across the globe it is not governed by regulation or enforced by mandatory laws. It is a voluntary initiative of manufacturers and carriers who have chosen to work together.[139]

4.7.4.1 Summary

MobileMuster is a voluntary, not-for-profit mobile phone recycling programme in Australia. It has been funded by the mobile phone industry since 1998, and in 2014 became the first voluntary programme to be accredited by the Australian Government under the Product Stewardship Act.

MobileMuster is managed by the Australian Mobile Telecommunications Association (AMTA) on behalf of its members. In 2013–14 AMTA estimated that 46% of available handsets were recycled. Following stakeholder criticism in the mid-2000s, the programme has evolved to become more proactive, transparent and accountable.

138 Hunt, G. (2015, June 10). *Overhaul of E-waste Scheme Will Protect Jobs and Deliver 32,000 Tonne Recycling Boost.* Media release. Retrieved from http://www. greghunt.com.au/Home/LatestNews/tabid/133/ID/3320/Overhaul-of-e-waste-scheme-will-protect-jobs-and-deliver-32000-tonne-recycling-boost.aspx
139 AMTA (2015). *Australia's Mobile Decade: 10 years of Consumer Insights into Mobile Use and Recycling.* Sydney: Australian Mobile Telecommunications Association, p. 7.

PHOTO 4.7   A MobileMuster retail collection point

Photo: AMTA

4.7.4.2 Drivers for product stewardship

The Mobile Phone Industry Recycling Programme, as it was then called, was founded by Telstra (the national telecommunications company) and handset manufacturers Nokia and Motorola.

When the programme was established in 1998 it was primarily driven by stakeholder and company concerns about the toxicity of nickel cadmium (NiCd) batteries. At the time most mobile phones contained two NiCd batteries, and mobile phone ownership was growing at around 15% per year.[140]

According to AMTA's previous Recycling Manager Rose Read, the industry wanted to "stay ahead of the regulatory curve … taking control of their destiny rather than have someone else control it".[141]

The introduction of the voluntary programme failed to stop the threat of regulation, however. In 2004 mobile phones and NiCd batteries were identified by the New South Wales (NSW) Government as two of the nine products that would be the focus of priority action under the government's EPR policy. The Department of Environment and Conservation "put relevant

140 *Ibid.*, p. 10.
141 Personal communication with R. Read, 1 November 2013.

industry sectors on notice to reduce the end-of-life impact of their products or face regulatory action".[142]

The programme was publicly criticized by environment groups in 2004. In one media report the Total Environment Centre (TEC) claimed that "mobile phones are very toxic cocktails of a whole lot of chemicals—you've got arsenic, cadmium, mercury, lead, different sorts of toxic plastics" and that the industry programme was "a seriously bad voluntary industry programme that has basically hit rock bottom". The CEO of Planet Ark argued in the same report that the performance of the mobile phone recycling programme was extremely poor.[143]

In 2005 there was more political pressure, with two important developments:

- In March the Victorian Environment Minister threatened the mobile phone industry with regulation, calling for a 50% collection target and a refundable deposit on phones to encourage their return

- In April environment ministers from the Commonwealth, states and territories directed their officials to negotiate a voluntary agreement with the mobile phone industry with clear targets and deliverables.[144]

Later that year the NSW Government's Expert Reference Group on EPR noted the "exponential" growth of mobile phone sales since the late 1990s. They suggested that if national negotiations failed to produce a "robust agreement" by April 2006, then:

> ... the Minister should initiate as soon as possible regulatory action to mandate EPR by the mobile telephone industry to ensure that the industry takes full physical and/or financial responsibility for the proper end of life management of mobile phones and batteries in NSW.[145]

142 DEC (2005). *Report on the Implementation of the NSW Extended Producer Responsibility Priority Statement*. Sydney: Department of Environment and Conservation, p. 1. Retrieved from http://www.epa.nsw.gov.au/resources/waste/050250-epr-expert.pdf

143 Bannerman, M. (2004). Phone recycling claims called into doubt. In *7.30 Report*. Australia: Australian Broadcasting Corporation (ABC).

144 TEC (2007). *Busted! The "Mobile Muster" Myth Exposed*. Sydney: Total Environment Centre.

145 DEC (2005), p. 5.

Despite a number of changes to the programme in 2005 to enhance its effectiveness, it continued to attract criticism from the environment movement. The Total Environment Centre (TEC), for example, ran a campaign calling for regulation of the industry. In a research report entitled "Busted! The 'Mobile Muster' myth exposed", TEC argued that the retail drop-off network for used phones was not as extensive or available as the industry claimed.[146] In a media release the Director of the TEC was highly critical of the industry: "After seven years in the game, all the industry can claim is a pathetic 3% recycling rate, despite collecting a levy on every new phone sold. MobileMuster is all spin and no substance".[147]

TEC called for EPR regulations with clear targets and a refundable deposit or prepaid envelope to provide consumers with an incentive to recycle. Their concerns about the voluntary scheme were as much about transparency as performance. They claimed, for example, that the industry's audits of their retail stores were not published, nor was there any public information on the total amount of levies collected and their disbursement.[148]

4.7.4.3 Stewardship strategies

After the programme was established in 1998 AMTA partnered with an environmental group, Planet Ark, to help build the profile of the programme under the name "Phones for Planet Ark". An extensive collection network was established through retail stores, and consumers were provided with a post-back option through Australia Post.

In 2004 AMTA members had become concerned about the lack of growth in the collection rate and decided to review the programme. They commissioned research that identified a low level of community awareness, a desire by consumers to hang on to their phones, and an "invisible" collection network. They were also under pressure from the federal government and state and territory governments to either improve their performance or risk regulation.

AMTA re-launched the programme in December 2005 under the new brand name "MobileMuster", aiming to get the programme "back on track".[149] To improve the programme's visibility to consumers, AMTA committed to:

146 TEC (2007).
147 *Ibid.*
148 *Ibid.*
149 AMTA (2008). *Mobile Telecommunications Industry Statement of Commitment to Mobile Phone Recycling.* Sydney: Australian Mobile Telecommunications

- Promote and advertise MobileMuster nationally

- Educate mobile phone users, local councils, retailer, recyclers and students on why and how they can recycle mobile phones

- Offer incentives and rewards to those who collect and recycle

The action plan for the programme included three-year targets to treble collections (from 50 tonnes per annum to 150 tonnes per annum), halve the rate of disposal to landfill (from 9% to 4.5%) and to boost community awareness (from 46% to over 80%) by 2008.

The strategy was updated again in 2008 when AMTA released a public "statement of commitment" that reiterated AMTA's vision of "an environ-mentally, socially and economically responsible, successful and sustainable mobile telecommunications industry in Australia".[150] Importantly, given the complaints by TEC about a perceived lack of transparency, AMTA commit-ted to publishing annual reports on progress.

The programme is funded by handset manufacturers, handset importers and carriers through an advance recycling fee (levy) of $0.42 per handset, which is split between the manufacturers (30 cents) and carriers (12 cents). In 2014–15 the participating manufacturers were Microsoft (Nokia), Sam-sung, Motorola, HTC, Huawei, ZTE and Alcatel ONETOUCH, who collec-tively represent around 45% of the market for new handsets. Participating network carriers were Telstra, Optus and Vodafone Hutchison Australia, and reseller Virgin Mobile.

The involvement of the carriers has helped to ensure a high level of partic-ipation by manufacturers. It also reflects the industry's approach to "shared responsibility". Rose Read explains the rationale for the funding split:

> This was done because of the symbiotic relationship between the carrier and the manufacturer. The carrier does benefit substantially from the handset, so when you come back to the definition of prod-uct stewardship ... whoever benefits from the product should take some responsibility for its environmental impacts. That includes us, the people who use the phones. We have a responsibility to make sure that when we're finished with it we don't throw it in the rubbish bin, that we put it in the recycling bin and do the right thing.[151]

Association, p. 4. Retrieved from http://www.mobilemuster.com.au/media/6023/mpirp_national_statement_271108.pdf

150 *Ibid.*, p. 3.
151 Personal communication with R. Read, 1 November 2013.

PHOTO 4.8   Environment Minister Greg Hunt announcing MobileMuster's accreditation by the Australian Government

Photo: AMTA

MobileMuster is managed by AMTA on a not-for-profit basis. Unlike some other phone recycling programmes, no revenue is raised from the sale of mobile phones for refurbishment or resale.

The phones are collected through a network of more than 3,500 public drop-off points, primarily in retail stores and local council sites. Consumers can also post back their old mobile phone and battery for free in a plastic satchel available with new phones or from Australia Post. A further 3,000 MobileMuster units are located in businesses, government agencies, schools, universities, manufacturers and distributors to enable their staff and students to recycle.

Collecting used phones for recycling has always been a challenge because many consumers prefer to store rather than dispose of their old phone. The estimated number of used mobile phones in storage in Australia increased from 12 million in 2006 to 22.5 million in 2015.[152]

The collected handsets are sent to MobileMuster's recycling partner TES-AMM, who separates them into various components: metals, batteries,

152   AMTA (2015), p. 23.

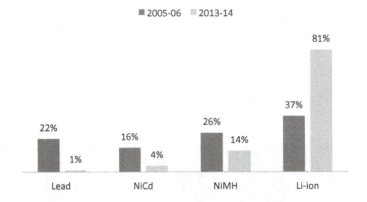

FIGURE 4.4   Battery types collected by MobileMuster as a percentage of all batteries collected by weight, 2005–06 to 2013–14

Source: Based on AMTA (2013). *Mobile Australia: A Report on How We Use and Recycle our Mobiles.* Sydney: Australian Mobile Telecommunications Association, p. 11

plastics, circuit boards and accessories. The various components are then further processed by downstream recycling partners to recover precious metals (gold and silver), cobalt, lithium, copper, aluminium, cadmium, lead and plastics. AMTA works with TES-AMM to ensure total transparency of all recycling processes and outcomes. The materials recycling rate (i.e. the estimated percentage of materials recovered) is 96%.[153]

In 2014 MobileMuster became the first voluntary stewardship scheme in Australia to be accredited by the federal government under the Product Stewardship Act. The Minister for the Environment announced this as a "green tick" for the programme.[154] One of the commitments that the programme made to achieve accreditation was to increase the collection rate for mobile phones from 50 to 55% over the next five years. Accredited schemes such as MobileMuster can use the official government logo.

4.7.4.4 Shared value outcomes
Changes to the design of mobile phones over the past 10–15 years have reduced their environmental impact in a number of ways. There has been a significant weight reduction, from around 10 kg for first generation models to around 80 g in 2005.[155]

153   *Ibid.*, p. 53.
154   AMTA (2014), p. 3.
155   Nokia (2005), p. 9.

The environmental impact of batteries has reduced, with the original lead acid batteries replaced by nickel cadmium (NiCd) and then by nickel metal hydride (NiMH). Most phones now have a lithium ion (Li-ion) or lithium polymer battery. These trends have reduced both energy consumption and potential toxicity of phones.[156] Changes in battery technology are evident in the data reported by MobileMuster, which shows the changing composition of batteries collected and recycled through the programme (Fig. 4.4).

MobileMuster monitors the collection rate for mobile phones, which is calculated as a percentage of phones "available for collection". The quantity available for collection is falling due to a downward trend in imports, an upward trend in exports and high storage rates as consumers increasingly want to hold on to their old phones. As result while the quantity of phones sent for recycling has fallen from its peak of 122 tonnes in 2011–12 to 74 tonnes in 2014–15, the collection rate has increased from 42.6% to 54.7%.[157]

Since the programme commenced in 1998 it has collected 1,168 tonnes of product, which has reduced the need to mine 29,000 tonnes of precious metals and saved 9,400 tonnes of CO_2 emissions.[158]

The benefits of the programme for AMTA members include being able to meet corporate CSR commitments for product recycling while "staying ahead of the regulatory curve". In other countries handset manufacturers and carriers tend to manage their own take-back programmes. Rose Read argues that MobileMuster adds significant value to companies compared with an individual producer responsibility programme:

> It's got brand presence, which is really important. [Our members] see it out there, it's very visible, and that's good for them because it gives them confidence. Plus it's effective. There is always a debate; they're always trying to save money ... But what they do is they start to compare ... if we wanted to do it ourselves how would we do it? "We wouldn't achieve the same spread or visibility". That's the thing about our program, we have that distribution network.[159]

156 *Ibid.*
157 AMTA (2014), p. 7.
158 *Ibid.*, p. 5.
159 Personal communication with R. Read, 1 November 2013.

5
Batteries

5.1 Introduction

Batteries are ubiquitous and diverse. They are found in many shapes and sizes; manufactured from a wide variety of materials and chemistries; and used in every home, business and institution. The rapid growth in consumption of battery-powered devices and concerns about toxicity of some components, have prompted calls for battery manufacturers to take greater responsibility for the environmental and social impacts of their products.

Like the previous two chapters on packaging and electrical and electronic equipment, this chapter follows the framework developed in Chapter 2 (see Fig. 5.1) to analyse why and how companies are taking more responsibility for the sustainability impacts of batteries. It begins with a brief description of some market trends that have implications for battery consumption, waste and recyclability. This is followed by an overview of stakeholder expectations (Section 5.3) and some of the key environmental and social impacts of batteries (Section 5.4); both of which are driving regulations and voluntary stewardship initiatives.

FIGURE 5.1   Product stewardship framework for batteries

Stewardship strategies pursued by battery producers have included significant and widespread changes to battery design and chemistry to reduce their toxicity. The extent to which producers have taken responsibility for batteries at end of life has varied, largely driven by legislation. Section 5.5 highlights some leading practice examples in policy, design, procurement and product take-back.

More detailed case studies are provided in Section 5.7. These describe the drivers, strategies and benefits of two quite different industry initiatives:

- **Call2Recycle** collects and recycles rechargeable batteries on behalf of brand owners and distributors in the US. Originally established in 1995 to meet regulations for nickel cadmium batteries, the programme has evolved to meet the needs of a changing market. The organization now collects all handheld rechargeable batteries, mostly on a voluntary basis, and is seeking back-up regulations to address free-riders.

- **Battery World** is a retail franchise network in Australia that decided in 2006 to offer its customers a free drop-off and recycling service for handheld batteries. There are no mandatory take-back requirements for batteries in Australia, and the initiative is entirely funded by the company and its franchisees. The programme has been successful in differentiating the Battery World brand from its competitors and increasing foot traffic in stores.

5.2 Market trends

The wide variety of batteries on the market is highlighted in Table 5.1. The range of users, applications and chemistries presents challenges for recycling because of the need for different collection channels and recycling processes.

The demand for portable batteries will continue to increase, driven by a shift to wireless communications platforms and the growing popularity of products such as mobile phones, tablets and laptops. Cordless power tools are becoming more popular because of their safety benefits in the workplace. The automotive sector is shifting from fossil fuel engines (petrol, diesel and gas) to electric motors, which require larger batteries with different chemistries. Demand for energy storage batteries is also increasing, driven

TABLE 5.1 Battery types and applications

Users	Chemistry	Typical uses	Portable/heavy	Single use/rechargeable
Household and commercial	Alkaline manganese (AlMn)	Clocks, portable audio and devices, torches, toys, cameras, remote controls and electronics	Portable (< 3kg) e.g. AAA, AA, C, D, PV, lantern, mobile phone, laptop	Single use
	Zinc carbon			
	Zinc air (button)	Hearing aids, pagers		
	Silver oxide (button)	Cameras, calculators		
	Lithium manganese (button)	Digital cameras, toothbrushes, MP3 players		
	Nickel cadmium (NiCd)	Cordless phones, power tools, emergency lighting		Rechargeable
	Nickel metal hydride (NiMH)	Mobile and cordless phones		
	Lithium ion (Li-ion)	Mobile phones, laptops, tablets and cameras		
	Lithium	Photographic equipment, remote controls, electronics		
	Lead acid	Hobby, small UPS for office use, alarms and emergency lighting ("sealed lead acid batteries")		
Large and industrial		Starting lighting and ignition (SLI) for cars, trucks and motorcycles	Heavy (more than 3 kg)	
		Motive power for industrial fork lifts		
		Standby power for photovoltaic systems and emergency back up		
	Nickel cadmium	Standby power for photovoltaic systems and emergency back up		
	Nickel metal hydride (NiMH)	Motive power for hybrid electric vehicles (HEV)		
	Lithium ion	Motive power for electric vehicles (EV), power storage for photovoltaic systems and mains power		
	Lithium polymer	Motive power for emerging EV, HEV		

by investments in renewable energy and lower battery manufacturing costs. These trends, which all have important implications for product steward-ship, are discussed further below.

5.2.1 Increasing proportion of rechargeable batteries

Detailed analysis of portable battery sales between 2004 and 2012 in four European countries—Belgium, Germany, France and Switzerland—high-lights a number of significant trends, including:

- An increase in the number of batteries consumed and the average weight of batteries per capita. New applications for heavier batter-ies (e.g. power tools) are expected to increase this further.

- An increase in the proportion of rechargeable batteries (by weight). Improved battery technologies will continue to drive their wide-spread adoption in a variety of applications including power tools and garden equipment, electric bikes and standby power packs, so this trend is expected to continue.[1]

5.2.2 Changing battery chemistries

Lead acid battery technology has been around for over 150 years, and its popularity is likely to continue because of its good performance and rel-atively low cost for automotive and industrial applications. Lead battery technologies will continue to evolve to meet market demands.

Increasing awareness and regulation of toxic heavy metals in products has seen the development of nickel metal hydride (NiMH) and lithium-ion (Li-ion) batteries to replace nickel cadmium (NiCd) in many applications. The performance advantages of Li-ion batteries, including energy density (power to weight ratio) and durability, are driving their rapid uptake in applications such as consumer electronics, power tools, emergency lighting and electric vehicles. New Li-ion technologies have been developed to meet specific needs, including lithium cobalt dioxide, lithium manganese spinel, lithium titanate and lithium iron phosphate.

---

[1] SRU, Perchards, & SagisEPR (2014). *Study into Market Share and Stocks and Flows of Handheld Batteries in Australia.* Report to the National Environmnet Protection Council Melbourne, pp. 40-44.

5.2.3 Growth in energy storage batteries

Demand for energy storage batteries is increasing as more households and businesses install solar systems for renewable power. Batteries allow the user to store surplus energy for their own use rather than exporting it to the grid, and in some cases to disconnect from the grid completely. The Rocky Mountain Institute analysed the economics of alternative energy supply scenarios for households and commercial consumers in five US cities.[2] They concluded that the economically optimal system is moving away from total reliance on the electricity grid towards a combination of solar power, battery storage and grid connection as back-up. In Westchester County, New York, for example, they found that the grid's contribution to power supply will reduce from 100% in 2015 for commercial customers to around 25% by around 2030 and to less than 5% by 2050.[3]

Lead acid batteries are commonly used for energy storage, but Li-ion batteries are emerging as the future chemistry of choice. There are many different Li-ion chemistries under development, as well as less hazardous alternatives including flow batteries and sodium ion batteries.[4] Lithium iron phosphate is attractive because of its enhanced safety performance.

Demand for these batteries is expected to increase exponentially in future as a result of ongoing investments in renewable power, combined with improved battery performance and lower costs of solar systems and storage batteries. The environmental and social impacts of these batteries, including their recyclability at end of life, will increasingly be considered along with safety and performance characteristics. Some examples of performance and sustainability trade-offs are shown in Table 5.2.

5.2.4 Batteries for electric vehicles

A similar transformation is taking place in the automotive industry, where internal combustion engines (ICE) are being replaced by electric power. The shift began with the introduction of hybrid electric vehicles (HEV), such as the Toyota Prius and Honda Insight, which combine an ICE with an

2   RMI (2015). *The Economics of Load Defection*. Boulder, CO: Rocky Mountain Institute.
3   *Ibid.*, p. 6.
4   Turner, L. (2015). Get the right energy storage: a battery buyers guide. *Renew*, 2015(131), 67-76.

TABLE 5.2   Performance and sustainability considerations for selected energy storage batteries

Battery chemistry	Performance	Sustainability
Lead acid (wet cell or sealed)	• Reliable, well-understood technology.	• Batteries need to be carefully managed because of the toxicity of lead and the acid electrolyte. • There are well-established infrastructures for collection and recycling, up to 99% recycling efficiency.
Lithium iron phosphate (LiFePO$_4$)	• Higher storage density, better charging efficiency and longer life-span than lead acid. • Most stable and safest of the Li-ion batteries.	• These are less toxic than lead acid at end of life but safety issues need to be carefully managed. • There are limited (but growing) infrastructures for collection and recycling. Recycling efficiency is more limited than lead acid, e.g. around 40–60%.
Lithium cobalt oxide	• Higher energy density than LiFePO$_4$ but less stable and more likely to catch fire if damaged.	• As above. These are more in demand for recycling than LiFePO$_4$ owing to the high value of cobalt.

Sources: Turner (2015); ABRI (2015). *Guide to Recycling Options for Large and Industrial Batteries.* Sydney: Australian Battery Recycling Initiative. Retrieved from http://www.batteryrecycling.org.au/wp-content/uploads/2015/03/Recycling-options-info-sheet-v4.pdf

electric drivetrain.[5] Improvements in design and technology have seen the introduction of a new generation of fully electric vehicles (EV) and plug-in hybrid electric vehicles (PHEV).

Battery technology for electric vehicles is also evolving towards Li-ion chemistries, particularly lithium iron phosphate (Table 5.3). Li-ion is the only commercially available option for EV because of its energy density, weight, recharge capability and energy efficiency.[6] Lead acid batteries will continue to be used in EV for the secondary electrical system that powers

5   Turner, L. (2015). Know your renewables: all about EVs. *Renew*, 2015(131), 38-42.

6   EUROBAT, ACEA, JAMA, KAMA, & ILA (2014). *A Review of Battery Technologies for Automotive Applications.* Association of European Automotive and Industrial Battery manufacturers (EUROBAT), European Automobile Manufacturers Association (ACEA), Japan Automobile Manufacturers Association (JAMA), Korea Automobile Manufacturers Association (KAMA), International lead Association (ILA). Retrieved from http://www.ila-lead.org/UserFiles/File/Newsletter%20files/A_Review_of_Battery_Technologies_for_Automotive_Applications_May_2014.pdf

TABLE 5.3 Examples of batteries in electric vehicles

Type of vehicle	Type of battery	Sub-category	Example
Hybrid electric vehicle	Nickel metal hydride		Toyota Prius, Camry hybrid, Lexus CT200h
Electric vehicle	Lithium ion	Lithium nickel cobalt aluminium (NCA)	Tesla Model S, Tesla Model X
		Lithium nickel manganese cobalt oxide (NMC)	Honda Accord hybrid, Nissan Leaf, BMW i3
		Lithium iron phosphate (LiFePO$_4$)	Coda, BYD E6
		Lithium manganese oxide (Spinel)	Mitsubishi i-MiEV

controls, comfort features, redundancy and safety features. The cost of a Li-ion battery pack is expected to fall by around 30% when Tesla's "Gigafactory" in the US is commissioned in 2017.[7]

5.3 Stakeholder expectations

Some common issues of concern to stakeholders are summarized in Table 5.4. The perspectives of consumers, battery manufacturers (producers), government regulators, environmental groups and municipalities are then explored further below.

There are significant differences between stakeholder interests and levels of engagement within and between countries, so companies are encouraged to undertake their own stakeholder analysis based on their business activities and locations in which they operate.

5.3.1 Consumers

With some notable exceptions, such as pollution from lead acid battery recycling (see Section 5.4.3 "Pollution from recycling"), environmental issues for batteries do not tend to have the same profile with consumers as those for packaging and e-waste. Consumers have therefore not been a major driver for battery design or recycling in the past.

---

7   Tesla (2015). *Tesla Gigafactory*. Retrieved from http://www.teslamotors.com/gigafactory

TABLE 5.4   Stakeholder interests in batteries and product stewardship

Stakeholder	Interests
Consumers	• Availability of recycling services • Toxicity of batteries in landfill • Safety concerns (risks to children from ingestion)
Producers	• Preference for regulated rather than voluntary stewardship schemes • Minimizing costs of compliance • Harmonization of extended producer responsibility (EPR) laws between jurisdictions
Retailers	• Corporate reputation and sustainability goals • Meeting compliance obligations under some EPR regulations (e.g. in the US) • Using battery recycling to boost "foot traffic" and sales
Government regulators	• Low recycling rates for handheld batteries • Potential leachate of toxic substances into groundwater • Pollution from lead acid battery processing • Risks to human health and safety (ingestion, explosion, fires, etc.)
Environmental groups	• Poor recycling rate • Toxicity in landfill

This is starting to change, however, as portable batteries become more ubiquitous and consumers start to look for recycling services. In a survey of Australian consumers in 2010, 80% said that end-of-life batteries should be recycled and 75% said they would "definitely" recycle batteries if there was an easy way to do it.[8] When asked who should be responsible for bearing the cost of battery recycling, the most commonly nominated group was battery manufacturers (nominated by 36% of respondents).

Consumers in the US are more likely to expect producers to take responsibility for recycling. When Call2Recycle asked people who should fund portable battery and mobile phone recycling, the answers were evenly split between consumers (48%) and product manufacturers (47%).[9] The survey also revealed strong interest in recycling, but significant barriers:

• The majority of consumers (81%) said that they were likely to recycle batteries, mobile phones and other small electronics, with the main reason being that "it's the environmentally responsible choice"

8   Planet Ark (2010). *Lead Acid Battery Use, Disposal & Recycling in Australia*. Sydney. Retrieved from http://recyclingweek.planetark.org/documents/doc-687-lab-report-2011-11-09-final.pdf

9   Call2Recycle (2015, April 21). "Green guilt" on the rise. *Newsletter*. Retrieved from http://www.call2recycle.org/green-guilt-on-the-rise/

- Seven out of ten consumers cited barriers to recycling these products, particularly not knowing how or where to recycle (33%), not being able to find a collection event (22%) or local retailers not offering programmes (20%)

While an estimated 97% of car batteries are recycled in the US, there are still important gaps in consumer knowledge. A survey by Johnson Controls found that seven out of ten consumers did not know how to recycle a car battery, highlighting the importance of ongoing consumer education.[10]

5.3.2 Producers

Product stewardship initiatives for batteries have largely been driven by regulation or threats of regulation. The key issue for government policy-makers has always been the toxicity of heavy metals such as lead, cadmium and mercury. In 1985 members of the European Portable Battery Association (EPBA) launched a voluntary programme to remove mercury from alkaline and zinc batteries. This was successfully completed by 1994, six years before regulations came into force.[11]

Take-back regulations in many jurisdictions have resulted in the establishment of industry-funded, take-back programmes for rechargeable batteries. The Rechargeable Battery Recycling Corporation (now Call2Recycle) was set up by battery manufacturers in 1994 after bills were introduced in a number of states making manufacturers responsible for collecting and recycling batteries (see Case study 5.7.1).

Outside the European Union (EU), however, there are very few jurisdictions that make producers responsible for recycling non-rechargeable (primary) batteries. There are many voluntary initiatives (see Section 5.5.4, "Reuse and recycling"), but these tend to operate on a small scale. Some manufacturers and industry associations argue that primary alkaline batteries are not hazardous and therefore do not need to be recycled. On its website the Battery Association of Japan states that:

10 Johnson Controls (2014). *New Survey Shows Knowledge Gap in Car Battery Recycling.* Retrieved from http://www.recyclingmybattery.com/en-us/whats-happening/news/new-survey-shows-knowledge-gap-in-car-battery-recycling/

11 EPBA (2011). *Sustainability Report 2010.* Brussels, Belgium: European Portable Battery Association. Retrieved from http://www.epbaeurope.net/Sustainabilityreport.html

BAJ believes that with the current level of technology, the collection and recycling of all dry batteries that do not contain mercury is not appropriate. This viewpoint basically conforms to the official position of the Japan, Europe, and United States trilateral work group of battery experts.[12]

Duracell advises its customers that alkaline batteries can be safely disposed of in household waste.[13] While encouraging customers to recycle rechargeable batteries, Duracell claims that "[p]roven cost-effective and environmentally safe recycling processes are not yet universally available for alkaline batteries". Energizer is more positive, advising that "Energizer strongly recommends proper disposal and recycling of all batteries".[14] Through a partnership with environment group Earth911, Energizer also provides consumers with a guide to recycling primary and rechargeable batteries.

The formation of the Corporation for Battery Recycling (CBR) in the US by battery manufacturers Energizer, Duracell, Panasonic and Rayovac, and their announcement that they would establish a voluntary national recycling programme for alkaline batteries, was driven in part by proposed extended producer responsibility (EPR) legislation in California.[15] Marc Boolish, president of CBR and technology manager at Energizer, noted that "We wanted to get in front of [the legislation]".[16] The decision by Rayovac to withdraw from the initiative was one of the factors that prompted CBR and its member companies, including Energizer, to start pushing for regulation instead of voluntary stewardship.

Consistent with industry views in many other sectors, battery producers are looking for regulatory certainty and consistency between jurisdictions. In its first sustainability report EPBA welcomed a "surge" of policy initiatives at a national, European and global level to address sustainability and environmental issues. The main concern was to ensure that these "do not result

12   BAJ (2012). *Dry Batteries and Lithium Primary Batteries: Disposal Methods.* Tokyo: Battery Association of Japan. Retrieved from http://www.baj.or.jp/e/recycle/recycle01.html

13   Duracell (2016). *Battery Care, Use and Disposal.* Retrieved from https://www.duracell.com/en-us/technology/battery-care-use-and-disposal/

14   Energizer (2015). *Proper Disposal, Storage, Care and Handling of your Batteries.* Retrieved from http://www.energizer.com/about-batteries/battery-care

15   Thomas, J. (2012). Batteries initiative faces tough challenges, *Resource Recycling.* Retrieved from http://resource-recycling.com/node/2925

16   *Ibid.*, p. 1.

in an increasingly fragmented policy approach".[17] For similar reasons the Mercury-Containing and Rechargeable Battery Act ("Battery Act") in the US was described by the industry's recycling body as "the fulfilment of a dream" because it replaced a patchwork of state laws and removed regulatory barriers to a national programme.[18]

5.3.3 Government regulators

Batteries containing heavy metals are now regulated in many jurisdictions around the world, primarily due to concerns about toxicity and pollution. The most common regulations are restrictions on the use of heavy metals and producer responsibility for collection and recycling (Table 5.5).

In the 1980s and early 1990s policy-makers became aware that heavy metals in batteries, particularly lead, mercury and cadmium, were problematic in waste, although energy and resource conservation were also considerations.[19] Seven states in the US introduced laws to reduce the environmental impacts of rechargeable batteries through a combination of landfill bans, requirements for batteries to be easy to remove from products, and requirements for labelling and collection.[20] These laws prompted manufacturers to establish a recycling programme for NiCd batteries.

Facing a patchwork of different state laws and restrictive hazardous waste requirements, producers pressured the US Environment Protection Agency to introduce a national framework.[21] This was achieved in 1996 with the introduction of the Mercury Containing and Rechargeable Battery Act (Battery Act), which established uniform national labelling requirements for NiCd and small sealed lead acid (SSLA) batteries, eased hazardous waste regulations for battery recycling through the "Universal Waste Rule", and prohibited the sale of mercury-containing batteries. It also established a national set of rules for battery recycling and enabled the Rechargeable

17   EPBA (2011), p. 5.
18   Call2Recycle (2014, May 15). *The 1996 Battery Act: The Fulfillment of a Dream.* Retrieved from http://www.call2recycle.org/1996-battery-act/
19   Lindhqvist, T. (2010). Policies for waste batteries: learning from experience. *Journal of Industrial Ecology*, 14(4), 537-540.
20   PSI (2010). *Battery Stewardship Briefing Document.* Boston, MA: Product Stewardship Institute. Retrieved from http://www.productstewardship.us/displaycommon.cfm?an=1&subarticlenbr=611
21   Fishbein, B. (1996, December). Industry takes charge: battery recycling. *Resource Recycling*, pp. 24-28.

TABLE 5.5   Examples of product stewardship laws and policies for batteries

Type of regulation	Detail	Purpose	Examples*
Mandatory take-back for portable batteries	Producers or distributors are physically or financially responsible for recovery of batteries at end of life.	To shift the costs of recycling from taxpayers to producers and consumers; to increase levels of recycling.	• Asia: Japan, Taiwan • Europe: EU Battery Directive (2006) and Switzerland • US: laws mandating collection of rechargeable batteries (CA, IA, FL, ME, MD, MN, NJ, NY, VT) and primary batteries (VT) • Canada: four provinces (Ontario, Manitoba, British Columbia and Quebec)
Mandatory or voluntary deposit on lead acid batteries	A deposit is paid by consumers and redeemed when they return the battery to a retailer or waste depot.	To promote return by consumers and to achieve higher recycling rates.	• US: 15 states
Disposal ban	Ban on disposal of automotive lead acid batteries to landfill	To reduce lead pollution from waste batteries; to support recycling initiatives	• US: more than 30 states • Europe: all EU members
Disposal ban	Ban on disposal of portable batteries to landfill	To reduce lead, cadmium and mercury pollution from waste batteries; to support recycling initiatives	• US: Eight states ban disposal of NiCd and SSLA* batteries (FL, IA, ME, MD, MN, NJ, RI, VT). Mercury-added batteries are banned from disposal in six states (MA, ME, MN, NH, RI, VT). California bans all batteries except carbon zinc.
Design requirements	These may include labelling requirements and/ or restrictions on the use of mercury and cadmium and design for easy removal from products	To reduce cadmium and mercury pollution from waste batteries; to support recycling programmes by ensuring that SSLA, NiCd and mercury-containing batteries are labelled	• Asia: Taiwan, Japan • Europe: all member states • US: federal legislation (Mercury Containing and Rechargeable Battery Act)

* Abbreviations: CA (California), CT (Connecticut), IA (Iowa), FL (Florida), MA (Massachusetts), ME (Maine), MD (Maryland), MN (Minnesota), NJ (New Jersey), NY (New York), VT (Vermont), RI (Rhode Island), NH (New Hampshire); SSLA, small sealed lead acid batteries

Battery Recycling Corporation to launch its first national recycling campaign (Case study 5.7.1).

Heavy metal restrictions were introduced in the European Union following the introduction of Directive 2006/66/EC on Batteries and Accumulators and Waste Batteries and Accumulators (2006) (the "Battery Directive"). Among the most significant provisions in the directive, member states must:

- Prohibit the disposal of industrial and automotive batteries in landfill or by incineration

- Prohibit batteries with more than 0.0005% mercury (excluding button cells with mercury content of no more than 2%)

- Prohibit batteries with more than 0.002% cadmium (with certain exemptions)

Member states must also ensure that appropriate collection systems are in place for portable batteries, and producers pay any net costs for collection, treatment and recycling of all portable batteries. Minimum collection rates of 25% were to be achieved by 2012 and 45% by 2016.

An evaluation of the Battery Directive was undertaken as part of a broader evaluation of recycling and waste policy.[22] The evaluation concluded that good progress had been made to improve recycling rates although some member states might struggle to meet the 45% collection rate by 2016. It found some violations on limits on hazardous substances, particularly mercury in imported Asian brands. The review recommended some changes including additional labelling by chemistry type to improve sorting efficiencies and changes to the way that collection rates are calculated to take into account battery lifetimes and hoarding.[23]

Laws that would mandate producer responsibility for recycling batteries are gradually being introduced in the US and Canada. Companies that sell portable batteries in Quebec, for example, must either implement an individual recovery programme, or join an organization that will recover and recycle batteries on their behalf. The Regulation Respecting the Recovery and Reclamation of Products by Enterprises (2011) applies to primary and rechargeable batteries sold separately as well as batteries sold as components of other products.

22 Bio Intelligence Service, Arcadis, & Institute for European Environmental Policy (2013). *Ex-post Evaluation of Certain Waste Stream Directives*. Report to the European Commission—DG Environment.

23 *Ibid.*

Take-back laws for rechargeable batteries have been passed in California (2006), Florida (2008) and New York State (2010). In 2014 Vermont became the first state to introduce a law regulating primary batteries (2014), with others likely to follow. A model bill that would mandate producer responsibility for all portable batteries was under negotiation in a number of states in 2015, including California, Connecticut, Texas and New York.

Japan and Taiwan both have EPR laws for portable batteries, but they operate quite differently. The Japanese Law for the Promotion of the Effective Utilization of Resources (2000) requires all manufacturers and importers of rechargeable batteries (NiCd, NiMH, Li-ion and SSLA) and equipment utilizing rechargeable batteries, to implement a system to recover them. Producers meet their recycling obligation through a single producer responsibility organization, the Japan Portable Rechargeable Battery Recycling Center (JBRC). The designated batteries must be labelled with the relevant chemical symbol and chasing arrow. In Taiwan manufacturers and importers pay for collection and recycling of all dry cell batteries through a tax but, unlike in Japan, the programme is managed by the government through the Environment Protection Authority.

The recovery of lead acid batteries (automotive and industrial) tends to be less regulated than portable batteries because they generally have a commercial value in the market due to their high lead content. Thirty US states have introduced legislation for lead acid batteries based on a model Bill developed by the Battery Council International.[24] Most ban the disposal of these batteries from landfill and 15 have introduced a refundable deposit to boost collection rates. In India, manufacturers, importers, assemblers and reconditioners of lead acid batteries must ensure that used batteries are collected and sent only to registered recyclers. Dealers must give a discount for every used battery returned by the consumer.

In addition to EPR regulations in some jurisdictions, recycling programmes must comply with regulations governing the transport of hazardous wastes and dangerous goods. This particularly applies to rechargeable batteries such as lead and Li-ion. In the US, Department of Transportation (DOT) regulations require certain types of batteries to be bagged or have their terminals taped to avoid the risk of a short-circuit. For this reason the Call2Recycle programme requires all individual batteries to be placed in a plastic bag before going into the collection box.

24 BCI (2013). *Battery Recycling*. Chicago: Battery Council International. Retrieved from http://batterycouncil.org/?page=Battery_Recycling

In Europe the relevant dangerous goods code (referred to as "ADR 2011") has been amended to accommodate used batteries being transported from a consumer collection point to an intermediate processing facility for recycling or disposal, and requirements are less onerous.[25]

The international transport of used batteries is controlled by the Basel Convention on the Control of Trans-Boundary Movements of Hazardous Wastes and their Disposal ("Basel Convention"). This treaty is designed to reduce the movements of hazardous waste between nations, specifically to prevent transfer of hazardous waste from developed to less developed countries. According to the National Electrical Manufacturers Association in the US, only batteries containing mercury, cadmium and lead are classified as hazardous under the Basel Convention.[26] Alkaline manganese and carbon zinc batteries are therefore considered to be non-hazardous. This interpretation is consistent with those of the EU—the European Waste List 2000/532/EC classifies hazardous and non-hazardous wastes—and the OECD.[27]

5.3.4 Environment groups

Unlike packaging and e-waste, batteries have not been a major or ongoing focus for environment groups. In 2013 27 organizations in the US ran a campaign to convince one producer, Rayovac, to take back its batteries for recycling.[28] This followed the company's decision to withdraw from the Corporation for Battery Recycling, which it had established with its competitors Duracell, Energizer and Panasonic.

25 United Nations Economic Commission for Europe (2010). *European Agreement concerning the International Carriage of Dangerous Goods by Road.* Retrieved from http://www.unece.org/trans/danger/publi/adr/adr2011/11contentse. html

26 National Electrical Manufacturers Association (2009). *Treatment of Batteries within the Basel Convention.* Rosslyn, VA: NEMA. Retrieved from http://www. nema.org/Policy/Environmental-Stewardship/Documents/Treatment%20 Basel%20Convention.pdf

27 OECD (2001). *Decision of the Council C(2001) 107/Final Concerning the Transboundary Movement of Wastes Destined for Recovery Operations.* Paris, France: Organisation for Economic Cooperation and Development. Retrieved from http://www.oecd.org/env/waste/30654501.pdf

28 Texas Campaign for the Environment (2013, August 1). Environment groups press Rayovac for battery recycling. *Waste and Recycling News.* Retrieved from https://www.texasenvironment.org/environmental-groups-press-rayovac-for -battery-recycling/

Other groups have worked at a local, national or international level to reduce the environmental and health impacts of lead acid battery recycling, including lead poisoning of workers and communities (see Section 5.4.3 "Pollution from recycling"). A San Francisco-based, not-for-profit association, Occupational Knowledge International (OK International), is working to promote environmental improvements in what it claims to be "one of the world's most polluting industries, affecting the health and educational opportunity of millions of children around the globe".[29] OK International has developed a certification standard ("Better Environmental Sustainability Targets" or BEST) in collaboration with government and industry groups in India. The standard recognizes recyclers that meet minimum emission standards and agree to take back used batteries for "environmentally sound" recycling.

There are also groups that operate at a local level. In the US, for example, an organization called Communities for a Better Environment fought for many years to have the Exide Technologies battery recycling plant in Los Angeles closed because of concerns about its health and environmental impacts.[30]

5.3.5 Municipalities

In most jurisdictions local governments have responsibility for waste management systems including landfill, incineration and recycling. They primarily support recycling programmes for batteries because they divert toxic materials from landfill (see Section 5.4.1 "Toxicity in waste"). Lead acid batteries are separated for recycling at waste management centres and landfill sites, both to divert them from landfill and to obtain financial return.

Local government involvement in recycling varies. In the US and Canada governments pay for collection and recycling of batteries not covered by the Call2Recycle programme for rechargeable household batteries (mainly alkaline primary batteries) if they are required or choose to collect them.[31] Municipalities also pay for disposal of batteries to landfill where there is

29   OK International (2016). *Lead Battery Background*. San Francisco, CA: Occupational Knowledge International. Retrieved from http://www.okinternational.org/lead-batteries/Background

30   Barboza, T., & Vives, R. (2015, March 12). Regulators detail Exide battery plant closure after decades of pollution. *Los Angeles Times*. Retrieved from http://www.latimes.com/local/lanow/la-me-ln-exide-plant-closure-20150312-story.html

31   PSI (2010). *Battery Stewardship Briefing Document*.

PHOTO 5.1 Battery collection point in a city library, Sydney

Photo: Helen Lewis

no recovery programme available. The Product Stewardship Institute has highlighted the financial benefits of producer-funded programmes such as Call2Recycle:

- Municipalities that already provide a recycling service for batteries gain a direct cost saving if producers take over costs that the municipality is already paying for collection, transport and reprocessing

- Those without a recycling programme enjoy a new service at no or minimal cost[32]

In Western Australia local councils provide an extensive network of permanent and temporary sites that collect portable batteries for recycling, with financial support from the state government. The programme aims

32 PSI (2010). *Financial Benefits to Local Governments from Product Steward-ship*. Boston, MA: Product Stewardship Institute. Retrieved from http://www.productstewardship.us/associations/6596/files/Financial_Benefits_Fact_Sheet_5_06_10.pdf

to divert hazardous materials from landfill and alternative waste management facilities, and to educate the community not to place batteries in their kerbside recycling bin for paper and packaging. According to the waste authority, batteries are one of the most hazardous wastes placed in kerbside recycling bins.[33]

The City of Sydney has introduced a recycling service for portable batteries, mobile phones and compact fluorescent lamps in public buildings (Photo 5.1). The main concern is the potential hazards from disposal in landfill: "If they end up in landfill they can leach toxic chemicals into our soil and possibly even contaminate the groundwater table, the source of our drinking water ... Some also contain valuable resources, like precious metals".[34]

5.4 Product impacts

5.4.1 Toxicity in waste

Unlike packaging, concerns about batteries in the waste stream are related to toxicity rather than the volume of waste going to landfill.

Most batteries contain substances that are potentially hazardous, including heavy metals and corrosive electrolytes (Table 5.6). The metals are contained within the battery casing and pose no real risks while the battery is in use. However, some of the metal components are toxic to human health and/or have eco-toxicity impacts if they exceed minimum concentrations in the natural environment. Lead, mercury and cadmium are the most toxic of the heavy metals in batteries, but other metals such as zinc can also be a concern if they leach into water or soil. The US EPA has also expressed concern about the neurotoxicity and developmental toxicity impacts of lithium.[35]

33   Waste Authority WA (2016). *Battery Collection*. Retrieved from http://www.wasteauthority.wa.gov.au/programs/wws/waste-wise-in-action/recycling

34   City of Sydney (2014). *Battery, Mobile and Light Bulb Recycling*. Retrieved from http://www.cityofsydney.nsw.gov.au/live/waste-and-recycling/e-waste-and-chemicals/battery-mobile-and-light-bulb-recycling

35   Amarakoon, S., Smith, J., & Segal, B. (2013). *Application of Life Cycle Assessment to Nanoscale Technology*. Washington, DC: Report by Abt Associates for the United States Environmental Protection Agency.

TABLE 5.6   Hazards associated with different battery types

Battery type	Hazard
Lead acid	• Lead toxicity can cause paralysis, anaemia, abdominal pain, brain or kidney damage in humans. It can affect a child's mental and physical growth. • Exposure to lead can be fatal for animals. • Sulphuric acid is a corrosive chemical, which can leak if batteries fall over or are damaged.
Alkaline manganese	• Zinc toxicity is relatively minor except at high concentrations. • Manganese is a neurotoxin in humans. • Potassium hydroxide is a corrosive chemical, which can leak if batteries are damaged. • If batteries become wet the potassium hydroxide can react with metals to produce flammable and explosive hydrogen gas.
Nickel cadmium	• Cadmium is a "probable carcinogen". It is highly persistent in the environment and will concentrate or bioaccumulate in aquatic animals. • Nickel has only minor health effects on humans but can be highly toxic to aquatic life.
Nickel metal hydride	• Nickel has only minor health effects on humans but can be highly toxic to aquatic life.
Lithium and Lithium-ion	• There is potential for fires or explosions if lithium batteries are damaged or become over-heated, for example if they short-circuit.
Mercuric oxide batteries	• Mercury is highly toxic. It can permanently damage the nervous system, brains, kidneys or developing foetus. In the environment it has acute (short-term) and chronic (long-term) effects on aquatic life. It is highly persistent in water and will bioaccumulate in the tissues of fish.

Use of mercury and cadmium is restricted under the European Union's Battery Directive. Mercury has been phased out of most household batteries but is still found in some batteries being collected for recycling, including alkaline and zinc carbon batteries.[36]

While there is still considerable uncertainty about the environmental impacts of batteries in landfill, there is some evidence that heavy metals from electronic products, including batteries, mobilize to some extent in landfill leachate. This process may take decades or much longer, depending on environmental conditions (such as temperature, rainfall and landfill design).

If leachate is not properly managed it can contaminate surface and groundwater. Well-designed modern landfills control leachate through the

---

36   Terazona, A., Oguchi, M., Lino, S. & Mogi, S. (2015). Battery collection in municipal waste management in Japan: challenges for hazardous material substance control and safety. *Waste Management*, 2015(39), 246-257 (p. 249).

use of landfill liners and leachate collection systems. However, many older or poorly managed landfills are still in use.

Researchers have identified 14 kinds of heavy metal in contaminated water draining from landfill sites in Australia.[37] The source of these is likely to be electronic waste (e-waste), which includes old computers, televisions, mobile phones and batteries. Toxic metals measured by the researchers included arsenic, cadmium, cobalt, chromium and zinc. One of the research leaders, Professor Ravi Nadu, stated that: "When groundwater is contaminated it in turn contaminates soil. Both water and soil can be used for growing crops, with the result that the toxins may enter the food chain".[38]

A study of northern hemisphere landfills noted that batteries and appliances are a potential source of cadmium, nickel, zinc, lead and mercury in landfill leachate.[39] While the authors did not consider heavy metals to be a groundwater pollution threat, they noted that concentrations in leachate sampled in the United States and Eastern Europe exceeded legislative permits and drinking water limits.

A small number of studies indicate that heavy metals do leach out of batteries in landfill, although the timeframe may be anywhere from decades to thousands of years.[40]

There are also environmental risks for communities that rely on incinerators rather than landfill for waste disposal.[41] Metals such as cadmium and lead concentrate in the ash produced by combustion and may leach into

---

37   Twomey, D. (2011, September 13). Toxins, heavy metals escaping from Australian landfills. *Eco-news*. Retrieved from http://econews.com.au/news-to-sustain-our-world/toxins-heavy-metals-escaping-from-australian-landfills/

38   *Ibid.*

39   Slack, R.J., Gronow, J.R., & Voulvoulis, N. (2005). Household hazardous waste in municipal landfills: contaminants in landfill. *Science of the Total Environment*, 337(2005), 119-137.

40   See Rydh, C., & Karlstrom, M. (2002). Life cycle inventory of recycling portable nickel-cadmium batteries. Resources. *Conservation and Recycling*, 34(2002), 289-309; Xara, S., Delgado, J., Almeida, M. & Costa, C. (2009). Laboratory study on the leaching potential of spent alkaline batteries. *Waste Management*, 29(2009), 2121-2131; Karnchanawong, S., & Limpiteeprakan, P. (2009). Evaluation of heavy metal leachate from spent household batteries disposed in municipal solid waste. *Waste Management*, 29, 550-558.

41   United States Environment Protection Agency (1997). *Implementation of the Mercury-Containing and Rechargeable Battery Management Act*. Washington, DC: USEPA. Retrieved from http://www.epa.gov/osw/hazard/recycling/battery.pdf

the environment when this ash is disposed to landfill. They can also enter the atmosphere through smokestack emissions.

Removal of batteries and other electronic products from household waste helps to support the production of high quality organic products from alternative waste facilities; something that will become more common in future as landfills are phased out. These facilities process mixed household waste and/or source-separated organic wastes to produce organic products such as soil conditioners and mulch.

5.4.2 Resource conservation

The disposal of batteries to landfill represents a loss of valuable, non-renewable resources, particularly as ore grades are in terminal decline for a range of metals including nickel and lead-zinc-silver ores.[42] As the most accessible and higher grade ores are depleted, mining operations target deeper or lower grade deposits, which tend to have higher social and environmental costs. Recycling has the ability to generate a substantial and growing resource and will become more economically viable as virgin resources are depleted and become more expensive.

The typical composition of the different battery types is shown in Table 5.7 (rechargeable batteries) and Table 5.8 (single use batteries).

The use of recycled metals to manufacture new products, including batteries, has significant environmental benefits over the life-cycle. It has been estimated, for example, that 46% and 75% less energy is required to recycle cadmium and nickel, respectively, compared with the extraction and refining of virgin metal.[43]

Some of the metals contained in batteries have very low global recycling rates (Table 5.9). This is a particular concern given that some appear to have very limited reserves, such as the rare earth metals. Rare earth metals—cerium (Ce), lanthanum (La), neodymium (Nd) and praseodymium (Pr)—comprise around 7% of a nickel metal hydride battery. Lithium—an essential raw material for the latest generation of consumer electronics—is also relatively rare.

Lead acid batteries are already recovered at high rates in many countries because of the relatively high price of lead, which is driven by the demand

---

42   Giurco, D., Prior, T., Mudd, G., Mason, L. & Behrisch, J. (2010). *Peak Minerals in Australia: A Review of Changing Impacts and Benefits*. Sydney: University of Technology Sydney and Monash University for CSIRO Minerals Down Under Flagship.

43   Rydh, C., & Karlstrom, M. (2002).

TABLE 5.7 Composition of rechargeable batteries

Material	Nickel cadmium (%)	Nickel metal hydride (%)	Lithium ion (%)	Lead acid (%)
Aluminium			5.0	
Cadmium	15.0			
Cobalt		4.0	18.0	
Iron and steel	35.0	20.0	22.0	
Lead				65.0
Manganese		1.0		
Nickel	22.0	35.0		
Lithium			3.0	
Zinc		1.0		
Other metals		10.0	11.0	4.0
Alkali	2.0	4.0		
Carbon			13.0	
Plastics	10.0	9.0		10.0
Water	5.0	8.0		
H_2SO_4				16.0
Other non-metals	11.0	8.0	28.0	
Other material				5.0

H_2SO_4 = sulphuric acid

Source: Based on data from Fisher, K., Wallén, E., Laenen, P. & Collins, M. (2006). *Battery Waste Management Life Cycle Assessment*. Report by Environmental Resources Management for UK Department for Environment Food and Rural Affairs (DEFRA), London, pp. 57-58

for lead to make new batteries. The recovery of used batteries is therefore an essential part of the supply chain and not something that necessarily needs to be encouraged through regulation, assuming that high prices continue to drive demand. Johnson Controls claims that with an estimated recycling rate of 97%, lead acid batteries are the most recycled consumer product in the US.[44]

In contrast, portable batteries are recovered at very low rates in many countries, and there is significant potential for improvement. In California, for example, only 6% of alkaline batteries sold were collected for recycling in

44 Johnson Controls (2015). *Recycling Process*. Retrieved from http://www. recyclingmybattery.com/en-us/whats-the-process/

TABLE 5.8   Composition of single use batteries

Material	Alkaline manganese (%)	Zinc carbon (%)	Mercuric oxide (button) (%)	Zinc air (button) (%)	Lithium (button) (%)	Alkaline (button) (%)	Silver oxide (button) (%)	Lithium manganese (%)
Iron and steel	24.8	16.8	37.0	42.0	60.0	37.0	42.0	50.0
Lead		0.1						
Manganese	22.3	15.0	1.0		18.0	23.0	2.0	19.0
Nickel	0.5		1.0		1.0	1.0	2.0	1.0
Lithium					3.0			2.0
Silver							31.0	
Zinc	14.9	19.4	14.0	35.0		11.0	9.0	
Mercury			31.0	1.0		0.6	0.4	
Other metals	1.3	0.8		4.0			4.0	
Alkali	5.4	6.0		4.0		2.0	1.0	
Carbon	3.7	9.2	1.0	1.0	2.0	2.0	0.5	2.0
Paper	1.0	0.7						
Plastics	2.2	4.0	3.0	4.0	3.0	6.0	2.0	7.0
Water	10.1	12.3	3.0	10.0		6.0	2.0	
KOH			2.0					
Other non-metals	14.0	15.2		3.0	13.0	14.0	4.0	19.0
Other material			7.0					

KOH = potassium hydroxide

Source: Based on data from Fisher et al. (2006), pp. 55-57

TABLE 5.9   Global recycling rates for metals commonly used in batteries

Type of metal	Metal	Recycling rate (%)
Ferrous	Manganese (Mn)	> 50
	Iron (Fe)	> 50
	Nickel (Ni)	> 50
Non-ferrous	Zinc (Zn)	> 50
	Lead (Pb)	> 50
	Aluminium (Al)	> 50
	Cobalt (Co)	> 50
Precious	Silver (Ag)	> 50
Speciality	Cadmium (Cd)	10–25
	Mercury (Hg)	1–10
	Lithium (Li)	< 1
	Lanthanum (La)	< 1
	Cerium (Ce)	< 1
	Praseodymium (Pr)	< 1
	Neodymium (Nd)	< 1

Source: UNEP International Resource Panel (2011). *Recycling Rates of Metals: A Status Report*. Nairobi: United Nations Environment Programme, p. 19

2010.[45] In 2010 the recycling rate for all portable batteries was around 3% in the UK before the implementation of the recycling regulations.[46] Collection rates of up to 50–60% have been achieved in European countries that have had a programme in place for many years (Fig. 5.2). The highest recorded rate is in Switzerland, with an estimated recovery rate of 70%.[47]

45   Masanet, E., & Horvath, A. (2012). *Single-use Alkaline Battery Case Study: The Potential Impacts of Extended Producer Responsibiity (EPR) in California on Global Greenhouse Gas (GHG) Emissions.* Report by University of California, Berkley, for the California Department of Resources Recycling and Recovery: Sacramento, CA, p. 7. Retrieved from http://www.calrecycle.ca.gov/publications/Documents/1433%5C20121433.pdf
46   Hickman, M. (2010, February 1). Battery-recycling law in force. *The Independent.* Retrieved from http://www.independent.co.uk/news/uk/home-news/batteryrecycling-law-in-force-1885170.html
47   Perchards, D., & SagisEPR (2013). *The Collection of Waste Portable Batteries in Europe in View of the Achievability of the Collection Targets set by the Batteries Directive 2006/66/EC.* Report to the European Portable Battery Association. Retrieved from http://www.epbaeurope.net/documents/Perchards_Sagis-EPBA_collection_target_report_-_Final.pdf

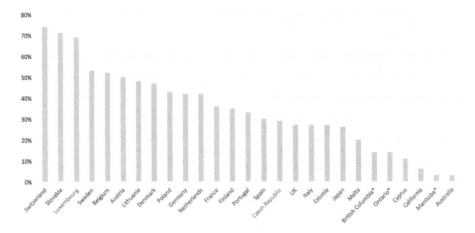

FIGURE 5.2 Collection rates for portable batteries in selected countries and provinces, 2011–2012

* Canadian province, primary batteries only. Note: time periods and methodologies vary between jurisdictions, so data may not be directly comparable.

Sources: Perchards, & SagisEPR (2013), p. 5; CM Consulting (2012). *Managing Canada's Waste Batteries*. Peterborough, Ontario, Canada: CM Consulting, p. 15; SRU *et al.* (2014); Terazona *et al.* (2015)

A number of life-cycle assessment (LCA) studies have explored the environmental costs and benefits of recycling batteries compared with disposal to landfill. LCA studies on alkaline batteries, for example, indicate that recycling may generate a net environmental cost *or* benefit depending on:

- Which environmental impact criterion is considered, for example energy consumption, global warming potential, eco-toxicity or health impacts

- The type of collection system and consumer behaviour, for example whether consumers make a special trip to a retail store to drop off their batteries

- The materials recovered and their end market

A study on the potential impacts of a take-back scheme for alkaline batteries in California on global greenhouse gas (GHG) emissions concluded that kerbside collection and retail drop-off schemes for used batteries both generate a GHG saving.[48] The saving is due to the avoided production of new ("virgin") metals.

48   Masanet & Horvath (2012).

PHOTO 5.2 Lead recovered from used batteries

Photo: Helen Lewis

A more detailed study of recovery options for alkaline batteries was conducted by the Massachusetts Institute of Technology for the National Electrical Manufacturers Association in the US.[49] Figure 5.3 shows the estimated impacts measured against one criterion, cumulative energy demand (CED), highlighting the dominance of raw materials extraction and processing. The life-cycle impacts are dominated by the production of raw materials, particularly manganese dioxide, zinc and steel.

On the basis of that study the Corporation for Battery Recycling (CBR), whose members at the time included Duracell, Energizer, Panasonic and Spectrum Brands, decided to establish a voluntary national recycling programme for primary batteries in the US. In their request for proposals from potential stewardship organizations CBR noted that the LCA report "… showed that a carefully designed physical system can be net environmentally positive compared to landfill".[50]

49 Olivetti, E., Gregory, J., & Kirchain, R. (2011). *Life Cycle Impacts of Alkaline Batteries with a Focus on End-of-life*. Report by Massachusetts Institute of Technology for the National Electrical Manufacturers Association. Retrieved from http://www.epbaeurope.net/documents/NEMA_alkalinelca2011.pdf
50 The Corporation for Battery Recycling (2012). *Request for Proposal for Stewardship Organization*. Rosslyn, VA: Corporation for Battery Recycling, p. 3.

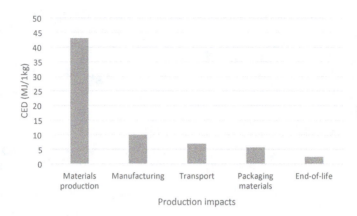

FIGURE 5.3   Life-cycle impacts of 1 kg weighted average alkaline battery

Source: Based on Olivetti *et al.* (2011), pp. 23-24

Another LCA funded by the UK Department for Environment Food and Rural Affairs, which modelled a number of different collection and recycling scenarios for mixed portable batteries concluded that: "… increasing recycling of batteries is beneficial for the environment, due to the recovery of metals and avoidance of virgin metal production. However, it is achieved at significant financial cost when compared to disposal".[51]

Recycling impacts were strongly influenced by the technology used for recycling. From a climate change perspective, for example, the best outcomes were those involving hydrometallurgical recycling in the UK and EU.

The environmental impacts of recycling the more hazardous rechargeable batteries appear to be less equivocal. Research on the environmental impacts of recycling portable NiCd batteries in Sweden concluded that recycling was environmentally positive; in fact the study concluded that "[f]rom an environmental perspective, the optimum recycling rate for NiCd batteries tends to be close to 100%".[52]

5.4.3 Pollution from recycling

Lead is highly toxic, so there are environmental and safety risks that need to be managed throughout the supply and recovery chain. Unregulated or uncontrolled recycling of used lead acid batteries can cause significant pollution and health impacts, particularly in developing countries. The

51   Fisher *et al.* (2006), p. 3.
52   Rydh, & Karlstrom (2002), p. 289.

Blacksmith Institute developed a list of the top ten polluting industries, ranking industries based on the contribution of toxic pollutants to the global burden of disease.[53] Lead acid battery recycling, particularly in low and middle income countries, was ranked as the most polluting.

In 2011 the Chinese Government ordered the closure of around 83% of companies covered by an environmental and safety audit of battery manufacturers and recyclers.[54] Some of these closures were expected to be permanent because of their poor operating practices and proximity to residential areas. Industry sources have estimated that around 32% of lead consumed for battery manufacturing in China is lost to the environment compared with an "infinitesimal" amount in the United States.[55]

This is an issue in all developing countries, where battery recycling is still often undertaken by "backyard smelters" in the informal sector. The International Lead Association (ILA) has highlighted a number of unsustainable practices, including:

- Few or no facilities for neutralization and safe disposal of the acidic electrolyte, which can enter the water table, rivers and sewerage system

- Inadequate protection of workers

- Inadequate or non-existing exhaust control systems on furnaces to prevent air pollution

- Location close to shops and homes, increasing the risks of lead exposure[56]

53 Blacksmith Institute, & Green Cross Switzerland (2012). *The World's Worst Pollution Problems: Assessing Health Risks at Hazardous Waste Sites.* Zurich, Switzerland: Green Cross. Retrieved from http://www.worstpolluted.org/files/FileUpload/files/2012%20WorstPolluted.pdf

54 Lin, L. (2011, August 4). China halts 1,598 battery makers, recyclers after a 5-month probe. *Metal Bulletin.* Retrieved from http://www.metalbulletin.com/Article/2878332/China-halts-1598-battery-makers-recyclers-after-5-month-probe.html

55 BCI, & the Lead Acid Battery Branch of CEEIA (2011). *Lead Battery Health Safety and Environmental Summit, September 7–8 2011.* Retrieved from http://www.nepodc.com/summit/

56 ILA (n.d.). *Recycling in the Informal Sector. Lead Action 21.* London: International Lead Association. Retrieved from http://www.ila-lead.org/UserFiles/File/Recycling%20in%20the%20Informal%20Sector.pdf

The ILA has expressed strong opposition to the informal recycling sector on behalf of the "global regulated lead industry" and is working with stakeholders to improve global practices.[57] The International Lead Management Center, which was established by lead producers in 1996, "offers advice and assistance across the industry and throughout the lead lifecycle from mining, smelting and refining through to recycling".[58]

While environmental, health and safety impacts of lead acid battery recycling are highly regulated in most developed countries, some legacy issues are still being dealt with. In 2015 the US-based Exide Technologies entered bankruptcy and permanently closed its lead acid battery recycling factory in Vernon, Los Angeles, under an agreement with local regulators to avoid criminal prosecution. Exide agreed to pay US$50 million to clean up the site and the neighbourhood, and to continue testing residents for lead poisoning. According to one media report, the company had polluted the surrounding soil and groundwater with high levels of lead, arsenic, cadmium and other toxic metals over many decades of operation.[59]

5.5 Corporate strategy for batteries

5.5.1 Policy

Battery manufacturers are less proactive on sustainability and product stewardship issues (or less transparent about their policies) than companies in other sectors. Exide Technologies, for example, has a brief Environmental, Health and Safety policy that states the company will "[m]onitor emerging issues with respect to environment, health, and safety aspects, keeping ourselves informed and up-to-date on regulatory changes and technological innovations".[60] The terms "product stewardship" and "corporate social responsibility" are not mentioned in the policy or on the website.

57   *Ibid.*, p. 1.
58   International Lead Association (2016). *ILMC—Assistance to Industry and Governments Around the World.* Retrieved from http://www.ila-lead.org/responsibility/the-international-lead-management-center
59   Barboza & Vives (2015).
60   Exide Technologies (2015). *Environment, Health and Safety Policy.* Milton, GA: Exide Technologies. Retrieved from http://www.exide.com/Media/files/EHS-Policy.pdf

The company does have a strong commitment to lead acid battery recycling, primarily driven by its supply chain requirements for recycled lead.

Manufacturers of portable batteries, such as Spectrum Brands (Rayovac and Varta brands), Duracell and Energizer, provide consumers with contradictory messages on recycling in different markets. This suggests a reactive approach driven by regulations, rather than a strong corporate commitment to product stewardship or recycling. Spectrum Brands' environmental statement, for example, provides equivocal support for recycling:

> Waste, whether produced in the manufacturing plant, office, or home, represents environmental and economic inefficiency. Accordingly, we should dispose of resources intelligently, recycling those that can be utilized economically in a different form. We must recognize, however, that recycling is not without costs, and that some recycling processes consume more resources than they save.[61]

The company does, however, express support for industry efforts to introduce take-back regulations:

> Spectrum Brands and Rayovac, through our long-term partnership with Call2Recycle, look forward to participating in industry efforts in 2015 and working with more than 200 other product and battery manufacturers on an all battery product stewardship bill.[62]

On its US website Rayovac responds to the question "How should I dispose of my alkaline batteries?" by saying that "[a]lkaline batteries can be disposed in your household waste".[63] In contrast, a brochure published by the company in the UK encourages consumers to recycle:

> Throwing batteries in the bin to end up in landfill is harmful to the environment as well as a waste of a resource. To tackle this problem, new regulations have come into force to encourage the recycling of all types of batteries—including hearing aid batteries.
> … Battery users have a key role to play by recycling used batteries. To help you do this Rayovac has partnered with BatteryBack to provide easily accessible collection points throughout the country.[64]

61 Spectrum Brands (2015). *Environmental Statement*. Retrieved from http://www.spectrumbrands.com/aboutus/environmentalstatement.aspx
62 *Ibid.*
63 Rayovac (2015). *Frequently Asked Questions*. Retrieved from http://www.rayovac.com/contact/faqs.aspx
64 Rayovac (n.d.). *Be Positive Recycle Batteries*. Retrieved from http://www.rayovac.eu/assets/filemanager/Brochures/UK/RayovacBatteryDirective.pdf

Energizer is more positive about recycling, stating on its website that: "Recycling is a positive alternative. Please do the responsible thing. Energizer strongly recommends proper disposal and recycling of all batteries".[65]

Unlike Rayovac or Spectrum Brands Energizer also has a policy on sustainability:

> Essentially, our approach to sustainability all boils down to one simple thought: "Do the right thing." Not just because we're decent, good-hearted folks—which we are—but because we're staunch believers in the idea that doing the right thing affords us tremendous opportunity to make a positive impact on the well-being of our communities, our environment, and our shareholders ...
>
> First is a focus on reducing the impact our company and its products have on the environment. Through various efforts including product development, packaging, recycling and outreach programs, we are careful to make choices that ensure the availability of natural resources for generations to come.[66]

Japanese battery manufacturer FDK Group is one of the few portable battery manufacturers to publish an environmental report. In its most recent report the company states that "[w]e will promote the development of environmentally compatible products by eliminating the use of harmful materials, reducing the energy required for product use, and increasing product longevity".[67]

5.5.2 Design

Battery technologies have continued to evolve to reduce their environmental and safety impacts and to support the global transition to more sustainable fuel sources for automotive (e.g. hybrid electric vehicles) and stationary energy (renewable power). According to Johnson Controls, the world's largest manufacturer of automotive batteries, improved battery technologies are achieving significant fuel savings in vehicles (Table 5.10).[68]

65   Energizer (2015). *Proper Disposal, Storage, Care and Handling of your Batteries.* Retrieved from http://www.energizer.com/about-batteries/battery-care

66   Energizer (2015). *Sustainability Done Right.* Retrieved from http://www. energizer.com/about-energizer/sustainability

67   FDK Group (2010). *Environmental Report 2010.* Kosai City, Shizuoka, Japan: FDK Group, p. 2. Retrieved from http://www.fdk.com/kankyou-e/2010report_e.pdf

68   Johnson Controls (2015). *The Johnson Controls Way: 2014 Business and Sustainability Report.* Retrieved from http://www.johnsoncontrols.com/-/media/ jci/corporate-sustainability/reporting-and-policies/files/2014_bsr.pdf?la=en, p. 16.

TABLE 5.10 Estimated vehicle fuel savings across vehicle powertrains

Battery technology		Approximate fuel saving (%)
Conventional	Starting, lighting, ignition (SLI)	Baseline
Start-stop	Enhanced flooded batteries	Up to 5
	Absorbent glass mat	5+
Micro hybrid	Duel battery system: 48 V Li-ion battery and 12 V lead acid battery	12–15
Hybrid	Advanced Li-ion energy storage system	20
Plug-in and electric	Advanced Li-ion energy storage system	50+

Source: Based on Johnson Controls (2015), p. 16

Lithium-ion batteries, which are becoming the technology of choice for consumer electronics, electric vehicles and energy storage, also have potential to catch fire if they get damaged or short-circuit. This is because Li-ion batteries have more power than other batteries on a weight-for-weight basis, and lithium is highly reactive.[69] Manufacturers are working to improve safety through the development of new Li-ion chemistries, as well as the use of smart control systems.

Significant progress has been made in reducing, and in most cases eliminating, mercury and cadmium components in portable batteries.

Mercury is no longer used in general purpose household batteries (alkaline and carbon zinc) manufactured by major brand owners in Europe and the United States. In 1998 the European Commission banned primary batteries containing more than 5 ppm of mercury (Directive 98/101/EC). It was also banned in the US in 1996 with the passage of the Mercury-Containing Battery Management Act. However, a study by UK authorities in 2007 found some batteries that still contain high levels of mercury.[70] A study of used batteries in the US found low levels of mercury in a small percentage of alkaline batteries, and these figures are declining each year as older batteries reach the end of their life.[71]

Mercury is also still used as an electrode in mercuric oxide button cells. Its purpose is to suppress zinc corrosion, which can cause the generation

69 *The Economist* (2014, January 27). Why lithium batteries keep catching fire. *The Economist*. Retrieved from http://www.economist.com/blogs/economist-explains/2014/01/economist-explains-19

70 EPBA (2011), p. 22.

71 Olivetti *et al.* (2011).

of hydrogen gas in the canister. This can cause the battery to leak, limiting its ability to function. These types of button cells can contain up to 0.005 grams of mercury. Mercury free alternatives are available but they are more expensive and not commercially available everywhere.[72] Button cells with no more than 2% mercury were originally exempt from restrictions on mercury in the EU Battery Directive, but under later amendments (2013/56/EU) the exemption was removed. Leading brand owners in the US committed to a voluntary phase-out of mercury-added button cells and a few states in the US have passed legislation to ban their sale.[73]

The use of cadmium in rechargeable batteries is also being phased out in line with regulatory requirements. Batteries for cordless power tools were exempt from the restriction on cadmium in the EU Battery Directive to give manufacturers time to find commercially viable alternatives. When the Directive was amended in 2013, this exemption was removed from 31 December 2016 because alternatives are now available including nickel metal hydride (NiMH) and lithium-ion.

NiMH batteries have significantly lower environmental impacts over their life-cycle compared with NiCd batteries. A life-cycle assessment concluded that the use of NiMH batteries instead of NiCd resulted in an 18% benefit for human health, a 13% benefit for ecosystem quality and a 4% benefit for resources.[74] This was due to both the elimination of cadmium and their higher energy efficiency.

The trends for mobile phones are typical of a broader shift away from NiCd batteries towards less hazardous chemistries (Fig. 5.4). The most significant change has been the growth in Li-ion batteries since 2005–06, replacing almost all of the other chemistries.

With mercury and cadmium largely eliminated from new household batteries, producers are starting to focus on other environmental initiatives. In February 2015 Energizer announced the launch of EcoAdvanced™, its

72 NEWMOA (2010). *Mercury Use in Batteries*. Boston, MA: Northeast Waste Management Officials' Association. Retrieved from http://www.newmoa.org/ prevention/mercury/imerc/factsheets/batteries.cfm

73 NEMA (2006, March 2). *NEMA Announces Battery Industry Commitment to Eliminating Mercury in Button Cells*. Retrieved from https://www.nema.org/ news/Pages/2006-03-02-NEMA-Announces-Battery-Industry-Commitment-to-Eliminating-Mercury-in-Button-Cells.aspx

74 Parsons, D. (2007). The environmental impact of disposable versus re-chargeable batteries for consumer use. *International Journal of Life Cycle Assessment*, 12(3), 197-203 (p. 201).

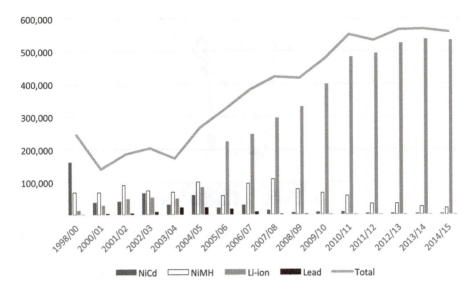

FIGURE 5.4   Number of batteries used for mobile phones in Australia, 1998/99–2014/15, total and by chemistry

Source: AMTA (2015). *Australia's Mobile Decade: 10 Years of Consumer Insights into Mobile Use and Recycling.* Sydney: Australian Mobile Telecommunications Association

"highest performing alkaline battery and the world's first AA battery made with four percent recycled battery material".[75] Energizer is working with battery recyclers to generate higher value through "closed loop" recycling:

> Innovations such as *Energizer*® EcoAdvanced™ batteries have created a use—and a value—for recycled battery materials (which until today had little use or economic value). By 2025, our vision for *Energizer*® EcoAdvanced™ is to increase the amount of recycled battery material ten-fold to 40%.[76]

Other companies promote the environmental credentials of their alkaline batteries on the basis of different measures and varying levels of transparency. Canadian company LEI Electronics claims that its Eco Alkalines™ battery lasts as long or longer than competing brands and contains absolutely no heavy metals; every purchase is "carbon neutral"; and the battery

75   Energizer (2015, February 3). Energizer introduces world's first high performance battery made with recycled materials. *Business Wire.* Retrieved from http://www.businesswire.com/news/home/20150202006219/en/Energizer-Introduces-World%E2%80%99s-High-Performance-Battery-Recycled-Batteries

76   Energizer (2015). *The Energizer® EcoAdvanced™ Story.* Retrieved from http://www.energizer.com/ecoadvanced

FIGURE 5.5   All batteries sold in the EU must show the "wheelie bin" symbol

and packaging can both be recycled.[77] Information and third-party certifi-
cations are provided for most of these claims.

All batteries sold in the EU must be labelled with the "crossed out wheelie
bin" (Fig. 5.5) to indicate separate collection. Batteries containing more
than 0.0005% mercury, more than 0.002% cadmium or more than 0.004%
lead, also have to be marked with the chemical symbol for the relevant
metal concerned.[78]

5.5.3 Procurement

Battery manufacturers appear to be under less pressure from customers to
manage sustainability issues in their supply chain than producers in the
electrical and electronic equipment sector, where most of the larger brands
impose strict and detailed requirements for product and packaging design.
One of the few issues that battery producers have been forced to address is
the use of "conflict minerals". This is primarily driven by regulation in the
US, where the Dodd-Frank Wall Street Reform and Consumer Protection Act
2010 requires producers to report on the use of minerals from conflict or
high risk areas that may be contributing to human rights abuses.

Spectrum Brands has implemented processes to ensure that its suppliers
comply with the regulation:

77   LEI Electronics (2015). *The Eco Alkalines™ Difference*. Retrieved from http://
www.leiproducts.com/eco-alkalines/eco-alkaline-difference

78   European Commission (2013). *Directive 2006/66 EC of the European Parliament
and the Council on Batteries and Accumulators and Waste Batteries and Accumulators*. Brussels, Belgium: EC.

> Spectrum's Supplier Code of Conduct requires suppliers to implement a policy and process to reasonably assure that the mining of the tantalum, tin, tungsten and gold in the products they manufacture does not directly or indirectly finance or benefit armed groups that perpetrate human rights abuses in the Democratic Republic of the Congo or an adjoining country ...[79]

Exide expects its suppliers to "ensure materials used in their products are sourced in an ethical manner, and expect a similar commitment from their global supply chain partners", and is prepared to change suppliers if their expectations are not met:

> To further this objective, we are requiring that each applicable supplier provide information on its use and sourcing of Conflict Minerals in the materials it supplies to Exide. To the extent any suppliers are unable to provide such assurance, Exide expects to initiate appropriate action to transition to alternative suppliers that can provide assurances that any Conflict Minerals supplied to Exide are not sourced from the Conflict Countries.[80]

Battery producers including Energizer, Johnson Controls and Panasonic have joined the Conflict Minerals Reporting Initiative, which was founded in 2008 by members of the Electronic Industry Citizenship Coalition and the Global E-sustainability Initiative.[81] The initiative provides its members with a reporting template and a third party auditing process which determines which smelters and refineries are "conflict free" according to global standards.

5.5.4 Reuse and recycling

Reuse (or "repurposing") can extend the life of some larger batteries, particularly those used for electric vehicles (EV). Bosch, for example, has

---

79 Spectrum Brands (2015). *Policy Regarding Conflict Minerals*. Retrieved from http://www.spectrumbrands.com/corporate-responsibility/conflict-minerals.aspx

80 Exide Technologies (2014). *Exide Technologies Policy Statement Regarding Conflict Minerals*, p. 1. Retrieved from http://www.exide.com/Media/files/Conflict-Minerals-Policy(1).pdf

81 Conflict Free Sourcing Initiative (2013). *Reasonable Practices to Identify Sources of Conflict Minerals: Practical Guidance for Downstream Companies*. Electronic Industry Citizenship Coalition and the Global e-Sustainability Initiative. Retrieved from http://www.conflictfreesourcing.org/media/docs/news/CFSI_DD_ReasonablePracticesforDownstreamCompanies_Aug2013.pdf

announced a partnership with BMW and Vattenfall, called the Second Life Batteries Alliance, to develop a large-scale energy storage system in Germany.[82] BMW will supply more than 100 second-hand Li-ion batteries from its ActiveE and i3 electric vehicles.

While reuse can generate significant environmental benefits by extending the life of a product, recycling is the only realistic option for most batteries when they reach the end of their life. The market for used batteries and the availability of a recycling infrastructure—both of which determine their recyclability—are driven by the value of their component materials, which varies significantly between the various battery types.

Lead acid automotive batteries contain a high percentage of lead (around 65%). Strong demand for lead and its relatively high commercial value means that recycling is largely driven by the market. Disposal or recycling is also regulated in many jurisdictions owing to the toxicity of lead and its impacts in landfill. As a result of regulation and market drivers recycling rates are generally high—the Battery Council International estimated that around 98% of used lead acid batteries were recycled in the US in 2011.[83]

In contrast, the components of an alkaline portable battery are less hazardous and most of their constituents don't have a high commercial value. For these reasons recovery rates tend to be low in the absence of regulation. Recycling generally requires a "fee for service" because the value of the recovered materials is less than the costs of collection, transport, sorting and reprocessing. This cost is met by producers where there is an EPR scheme in place, or by the organization providing the service (e.g. a retailer or government agency).

Historically Li-ion battery recycling has focused on recovery of cobalt because its value has risen in response to increased demand for battery manufacturing.[84] However, the use of cobalt in batteries is projected to decline as battery technology evolves.[85] In addition to cobalt, battery recyclers may recover lithium, nickel and other materials. Demand for lithium is expected to grow significantly as a result of increased use of Li-ion batteries in electric vehicles.[86]

---

82   Bosch (2015, January 21). *Second Life Batteries Project*. Retrieved from http://www.bosch.fr/en/fr/newsroom_7/news_7/news-detail-page_60994.php
83   BCI (2013).
84   Amarakoon *et al.* (2013).
85   *Ibid.*
86   *Ibid.*

There are other challenges associated with battery recycling apart from their material make-up:

- The wide variety of battery types (size, chemistry and application) require multiple collection channels and recycling solutions

- Many batteries remain inside the product until the end of its life, and will only be recycled if the product itself is recycled

- It may take many years for a battery to reach the end of its life. This makes it difficult for regulators and recyclers to know how many batteries are available for collection at any time

The EU Battery Directive has established targets for the "collection rate" of used batteries, which is calculated by dividing the weight of batteries collected in a year by the average weight of batteries put on the market during that year and the preceding two years. Research on battery life indicates that this is not an accurate measure of recycling performance because of the time lag between sale and disposal.[87] This is due both to the life of the product and to "hoarding" behaviour. Hoarding describes the tendency of many consumers to keep batteries and appliances in their home after they have reached the end of their life.

Bebat, the compliance organization for the collection and recycling of portable and industrial batteries in Belgium, sampled approximately 30,000 batteries in 2012 to investigate the typical time period for battery usage and hoarding.[88] Each battery was weighed and photographed, and manufacturers were asked to provide the production date. The results for the 17,000 batteries with a known production date are shown in Figure 5.6. Because portable batteries take significantly longer than three years to be discarded, Bebat is developing a calculation method for batteries "available for collection" and hopes to integrate this into the revision of the Battery Directive.[89]

The European Battery Recycling Association (EBRA) is working on a certification standard for battery recycling to achieve a "worldwide level

---

87 See Takao, M. (2013). *Update of Rechargeable Batteries Collection & Recycling Activity and the Latest Survey for Average Life of Batteries Returned in Japan*. International Congress for Battery Recycling. September 11–13, 2013, Dubrovnik, Croatia; Desmet, B., Mertens, A.-S., & Coonen, P. (2014). *How the Battery Life Cycle Influences the Collection Rate of Battery Collection Schemes*. International Congress of Battery Recycling. September 24–26, 2014, Hamburg, Germany.

88 Desmet *et al.* (2014).

89 *Ibid.*

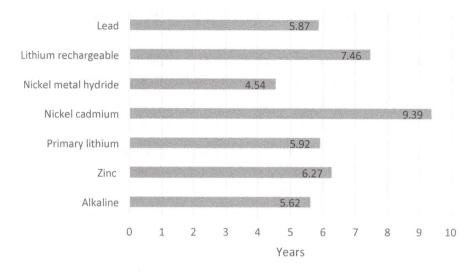

FIGURE 5.6   Average usage and hoarding term for batteries (years), Belgium, 2012

Source: Based on Desmet *et al.* (2014)

playing field".[90] The association has argued that there is no systematic way to ensure that recyclers are meeting the requirements of the Battery Directive, such as meeting minimum levels of recycling efficiency. The standard will address quality, environmental issues and health and safety in collection and recycling.

5.5.4.1 Voluntary take-back

Automotive and industrial batteries

Manufacturers of automotive and industrial batteries often take individual responsibility for taking back used batteries from customers for recycling. There are some collective programmes such as the Canadian Battery Association (CBA), which undertakes a collective stewardship programme for used lead acid batteries to meet regulatory requirements. In British Columbia, for example, all battery producers must have an approved product stewardship plan or appoint a third party organization to carry out its duties under a product stewardship plan. CBA has developed a plan to meet this obligation on behalf of producers. This includes:

---

90   Vassart, A. (2014). *The Why and How of the Certification Initiative for Recycling Plants.* International Congress for Battery Recycling. September 24–26, 2014, Hamburg, Germany.

- A network of 150 retail return facilities

- Events to collect used lead acid batteries from remote communities

- A website to promote collection points

- A pamphlet for all consumers that purchase a battery

- Standard recycling labels on all lead acid batteries sold in British Columbia

- Training and education for collection facilities and transporters on protecting the environment and worker safety

- Guidelines for safe collection, storage and transport

- An audit programme[91]

A similar plan has been submitted by CBA to the Government of Manitoba and other provinces on a voluntary basis.

While there are well-established systems in place in most countries to collect and recycle automotive batteries, consumers do not necessarily know how to recycle.[92] For that reason some producers focus on consumer education rather than (or in addition to) take-back programmes. Johnson Controls, for example, has created a website (www.recyclingmybattery.com) that allows consumers to enter their postcode to find out where they can recycle locally.

Johnson Controls also recycles used automotive batteries from Ghana, with sponsorship from the German Federal Ministry of Education and Research.[93] Managed by the independent Öko-Institut, this programme identifies opportunities in Africa to reduce environmental and health risks from improper recycling.

Portable batteries

In contrast to lead batteries, most recycling programmes for portable batteries have been introduced in response to legislation (e.g. Europe)

---

91   Canadian Battery Association (2011). *British Columbia Stewardship Plan for Lead-Acid Batteries*. Toronto: Canadian Battery Association. Retrieved from http://www2.gov.bc.ca/assets/gov/environment/waste-management/recycling/recycle/batteries/cbastewardshipplan.pdf

92   Johnson Controls (2014, April 17). *New Survey Shows Knowledge Gap in Car Battery Recycling*. Retrieved from http://www.recyclingmybattery.com/en-us/news/new-survey-shows-knowledge-gap-in-car-battery-recycling

93   Johnson Controls (2015).

PHOTO 5.3 Used batteries ready for collection

Photo: Helen Lewis

or regulatory threats (e.g. in the United States). After strict EPR laws for rechargeable batteries were introduced in New Jersey and Minnesota in 1991, manufacturers introduced a voluntary national programme to avoid further state or federal regulations. This strategy worked:

> Creation of this nationwide voluntary program effectively dissuaded additional states from enacting laws with stringent requirements. Laws enacted in Maryland in 1993 for mercuric oxide batteries ... and in Maine in 1995 for rechargeable batteries ... lack the performance goals and reporting requirements included in the New Jersey and Minnesota laws. No further EPR legislation was enacted at the state level for more than a decade.[94]

The programme established by manufacturers through the Rechargeable Battery Recycling Corporation (since renamed Call2Recycle) is described in Case study 5.7.1. While Call2Recycle has been successful in gaining industry support and providing a convenient collection programme for consumers, the recycling rate remains low. Nash and Bosso argue that "[a]s legislative

94 Nash, J., & Bosso, C. (2013). Extended producer responsibility in the United States: full speed ahead? *Journal of Industrial Ecology*, 17(2), 175-185 (p. 178).

pressure waned, so did the RBRC's programme goals".[95] The original goal
of recycling 70% of discarded batteries by 2001 is no longer mentioned,
and performance is reported as pounds of batteries collected rather than
collection rates.[96] As a result of major changes in the battery market since
the programme was introduced in 1994, including more battery-powered
devices and increased imports, the industry itself is now calling for supporting regulations.[97]

Battery stewardship is not regulated in Australia but some companies
have implemented voluntary take-back programmes. One of these is the
Battery World retail franchise network (Case study 5.7.2), which funds a
collection and recycling service through each of its stores. This case study
demonstrates that a voluntary battery recycling programme can generate
business benefits. While hard to measure, the benefits include enhanced
brand awareness and value and increased sales.

Another voluntary example from Australia is ALDI, the first supermarket
in the country to offer a free recycling service for portable batteries in all
of its stores. The programme was launched in October 2012 in partnership
with environment group Planet Ark, which provided marketing and promotional support. The design of the collection bin is based on ALDI's own-
brand "Activ Energy" batteries, clearly linking the recycling programme to
marketing (Photo 5.4). According to the company's Australian website, the
rationale for the programme is that: "Unlike Europe, there is no compulsory
battery recycling program for household batteries in Australia. As such, over
300 million household batteries end up in landfill each year".[98]

The programme appears to be based on a strong business case as well as a
sense of corporate responsibility. ALDI's corporate responsibility statement,
which is consistent with its global policy, states that "We are convinced
that long-term business success can only be achieved only if we … assume
responsibility for people, nature and the environment."[99]

95 *Ibid.*, p. 178.
96 *Ibid.*
97 Call2Recycle (2013). *2012 Annual Report*. Atlanta, GA. Retrieved from http://
    www.call2recycle.org/annual-report/
98 ALDI (2013). *Do your Bit and Recycle Batteries at ALDI!* Retrieved from https://
    corporate.aldi.com.au/en/corporate-responsibility/operations/battery
    -recycling/
99 ALDI (2015). *ALDI Corporate Responsibility*. Retrieved from https://corporate.
    aldi.co.uk/en/responsibility/corporate-responsibility/

PHOTO 5.4   ALDI's battery recycling bin in Australia

Photo: Helen Lewis

Canadian company LEI Electronics, which manufactures the EcoAlkaline brand, encourages consumers to return any of their used EcoAlkaline batteries to the company free of charge.[100] LEI Electronics arranges for any returned batteries to be recycled by local Ontario recycler, Raw Materials Company (RMC).

5.5.4.2 Compliance with EPR regulations

Take-back and recycling of used batteries is mandatory in many jurisdictions but producers' obligations vary. In some countries responsibility for recycling is only financial. In Taiwan for example, producers pay a tax to the government to pay for recycling, which is managed by the Environment Protection Administration (EPA).

In EU countries producers have partial or full responsibility for the collection and recycling of batteries. The UK Waste Batteries and Accumulators Regulations (2009) require portable battery manufacturers and importers to join a producer compliance scheme. The costs of participating are

---

100 LEI Electronics (2015). *Recycle Your Batteries*. Retrieved from http://www. leiproducts.com/eco-alkalines/recycle-your-batteries

TABLE 5.11   Comparison of EPR schemes for portable batteries in selected countries in the EU, 2014

Member state	Number of collective PROs	Costs covered by producers	Producer fees (€/tonne of batteries recovered)	Collection rate (%)
Austria	4	Full costs	1,143	49
Belgium	1	Full costs	9,065	52
Denmark	4	Partial (most portable batteries are collected by municipalities and provided to the PROs)	181	47
France	2 PROs + 1 individual scheme	Full costs	650	36
Netherlands	1	Full costs	1,595	42
Czech Republic	1	Full costs	5,074	72

Source: Based on Bio Intelligence Service, Arcadis, & Institute for European Environmental Policy (2013), pp. 55-63

determined by the compliance organization, based on the costs of recycling, marketing and administration.

Recycling fees vary widely across Europe. Recycling of automotive and industrial batteries is generally financed by revenue from recycled materials and producers don't need to pay a fee.[101] In Belgium there is a producer responsibility organization (PRO) for automotive and industrial batteries (RECYBAT), but producers only have to pay an administrative fee to cover the operating costs of the organization, such as data collection and reporting.

The situation is very different for portable batteries. Analysis of six case studies in the EU (Table 5.11) estimated that fees paid per tonne of batteries recovered ranged from €181/t in Denmark to €9,065/t in Belgium. In Denmark fees paid to the PROs are lower because they only have to cover part of the costs of collection and recycling, with municipal costs reimbursed through a separate levy on producers. However, a lack of transparency means that the total costs of collection and recycling are unclear.[102]

The PRO in Belgium (Bebat) has argued that its costs have been particularly high because the former federal tax did not reflect the true costs of

101 Bio Intelligence Service, Arcadis, & Institute for European Environmental Policy (2013).
102 *Ibid.*

collection and recycling. As a result the PRO has invested heavily in the collection infrastructure, communication and education, which has enabled it to reach a relatively high collection rate of 52%. The tax has now been replaced by an environmental fee, and the cost to producers is expected to fall.[103]

In France the PROs (COREPILE and SCRELEC) are required to introduce differential fees to encourage the design of batteries with reduced environmental impact. The criteria used to calculate their "eco modulated fees" are capacity (efficiency), the number of recharge cycles, risks (e.g. safety) and an estimate of "eco-costs" at end of life.[104]

The Battery Directive applies to all producers placing a battery on the market, including those sold in an appliance or vehicle. Because of overlap with the Directives for Waste Electrical and Electronic Equipment (WEEE) and End of Life Vehicles (ELV), member states have to ensure that there is no double charging.[105] Member states also have to ensure that manufacturers design appliances in such a way that waste batteries can be readily removed.

In some jurisdictions retailers also have obligations. In the UK retailers and distributors do not have a financial obligation, but they are required to assist in the collection and recycling of used batteries. Any retailer selling more than 32 kg of batteries a year has to provide recycling bins or facilities. In New York state retailers that sell rechargeable batteries (weighing less than 25 pounds [approximately 11 kg]) are required to collect used batteries of the same type from customers for recycling.

Battery recycling fees in Switzerland are passed on to consumers through an advanced recycling fee (ARF), which is visible to consumers on their retail sales docket. The amount of the ARF is regulated through the annex on batteries to the Ordinance on the Reduction of Risks Linked to Chemical Products (2005). The recycling programme is managed by INOBAT, a cooperative of battery producers, manufacturers and retailers. INOBAT invoices battery producers for the ARF based on their self-declared sales.

103 *Ibid.*, p. 64.
104 Hedouin, F. (2013). *French Battery CRO's: Implementation of an Eco-modulated 2013 Price List*. International Congress for Battery Recycling. September 11–13, 2013, Dubrovnic, Croatia.
105 Lee, R.G. (2008). Marketing products under the extended producer responsibility framework: a battery of issues. *Review of European, Comparative & International Environmental Law*, 17(3), 300-307.

5.6 Conclusion

Portable batteries are a prime target for take-back regulations because of rapid growth in the market for battery-powered products and the presence of hazardous materials such as lead, cadmium, mercury and lithium. A fee is generally required to cover the costs of collection and recycling, and companies are often unwilling to bear the cost unless required to do so by regulation. Despite significant achievements over a 20 year period the largely voluntary Call2Recycle programme in North America is now calling for regulations to address a free-rider problem.

The situation for automotive and industrial batteries is very different, with strong international demand for lead driving high collection and material recovery rates in recent years. This is likely to change in the future as lithium-ion batteries become more common in automotive and energy storage applications. As these larger non-lead batteries start to reach the end of their life in larger volumes, more formal product stewardship solutions may be required to ensure that they don't end up in landfill.

Municipalities, government policy-makers and regulators will increasingly focus on hazardous products such as batteries, used paint and mercury-containing lights because of their environmental impacts in landfill and increasing waste management costs. The additional risks associated with management of lithium-ion batteries, because of the potential for a fire or explosion, will only add to calls for greater producer responsibility, particularly at end of life. For producers this will mean more regulation and a greater need for industry collaboration on issues such as voluntary standards and certification for recyclers.

5.7 Case studies

Case study 5.7.1 Call2Recycle portable battery recycling

> How we address some overarching market trends will determine our
> success tomorrow. Products are becoming increasingly mobile, their
> batteries integrated into the design and packaging. That's a challenge
> to a standalone battery collector with limited capability. And that's
> why Call2Recycle will be so much more ... We have to look broadly
> and confidently at new turf that includes all battery-powered devices
> (Carl Smith, CEO and President, Call2Recycle, Inc.).[106]

5.7.1.1 Summary

Call2Recycle, Inc. is a not-for-profit battery stewardship organization operating in the US and Canada. Founded in 1994 in response to government
legislation, the organization began by collecting NiCd batteries. It has
evolved to meet changes in technology and regulatory requirements, adding additional types of batteries and mobile phones to its Call2Recycle® collection programme. Over the 20 years to 2014 Call2Recycle has recycled a
cumulative 45 million kilograms of batteries.[107]

5.7.1.2 Drivers for product stewardship

According to its official history, the Rechargeable Battery Recycling Corporation (RBRC), now Call2Recycle, Inc., was established in 1994 in response
to several regulatory developments.[108] In 1991 the US Environmental Protection Agency (EPA) announced that rechargeable NiCd batteries would be
classified as a hazardous waste and regulated under the Resource Conservation Recovery Act (RCRA). The RCRA delegated responsibility to the states
and instructed them to introduce recycling programmes. NiCd batteries
were singled out for regulation because they made up the bulk of batteries in use at the time, with the exception of small sealed lead acid batteries
(SSLA) that were already being recycled.[109]

Connecticut was the first state to implement a recycling mandate in 1989,
followed by Minnesota, Maine and Vermont in 1991. Six others followed
over the next two years. At the same time regulators in several states were

---

106 Dantini, B. (2015). *Our Story: The History of Call2Recycle, 20 Years*. Atlanta, GA:
     Call2Recycle Inc, p. 46.
107 Call2Recycle (2015). *Annual Report 2014: 20 Years of Product Stewardship*.
     Atlanta, GA. Retrieved from http://www.call2recycle.org/wp-content/uploads
     /2014-Annual-Report_English.pdf
108 Dantini (2015).
109 *Ibid.*

threatening to ban the sale of mercury and cadmium-containing products, including rechargeable batteries. The battery industry responded quickly:

> Rather than ban the sale of batteries containing these hazardous materials, it made more sense to collect them before they were sent to landfills. The founding fathers of what would become the Portable Rechargeable Battery Association (PRBA) and eventually RBRC, knew this. It would become the cornerstone of their proposals to address the safe disposal issue.[110]

In 1991 the five largest manufacturers of rechargeable NiCd batteries— Gates (later Energizer), Panasonic, Saft, Sanyo and Varta—established the PRBA. Its purpose was to develop a manufacturer-driven collection and disposal programme for NiCd batteries that "would dovetail with and facilitate EPA direction".[111] PRBA undertook several pilot recycling programmes, and in 1994 established the Rechargeable Battery Recycling Corporation as a new not-for-profit company. The initiative was designed to avoid the introduction of any further mandates.[112]

5.7.1.3 Stewardship strategies

In 1996 RBRC launched its first national consumer rechargeable battery recycling campaign, called Charge Up to Recycle. This was facilitated by other regulatory developments:

- The Universal Waste Rule (1995) redefined and simplified acceptable transport requirements for hazardous wastes. This meant that batteries could be transported by commercial shippers such as FedEx or UPS. However, the Universal Waste Law had to be adopted by individual states, and implementation was slow and ad hoc.

- The Mercury-Containing and Rechargeable Battery Management Act (1996) replaced a patchwork of state-based labelling and hazardous waste requirements. It required all states to comply with the Universal Waste Law for handling NiCd rechargeable batteries and sealed lead acid batteries. The Act also introduced mandatory labels for recyclability.[113]

---

110 *Ibid.*, p. 7.
111 *Ibid.*, p. 8.
112 Nash, & Bosso (2013).
113 Dantini (2015).

PHOTO 5.5   Call2Recycle
retail collection box

Photo: Call2Recycle

RBRC started collecting rechargeable NiCd batteries in the US in 1996 and in Canada in 1997. Its scope was extended to NiMH, SSLA and Li-ion batteries in 2001; mobile phones in 2004; and nickel zinc (Ni-Zn) batteries in 2008. The programme was re-branded Call2Recycle® (originally the name of its phone recycling programme) in 2004.

In most US states the programme is largely voluntary. Some states mandate collection of NiCd and/or SSLA batteries, and two states mandate collection of all rechargeable batteries. The scope of Call2Recycle has broadened further in recent years to include primary batteries where this is mandated by legislation or supported by governments, including Vermont in the US and several provinces in Canada (British Columbia, Manitoba, Quebec, New Brunswick and Prince Edward Island).

Rechargeable battery manufacturers and portable consumer electronics companies fund the programme by paying a licence fee to use Call2Recycle's battery recycling seal, which is printed on the batteries and/or product packaging. A toll-free number on the seal allows consumers to locate their closest collection site in the US and Canada.

Fees are based on the amount of product sold into the market. By 2014 Call2Recycle had around 300 participating companies (called "stewards"), who account for approximately 85% of the portable rechargeable battery market.[114]

Collection boxes such as the one shown in Photo 5.5 are placed in retail stores, offices and municipal facilities. Consumers are asked to place each rechargeable battery in a separate plastic bag before they put it in the box, to meet transport regulations for dangerous goods. There are about 34,000 public collection sites in the US and Canada.

The collected batteries are sorted by chemistry and sent to recycling partners in North America such as Wistron and INMETCO. According to CEO and President Carl Smith, Call2Recycle is one of the first organizations of its kind to have obtained Responsible Recycling (R2) and ISO 14001 certification, as well as e-Stewards recognition by the Basel Action Network (BAN).[115]

In 2014 Call2Recycle started to advocate for regulations to deal with an increasing number of free-riders. In 2014 and 2015 it collaborated with other industry bodies to develop a model state government bill that would mandate producer responsibility for all consumer batteries. In his testimony to Senate Committee hearings on Vermont's draft bill to mandate recycling of single use batteries, Carl Smith explained why:

> [F]or most of our 20 year existence, we have opposed mandatory product stewardship, believing that an inspired and diligent industry could successfully run an effective stewardship program. We certainly have. But over the last several years, it has become increasingly clear that voluntarily programs cannot survive long-term unless there is a strong mechanism to ensure that all players in the industry comply. It wasn't necessary for us in 1994; it is now.[116]

The same message was conveyed in testimony to the Connecticut Environment Committee during hearings on its battery recycling bill:

> Over the last few years, we've concluded that a purely voluntary program like ours cannot survive long-term without state requirements to participate. This not only ensures a level-playing field for the

114 Call2Recycle (2015). *Annual Report 2014*, p. 9.
115 Personal communication (interview) with C. Smith, CEO and President, Call-2Recycle, 3 September 2015.
116 Smith, C. (2014, April 11). *Statement before the Senate Committee on Natural Resources and Energy H.695—An Act Relating to Establishing a Product Stewardship Program for Primary Batteries*. Retrieved from http://legislature.vermont.gov/assets/Documents/2014/WorkGroups/Senate%20Natural%20Resources/Bills/H.695/H.695~Carl%20Smith~Testimony~4-10-2014.pdf

companies that do participate, it also guarantees that we have the money to handle the batteries we collect. We estimate that 30%–40% of what we collect is sold into the market by companies that do not participate in our program.[117]

In 2014 Call2Recycle started to explore opportunities to extend its stewardship model into new markets, such as pharmaceuticals and battery-powered products. This would benefit from the organization's existing expertise and collection network. As Smith has noted, "After all, nobody knows the recycling model in all its facets like Call2Recycle … during the next 20 years everything's on the table and anything's possible".[118]

5.7.1.4 Shared value outcomes

Call2Recycle does not calculate a recycling rate, instead measuring their performance in terms of volumes collected and consumer accessibility. On both of these measures the effectiveness of the programme has been steadily improving. In 2014 Call2Recycle collected 5.4 million kilograms of batteries and mobile phones, and recorded the 18th consecutive year of growth.[119] Around 90% of the population in North America have access to a drop-off or collection service.

From the point of view of most industry stewards—the battery manufacturers and importers—Call2Recycle is primarily a way to meet their compliance obligations in states that mandate product take-back. A single PRO like Call2Recycle can simplify the compliance process, particularly in a country such as the US with a multitude of different laws:

> Another tenet of stewardship is compliance with extensive state, provincial and federal regulations. Call2Recycle not only operates according to these regulations, but also streamlines the compilation and submission of the required reports to regulatory bodies. With the number and complexity of the regulations across North America, this task can be onerous for individual companies.[120]

117 Smith, C. (2015, March 11). Testimony before the Connecticut Environment Committee, Raised Bill 6957. Retrieved from https://www.cga.ct.gov/2015/ENVdata/Tmy/2015HB-06957-R000311-Carl%20Smith,%20Call2Recycle%20Inc.-TMY.PDF

118 Dantini (2015), p. 47.

119 Call2Recycle (2015). *Annual Report 2014*, p. 3.

120 Smith, C. (2015, June 18). Industry stewards: the hidden benefactors of recycling. *Environmental Leader*. Retrieved from http://www.environmentalleader.com/2015/06/18/industry-stewards-the-hidden-benefactors-of-recycling/

According to Smith, its benefits go beyond compliance for many organizations: "[Call2Recycle]… has also become a powerful advocate for product stewardship, bringing together the diverse interests of its stakeholders in pursuit of a shared goal to keep batteries out of landfills and protect the environment".[121]

Retailers participate in the programme for a variety of reasons, which may include regulatory compliance, meeting existing sustainability commitments or consumer expectations, and increased traffic and sales.[122] In 2012 Call2Recycle commissioned research on consumer recycling behaviour and the potential benefits for participating retailers. This found that while not necessarily a key driver of store traffic, recycling does increase visiting frequency. Recyclers typically either shop or browse the store when dropping off batteries or mobile phones.[123]

Case study 5.7.2 Battery World: achieving a competitive advantage through voluntary battery stewardship

5.7.2.1 Summary

Battery World is a retail battery franchise network in Australia, with 89 stores selling a wide range of automotive batteries and other portable power devices.[124] Its parent company, Century Yuasa, is an affiliate of GS Yuasa International, which is listed on the Tokyo Stock Exchange.

In 2005 a franchisee with one store in Townsville decided to start collecting handheld batteries for recycling as a way of differentiating his new business in a competitive retail environment. The success of the project led to it being rolled out nationally through all Battery World stores. This case study outlines the drivers for the franchisee and the Battery World network, the strategies that were used, and some of the shared value outcomes that have been achieved. It is based on a case study written by Phil Preston.[125]

---

121 *Ibid.*
122 Smith, C. (2013). From take-back to check out: the unseen value of in-store recycling programs. In *Australian Battery Recycling Initiative Retailer Forum, 2013, Melbourne, Australia.*
123 *Ibid.*
124 Battery World (2016). *About.* Retrieved from http://www.batteryworld.com.au/About
125 See Preston, P. (2013). Battery World: Successfully applying shared value concepts, executive summary (Unpublished). Phil Preston & Associates; Preston, P. (2013). *Creating Sustained Competitive Advantage: Battery World Case Study.*

PHOTO 5.6   Battery World franchisee, Greg Leslie (right)

Photo: Battery World

5.7.2.2 Drivers for product stewardship

When Greg Leslie purchased the Battery World franchise in Townsville, Queensland, it had been closed for four months. He reopened the store in July 2005, but found it difficult to compete in a crowded market. There were at least ten other stores selling automotive batteries in the same location. After trying conventional marketing approaches to build awareness and sales, he decided that he needed to find a new offering that would differentiate his business from competitors.

The strategy that Leslie chose was to collect and recycle household batteries:

> ... Greg's intuition told him that recycling might provide a level of brand differentiation and began assessing a strategy of collecting used batteries directly from households. It didn't make sense to him that his product stewardship stopped at point of sale—he thought he should at least be offering to recycle the batteries he sells.[126]

Managers of the franchise network took a keen interest in the initiative and decided to extend it to all Battery World stores. According to Kerry Hannah, Battery World's national marketing manager at the time, there were two drivers for the company: to "get people into a store" and the desire to be "socially responsible" by closing the loop on their products.[127]

5.7.2.3 Stewardship strategies

In Townsville Greg Leslie put a recycling bin in the store and in participating schools. He provided schools with education materials on battery recycling to complement their science curricula, and spoke at school assemblies.

The recycling initiative helped engage schools students in battery recycling and attracted a considerable amount of positive media. Media coverage was often driven by local political figures wanting to be seen to be associated with and supporting it.[128] The impact on sales was almost immediate: within two and a half years of acquiring the franchise, the Townsville store became the top performer out of 70 stores in the country.

Shared Value Initiative. Retrieved from http://sharedvalue.org/sites/default/files/resource-files/Battery%20World_FINAL.pdf

126 Preston, P. (2013). Battery World, p. 3.

127 Waters, C., & Stafford, P. (2012, October 9). Franchise innovation winners revealed: all their tips and tricks. *Smart Company*. Retrieved from http://www.smartcompany.com.au/growth/franchising/28421-franchise-innovation-winners-revealed-all-their-tips-and-tricks.html

128 Preston, P. (2013). Battery World, p. 4.

The recycling scheme in Townsville became the pilot for a national roll-out to other franchisees. In 2008 the network decided that a minimum level of recycling would become a "national pillar", with several elements:

- A collection bin in every store, with operational procedures for proper disposal

- The design of an optional schools programme with different levels of involvement depending on capacity and interest.[129]

At its highest level the schools programme provides web-based resources for teachers, posters, information sessions for staff, a school assembly talk, newsletter inserts, and a battery recycling bin.

There is no legislation in Australia that mandates producer responsibility for used household batteries, so the initiative is funded entirely by Battery World and its franchisees.

5.7.2.4 Shared value outcomes

At the Townsville store, foot traffic increased from the time Greg Leslie launched the recycling initiative and he recorded 20% rolling annual sales growth after the launch date.[130] The two appear to be linked: "It is hard to attribute precise value to the initiative, but in Greg's mind, the battery recycling initiative was the only variable that would logically explain the steady increases in business".[131]

The recycling programme has contributed to Battery World's brand value in the market, with the company now recognized as a steward of the products it sells. Research by the franchise network indicates that some people choose Battery World over similar retailers or suppliers because of its recycling offer.[132] In 2012 the franchise network won the National Innovator Award from the Franchise Council of Australia in recognition of its battery recycling programme.

The social outcomes have included engagement with local schools (224 schools involved nationally in 2014) and diversion of a hazardous waste from landfill. In 2012–13 the network collected 36 tonnes of household batteries and 1,880 tonnes of car batteries.[133]

129 *Ibid.*
130 Preston, P. (2013). *Creating Sustained Competitive Advantage*, p. 2.
131 Preston, P. (2013). Battery World, p. 6.
132 *Ibid.*
133 Preston, P. (2013). *Creating Sustained Competitive Advantage*, p. 2.

Part 3:
Conclusions

6
Strategies for success

6.1 Introduction

The previous chapters described how leading companies and stewardship organizations are taking action to reduce the environmental and social impacts of products through policy, design, procurement or recovery strategies. This chapter draws on these examples to identify some of the common lessons learned by these organizations, and strategies that have proven to be effective. Following Hart, these are divided into internal (competitive) strategies and external (cooperative) strategies for product stewardship practitioners (Table 6.1).[1]

As more companies take action to reduce the environmental and social impacts of their products, and as the number of product-related regulations continue to increase, more attention needs to be paid to professional development and capabilities within firms. This is starting to be addressed by organizations such as the Product Stewardship Society through the development of "core competencies" that it hopes will provide:

> … a foundation on which to build global knowledge of the profession, assist potential employers and employees in identifying opportunities to advance the profession, and defines the role of product stewardship in advancing environmental, health and safety protections and facilitating commercial supply chains.[2]

1   Hart, S. (1995). A natural-resource-based view of the firm. *Academy of Management Review*, 20(4), 986-1014.
2   Product Stewardship Society (2015). *Core Competencies*. Retrieved from http://www.productstewards.org/Resources/Pages/Core-Competencies.aspx

TABLE 6.1   Strategies for a successful product stewardship programme

Internal (competitive) strategies	External (cooperative) strategies
• Listen and respond to stakeholder expectations • Think about the total life-cycle • Identify the material issues for your organization • Align strategies with business goals • Look for multiple benefits • Understand and promote the business case • Integrate into business systems	• Develop effective partnerships • Understand the business case for partners • Establish and implement minimum standards • Start small and learn as you go • Engage with consumers • Start voluntarily and then think about regulation • Work with policy-makers on regulatory back-up

6.2 Seven internal (competitive) strategies

6.2.1 Listen and respond to stakeholder expectations

Successful companies listen to and respond to the expectations of important stakeholders, including customers, employees, regulators, shareholders and respected NGOs.

Some of the corporate initiatives outlined in this book were a direct response to stakeholder expectations. Foodstuffs New Zealand received negative media coverage after a public "naming and shaming" exercise by local environment group Wanaka Wastebusters (Case study 3.7.1). When the foamed polystyrene trays that Foodstuffs used for its own-brand products were nominated for a poor packaging award on the basis that they weren't recyclable, the company was proactive. Consultation with local councils and packaging suppliers resulted in a new design that achieves all of the functionality of a polystyrene tray, but with the added benefit of being recyclable.

Foodstuffs' Sustainability Manager Mike Sammons says that the problem was solved through better communication: "The chain [had previously] broken, no one spoke to each other. Auckland City Council said to me 'you're the first retailer who's ever come to speak to us about packaging, and about recycling'".[3]

Many leading companies have implemented a positive stakeholder engagement process to identify issues that affect stakeholder perceptions of the organization or brand. These inform the development of business strategies to address negative perceptions or to build on opportunities identified through consultation. Canon Oceania, for example, uses customer surveys,

3   Personal communication with M. Sammons, Sustainability Manager, Foodstuffs, 2 March 2015.

social media, conferences with partners, an employee engagement survey, tenders, media, community events and participation in regulatory consultation processes to compile a list of "material issues" for the business. Stakeholder engagement is underpinned by Canon's corporate philosophy, *Kyosei*: the idea of living and working together for the common good.[4]

Government regulators are an important stakeholder group for most organizations because of their ability to support or disrupt business activities. The overview of packaging, e-waste and battery regulations in the preceding chapters highlighted a trend to more product-related environmental regulations, and for the majority of these to impose some form of producer responsibility. For this reason practitioners must stay well informed and engaged in regulatory processes to ensure that their organization is meeting all relevant regulations and voluntary standards; and to identify regulations in other jurisdictions that may influence local requirements in the future.

6.2.2 Think about the total life-cycle

Product stewardship requires a whole-of-life approach that considers the extended footprint of a product, both "upstream" in the supply chain and "downstream" at end of life.

Life-cycle thinking opens up new possibilities to improve the sustainability of a product and its supply chain. Carpet manufacturer Interface has used life-cycle assessment (LCA) research to identify opportunities for product improvement. One of these studies identified yarn production as a major contributor to environmental impact, providing the impetus for designs with lower yarn weight. This change produced significantly lower carbon emissions while also reducing manufacturing costs.[5] LCA sometimes generates non-intuitive results, for example that lightweight packaging formats such as bags and pouches can have less environmental impact than more conventional, recyclable packaging formats, as long as they achieve comparable levels of product protection.[6]

---

4   Canon Oceania (2014). *Sustainability Report 2013*. Sydney, Australia: Canon Australia.

5   Hensler, C.D. (2014). Shrinking footprint: a result of design influenced by life cycle assessment. *Journal of Industrial Ecology*, 18(5), 663-669.

6   See for example Centre for Design at RMIT (2011). *Life Cycle Assessment of Nestle Nescafe Gold Coffee Packaging*. Retrieved from http://www.rmit.edu.au/about/our-education/academic-schools/architecture-and-design/research/research-centres-and-groups/centre-for-design-and-society/research-areas/sustainable-products-and-packaging/projects/life-cycle-assessment-of-nestl-nescaf-gold-coffe

Life-cycle thinking does not necessarily require expensive or time-consuming studies, such as a full LCA. A simple life-cycle mapping exercise, drawing on research and internal expertise (such as the one described in Chapter 2), can identify potential issues that need to be addressed in the product supply chain, during use or after disposal by the consumer.

6.2.3 Identify the material issues for your organization

Every product is associated with a wide variety of environmental and social issues over its total life-cycle. In the supply chain these might include land degradation from mining, extraction of scarce or unsustainably harvested raw materials, pollution from manufacturing, child labour or human rights abuses. As others have pointed out, companies are not necessarily responsible for *every* social issue.[7] The challenge is to identify the material issues for each organization, i.e. those that reflect the most significant economic, environmental and social impacts, or substantially influence the assessments and decisions of stakeholders.[8]

The Vinyl Council has used a combination of research and stakeholder engagement to identify material issues (Case study 2.6.2). When PVC came under pressure from Greenpeace in the 1990s because of concerns about harmful emissions, the Council commissioned a literature review from Australia's leading scientific research organization, CSIRO. This provided the scientific evidence they needed to design an evidence-based stewardship programme. External stakeholders continue to have input to the programme through membership of a Technical Steering Group and, according to CEO Sophi MacMillan, this has helped the Council to stay focused on the most significant issues.[9] In addition, stakeholder round tables have been held every two to three years following publication of the Vinyl Council's annual progress report:

> We invite stakeholders to a briefing, which is a very open discussion. This is normally about the performance of the industry, what the program's focused on, what it *should* be focused on, whether there are gaps in the program. They have been very, very useful discussions

7 See, for example, Porter, M., & Kramer, M. (2006, December). Strategy and society: the link between competitive advantage and corporate social responsibility. *Harvard Business Review*. Reprint pp. 1-16.

8 GRI (2013). *G4 Sustainability Reporting Guidelines: Implementation Manual*. Amsterdam, The Netherlands: Global Reporting Initiative.

9 Personal communication (interview) with S. MacMillan, Chief Executive, Vinyl Council of Australia, 3 June 2015.

for us. Very constructive. We've had people there who have held quite strong views about PVC but have provided really valuable input, and it has resulted in changes to the program.

In 2015 the Vinyl Council replaced the stakeholder round tables with a facilitated online discussion forum. This meant that the Council could invite a larger number of potentially interested stakeholders and made it easier for them to give feedback on the report and industry progress.[10]

6.2.4 Align product stewardship strategies with business goals

The most successful product stewardship strategies are those that align with and help to support the achievement of other business goals.

The President of Fuji Xerox, Tadahito Yamamoto, has said that "it is critically important to clarify the link between CSR and the mission and objectives of each organization and to achieve a full integration between CSR and our core business".[11] Mr Yamamoto described how this worked in practice for one project:

> … under the internal slogan "Challenge Eco No 1", Fuji Xerox launched a companywide initiative aimed at providing the world's top environmental value. In this program, individual employees on the front lines of operation identify problems intrinsic to our core business from the perspective of creating environmental value, such as resource saving, transport saving, and space saving, and endeavor to transform business processes and approaches to work.[12]

Within the packaging industry many companies have prioritized design changes that can reduce costs while also achieving environmental objectives. A good example is Walmart's drive to reduce supply chain costs by eliminating unnecessary packaging, such as deodorant boxes (see Chapter 3, Section 3.2.3).

In some cases companies have deliberately focused on design changes that have potential to achieve environmental *and* business goals. D&D Technologies, for example, initiated a packaging review in 2009 to reduce costs, after a request from one of its major retail customers.[13] When the

10 Personal communication (email) with Sophi Macmillan, 6 June 2016.
11 Fuji Xerox (2015). *Sustainability Report 2014*. Tokyo, p. 8. Retrieved from https://www.fujixerox.com/eng/company/sr/booklet/2014e.pdf
12 *Ibid.*, p. 10.
13 Crittenden, P., & Lewis, H. (2014). *The Business Case for Packaging Sustainability: D&D Technologies*. Sydney: Australian Packaging Covenant.

product development team consulted with internal stakeholders, they identified a range of other objectives that could be achieved at the same time, including:

- A new packaging concept that would be more efficient and compatible with increased automation

- An opportunity to meet the company's obligations under the Australian Packaging Covenant by reducing material consumption and waste

As a result of the review D&D Technologies shifted from a multi-component clamshell to a simple stand-up pouch, which achieved these objectives as well as other business benefits. The sales and marketing team was happy with the additional space on the pack to promote product features, and a reduced number of packaging types meant that inventory was significantly reduced.[14]

6.2.5 Look for multiple benefits

The D&D Technologies packaging example highlights the value of looking for multiple business benefits. Regardless of the original driver for a product stewardship initiative, companies often identify additional business benefits after the project has commenced. This was evident at Interface, whose market share increased as a direct result of its environmental improvements: "Interface did not initially pursue sustainability with the intention of gaining competitive advantage, but it quickly became clear that the marketplace would reward a company who was, as Ray Anderson would say, 'doing well by doing good'".[15] Environmental improvements, including the introduction of recycled yarn and a take-back programme for used carpet tiles, enabled Interface to capitalize on the growing market for "green" building products in the US (see Chapter 2, Box 2.1).

Chemson Pacific, a leading global manufacturer of PVC stabilizers, joined the Australian PVC industry's product stewardship programme in 2002 (Case study 2.6.2). The industry group committed to phase out the use of lead stabilizers, prompted by concerns about worker exposure in the manufacturing process and the possible release of lead to the environment from landfill waste. Chemson responded by formulating new carbon zinc organic

---

14   *Ibid.*
15   Hensler (2014), p. 664.

TABLE 6.2   Examples of multiple business benefits

Case study	Original driver for product stewardship initiative	Additional business benefits
Resene paint recycling (Case study 2.6.1)	Corporate commitment to environmental responsibility; "doing the right thing"	Improved brand reputation with consumers; awards for corporate responsibility
Foodstuffs redesign of their meat tray (Case study 3.7.1)	Negative publicity about non-recyclable packaging; corporate commitment to shift to 100% recyclable packaging	Positive consumer feedback; improved reputation with stakeholders
Fisher & Paykel appliance recycling (Case study 4.7.2)	Maintaining competitiveness; action by individual "champions" within the business	Marketing advantage by providing a recycling service to customers: "we can take back your used appliance"

stabilizers, which provided additional business benefits. Customers benefited from superior physical properties such as higher hoop-strength, while Chemson was able to move to a new, lead-free facility that had a number of benefits. These included avoiding stringent and costly procedures to protect workers from lead exposure, and a more flexible manufacturing process that no longer needed to keep lead and non-lead production separate.[16]

An important lesson from these and many of the other case studies in this book is that a systematic, evidence-based approach to product stewardship can achieve multiple business benefits. Some additional examples are listed in Table 6.2.

6.2.6 Understand and promote the business case for action

Practitioners within companies are more likely to get support for a product sustainability project if they understand and promote the business case for action. All of the potential benefits of the project, both for the organization and its stakeholders, need to be identified and evaluated against corporate goals and priorities. This is not to diminish or under-value the importance of sustainability goals in their own right; but rather to build a stronger case for product stewardship within firms.

16   Vinyl Council of Australia (n.d.). *PVC Stewardship Case Study: Best Practice in PVC Additives.* Melbourne, Australia: VCA. Retrieved from http://members. vinyl.org.au/images/Chemson_Best_Practice_additives_DRAFT_mod_JDK_ GH_JS_edit_for_web_V02.pdf

David Perchard, an experienced product stewardship consultant based in the UK, believes that while the business case for action depends on the individual company and product, there are a few common benefits:

> Consumers need to respect your company as well as your products. Bad or misleading products can taint the whole company, and there are many examples where this has happened. You want to be thought of as a good company that people want to join. Who do you work for? "I work for Shysters' Inc." or "I work for Good Guys Corporation". I want to say that I work for a respected company.
>
> Then as legislation comes along, if you've already moved ahead you are more likely to be in a position to shape it. You'll also find it easier to adjust. Now there are those who say "delay until the very last moment because you never know what you'll be forced to do". I don't really buy that, especially now that we've moved on from simple, quantified waste diversion targets, to rather more nebulous sustainability objectives that you can't legislate for specifically. It's what we call "soft law", which combines persuasion, "show-and-tell", and "naming and shaming".
>
> You've also got your customers—the retailers if you're a manufacturer. Your customers want to demonstrate their own credentials, for example by insisting their suppliers maintain certain standards. So they will put pressure on suppliers ... Walmart is an example. So it comes from a number of directions: from legislation, from the market, and from customers.[17]

Another commercial driver that will become more important for many companies in future is the need to maintain control of vital raw materials. Recycling Reinvented, an organization established by Nestlé Waters North America to promote take-back regulations for packaging, had argued that extended producer responsibility for products at end of life will become increasingly important to secure the supply of recycled materials (the organization ceased operating in 2015). This view was based on the observation that environmental and economic objectives were become more aligned:

- Companies are using more recycled materials because this is a measurable way to reduce their environmental footprint. At the same time, there is little political will for local and state governments to invest in recycling infrastructure.

- Global demand for packaging will also continue to increase, putting pressure on material supply. EPR would give companies

17 Personal communication (interview) with D. Perchard, Managing Director, Perchards Ltd., 2 October 2013.

more control over their supply chain when it comes to recycled materials.[18]

Manufacturers of electrical and electronic equipment are also using producer-funded recycling programmes to source quality raw materials from used products to go back into new products. Close the Loop (Case study 4.7.1) returns a proportion of the plastics recovered from used printer cartridges to its corporate partners for manufacturing new printer and copier parts. This helps the manufacturers maintain control of their raw materials while also meeting environmental performance targets. In 2013 Lexmark reported that its toner cartridge product line contained an average of 10% post-consumer recycled plastics, and the company was aiming to increase this to 25% by 2016.[19]

These examples are indicative of growing interest in the idea of a "circular economy" as population growth and economic development increase demand for resources. According to an industry think-tank in the US, the business case for action is clear: "If we continue with the business-as-usual approach, companies and society will witness a probable surge in price volatility, inflation of key commodities, and an overall decline—and in some cases, depletion—of critical material inputs".[20]

The corporate motivations for a circular economy, including stable supply chains, are discussed further in Chapter 7.

6.2.7 Integrate product stewardship into the business

To be successful a corporate commitment to product stewardship must be integrated into business systems and staff responsibilities. Many of the companies profiled in the previous chapters have a policy to consider environmental or sustainability impacts during design or procurement, and this is reflected in business procedures. Nestlé has a comprehensive, science-based approach to product stewardship in design, with all packaged

18   Gardner, P. (2013, February). *The Way Forward in EPR*. Portland, OR: Resource Recycling, pp. 35-60. Retrieved from http://resource-recycling.com/sites/default/files/4/Gardner0213rr.pdf

19   Lexmark (2013). *Corporate Social Responsibility Report 2012*, p. 49. Retrieved from http://csr.lexmark.com/pdfs/2012_lexmark_csr.pdf

20   US Chamber of Commerce Foundation (2015). *Achieving a Circular Economy: How the Private Sector is Reimagining the Future of Business*. Washington, DC, p. 4.

TABLE 6.3 Business functions and responsibilities for product stewardship

Business functions	Product stewardship responsibilities
In-bound logistics	Collaborate with suppliers and third party logistics contractors to optimize transport efficiency (loads, packaging, fuels etc.); recycle used packaging
Manufacturing	Optimize energy, water and material efficiency, reuse or recycle waste
Distribution	Optimize transport efficiency (loads, packaging design, fuels etc.), back-load used products from customers for reuse or recycling
After-sales service	Assist customers by providing or advising on repair, remanufacturing, reuse or recycling services
Marketing	Determine an optimal product mix (weighing up sustainability impacts and business opportunities), integrate sustainability criteria in design and procurement processes, survey customers on sustainability attitudes and behaviour
Procurement	Develop sustainability guidelines for suppliers, monitor compliance, collaborate with suppliers to develop more sustainable products
Corporate governance/legal	Monitor compliance with product-related laws including EPR (take-back) requirements, work with policy-makers to develop appropriate and acceptable laws
Product design	Consider environmental and social impacts during the design process to minimize life-cycle impacts. Comply with internal sustainability guidelines as well as any customer requirements.
Facilities management	Develop recycling systems for all facilities, optimize energy and water efficiency
Environmental management/ sustainability	Assist Marketing to evaluate product impacts, survey stakeholders to identify material issues, develop product stewardship goals and targets, monitor and report on progress, participate in industry-led recycling initiatives

products evaluated using its LCA-based design tool, EcodEX, to identify potential improvements.[21]

Not all companies have the resources (people and skills) to undertake this level of product evaluation. In contrast to Nestlé's environmental assessments, which must be undertaken for all new packaged products, an Australian company decided to develop more prescriptive guidelines to simplify the decision-making process for buyers. Officeworks, a retailer and supplier of office products, is a signatory to the Australian Packaging Covenant and therefore obligated to follow the Sustainable Packaging Guidelines. In 2013 Officeworks' environment manager decided that the most

---

21 Nestlé (2014). *Nestlé in Society: Creating Shared Value and Meeting Our Commitments 2014*. Retrieved from http://storage.nestle.com/nestle-society-full-2014/index.html#1/z

effective approach would be to develop a series of simple guidelines for each product category, based on the Sustainable Packaging Guidelines, and to integrate these in procurement processes.[22]

Integrating product stewardship in staff responsibilities and performance evaluation is also important. Canon, for example, has an Environmental Action Plan that aims to achieve environmentally conscious design, a reduction in CO_2 emissions during product use and increased product recycling. The environmental scorecard used internally to rank the different Canon companies recognizes environmental personnel and managers for their involvement in collaborative projects to improve the end of life recovery for Canon products.[23]

During a facilitated round table organized by the Product Stewardship Institute in 2015, the Senior Director Sustainability at EMC Corporation, Lisa Brady, commented on the need to integrate product stewardship goals in business processes:

> Driving sustainability into the business is key. We assess how our suppliers are performing against the goals we have set and the metrics we measure them by. We then feed that performance data into our decision-making process for the business. This fundamentally changes the way we manage corporate social responsibility in our supply chain, by integrating it into how our supply chain managers do their job.[24]

Product stewardship has implications for many different functions in a business, as shown in Table 6.3.

22   Lewis, H. (2014). *Officeworks: A Packaging Assessment Case Study*. Sydney: Australian Packaging Covenant. Retrieved from http://www.packagingcovenant. org.au/data/Case_study_Officeworks.pdf

23   Personal communication (interview) with J. Leslie, Manager Sustainability, Canon Australia, 13 November 2013.

24   Brady, L. (2015). How do producers view their responsibility for reducing product impacts? (facilitated round table). US Product Stewardship Forum, December 8–9, 2015, Boston, MA, http://www.productstewardship. us/?page=2015_ps_forum.

Government regulators   Industry associations   Community groups   Municipalities

Raw materials suppliers   Material & component suppliers   Product manufacturers   Distributors

Government funding agencies

Research organizations

Recyclers   Consumers   Retailers

FIGURE 6.1   Potential partners in the product chain

6.3 Seven external (cooperative) strategies

6.3.1 Develop effective partnerships

Collaboration is an obvious but important strategy for most successful product stewardship initiatives. In addition to other businesses in the product chain, such as raw material suppliers, component manufacturers, retailers and recyclers, potential partners may include municipalities, environmental groups or research organizations (Fig. 6.1). Finding the right partners and then working with them to achieve shared value (mutually beneficial outcomes) requires deliberate action.

Kimberly-Clark developed a positive working relationship with Greenpeace after the NGO ran a negative public campaign against the company's use of fibre from Canada's boreal forests for Kleenex tissues:

> The collaboration with Greenpeace furthered our appreciation of the value of—and need for—partnering with the right stakeholders. These partnerships deepen our understanding of environmental issues by seeing them through a different lens—this new perspective can create the impetus to change direction, accelerate plans or deploy improved practices. For us here at Kimberly-Clark, the collaboration with Greenpeace and other stakeholders such as the Forest Stewardship Council

has helped us gain insights into ways to improve the sustainability of
our products and supply chain.[25]

The support of suppliers is essential to the achievement of design or procurement objectives, given that most product manufacturers do not have
direct control over the tens or hundreds of materials and components that
make up their bill of materials. Almost every change, such as the elimination of a toxic substance, use of recycled materials or improved recyclability,
requires the active participation of suppliers. Successful product stewards
engage with suppliers through procurement guidelines, regular meetings,
training, incentives or purchasing policies that reward environmental innovation. This is recognized by Dell, for example, when it talks about the introduction of innovative packaging materials:

> It is very difficult for any one company to process all of the resources
> and knowledge needed to test and launch a game-changing idea into
> full-scale production. But by working with our partners to leverage
> their biotechnology expertise and Dell's own engineering industry
> experience, together we have dramatically accelerated time to market
> for new products like wheat straw and mushroom packaging.[26]

Successful product recycling initiatives often require the support of partners to provide reverse logistics, drop-off facilities and end-markets for the
collected materials. Depending on the product and the most appropriate
collection channels, recycling may need to involve suppliers, competitors,
recyclers, local governments, retailers or community groups. To develop a collection and recycling programme for soft plastic packaging, RED Group (Case
study 3.7.2) sought support from an industry association, the Australian Food
and Grocery Council, and then approached the association's members to
provide sponsorship. Other programme partners include a state government
agency, the Australian Packaging Covenant, two major supermarkets and a
recycler. Founder Liz Kasell highlighted the value of a collaborative approach:

> [Our programme] is founded in the understanding that we can't solve
> problems in isolation—that's where collaboration comes in. The
> model depends on everyone involved in the life-cycle of a product also
> being engaged in its recovery. We're dealing with a very low value mixed

25 Morden, L. (2014, October 6). What Kimberly-Clark learned from 5 years
    with Greenpeace. *GreenBiz.com*. Retrieved from http://www.greenbiz.com/
    blog/2014/10/06/kimberly-clark-and-ngos-building-sustainable-supply-chain
26 Dell (2014). *FY14 Corporate Responsibility Report: A Progress Report on Our 2020
    Legacy of Good Plan*, p. 32. Retrieved from http://i.dell.com/sites/doccontent/
    corporate/corp-comm/en/Documents/fy14-cr-report.pdf

material, which is why it [normally] goes to landfill. We had to develop
a model that looked at the product in a completely different way.[27]

When establishing a recycling programme it is important that stewardship
organizations consult with local government stakeholders. There are several reasons for this:

- In most jurisdictions local governments have responsibility for
  waste management and have a network of waste or recycling depots
  that could be utilized to collect specific products or materials

- They have a strong interest in diverting additional products and
  materials from landfill, particularly those that contain hazardous
  materials, and are often willing to support stewardship initiatives

- Local governments are in a good position to communicate with res-
  idents about the availability of recycling services and how to recycle

Non-government organizations can also play an important role in recycling programmes. The "Cartridges 4 Planet Ark" programme (Case study
4.7.1) was developed as a partnership between Close the Loop, original
equipment manufacturers (OEMs), retailers and environmental group
Planet Ark. The relationship with Planet Ark helped to attract brand owner
support and to raise awareness of the cartridge recycling programme with
consumers. Founder Steve Morriss highlights the benefits:

> Through a relationship with Planet Ark we were able to leverage off
> their trusted brand ... I can assure you it's a symbiotic relationship of
> the highest order. It's working for both parties. It's about parking your
> ego. Allowing your programme to be branded by someone else can
> sometimes increase the volume of product you get back, and there-
> fore improve the viability of the programme. Plus the Planet Ark brand
> helped us sign major multinational printer and photocopier brands in
> the first instance, because of that brand value.[28]

A key lesson from Close the Loop and many of the other case studies
described earlier, is that collaboration is very important to the success of
any product redesign or take-back programme. The challenge is to find the
right partners and to ensure that the needs and interests of all parties are
met.

27 Personal communication (interview) with L. Kasell, Director of Development,
    The RED Group, 14 August 2014.
28 Personal communication (interview) with S. Morriss, Founder and Director,
    Close the Loop, 4 May 2014.

6.3.2 Understand and promote the business case for partners

The business case for a product stewardship initiative needs to be understood and promoted to industry partners to encourage them to participate. This is particularly important if the initiative is entirely voluntary. Close the Loop's cartridge recycling programme is promoted to industry partners as a business opportunity as well as an environmental programme, because it provides valuable business intelligence data to OEMs.

There are many other examples of recycling programmes that generate significant business benefits. TerraCycle builds successful partnerships with companies to collect and recycle products that don't have an existing recovery system. Based in the US, TerraCycle operates around 125 recycling campaigns in 21 countries, with funding from consumer packaged goods manufacturers. Michael Waas, the company's Global Vice President for Business Development and Client Services, explains how campaigns also support their clients' business objectives through effective marketing:

> First and foremost ... our goal is to divert as much waste as possible from landfill and incineration. That's why we work only with non-recyclable waste, because if something is already recyclable there is no need for us to provide a solution. That's our number one return on investment. But because we work and are funded by marketing organizations, we also drive a marketing and retail communications return on investment by integrating our sustainability programme with the brand's marketing platform. [This] allows them to see real measurable positive impacts from our programmes, which allows them to continue investing in it.[29]

For example, TerraCycle developed a partnership with beverage manufacturer Tang to provide a recycling solution for used drink pouches in Brazil and in the process helped to increase product sales and brand awareness:

> That campaign ran for five years from 2009 to 2014, and had tremendous business results. [In] the first year of that programme sales increased by 40% compared to a 2% category-wide drop in sales for beverages. They also went from the top 50 to top 5 top-of-mind brands for Brazil, which is an indicator of a brand's visibility. They beat Coke for the first time. So this was an iconic campaign, [that was] then replicated in Mexico and Argentina.[30]

29 Personal communication (interview) with M. Waas, Global Vice President, Business Development and Client Services, 8 April 2015.
30 *Ibid.*

For retailers, one of the benefits of providing collection points for a recycling programme is that it can generate additional sales. There is some evidence that retailers who offer a recycling service may experience increased foot traffic and sales. A consumer survey in North America found that the availability of a retail drop-off service for batteries and mobile phones prompted 27% to 45% of consumers (depending on the retail store) to visit and shop more frequently.[31] A similar programme funded by a retail franchise network in Australia has helped to attract customers and build brand value (Case study 5.7.2). In California, more than half of the retail drop-off sites for used paint indicated that foot traffic had increased as a result of their participation in the PaintCare recycling programme, and 44% believed that customer loyalty had increased.[32]

Sometimes it can take time to identify the business benefits for industry partners and to convince them to come on board. When Liz Kasell initially met with Coles Supermarkets to seek their support for her plastics recycling programme, she had to find the right "fit" with their business:

> It was about understanding that the value for them overlaps several different areas of the business, and you have to engage the right stakeholders. It's absolutely critical. You have to find the person who's going to champion the project internally. [T]his programme covers everything from ... waste, sustainability, innovation, marketing [to] customer care, so I actually had to see every single one of those stakeholders and get them all in a room and find out where my programme was really going to fit in, where in their business it was going to land and who was going to drive it. It was a challenge at first![33]

6.3.3 Establish and implement minimum standards

There is increasing recognition that third-party certified standards for sustainability are important for both supply chain management and recycling programmes.

31   Call2Recycle (2012). *"Drop & Shop" Retail Recycling Programs Provide Great "Environment" for Consumers.* Retrieved from http://www.call2recycle.org/drop-shop-retail-recycling-programs-provide-great-environment-for-consumers/
32   PSI (2016). *California Paint Stewardship Program Evaluation: Final Report.* Boston, MA: Product Stewrdship Institute, p. 3. Retrieved from http://c.ymcdn.com/sites/www.productstewardship.us/resource/resmgr/Paint/2015.12.15_CA_Paint_Program_.pdf
33   Personal communication with L. Kasell (2014).

In the packaging sector, for example, corporate sustainability commitments are driving demand for fibre from responsibly managed forests. Certification by a credible organization such as the Forest Stewardship Council (FSC) provides companies with confidence that forest management and manufacturing processes meet minimum sustainability standards that have been endorsed by a wide range of stakeholders. McDonald's aims to have 100% of its fibre-based fast food packaging sourced from either certified or recycled sources by 2020.[34] Outdoor products retailer, Kathmandu, committed in 2012 to transition all of its paper-based packaging to FSC certified products.[35]

A common message from organizations involved in recycling is the need to ensure that products and materials are collected, transported and reprocessed responsibly. Recyclers are generally required to meet minimum standards for environment, health and safety management, with a priority placed on accreditation to recognized global standards. Examples for e-waste include the Responsible Recycling (R2) and e-Stewards® standards (see Table 4.9 in Chapter 4).

Call2Recycle (Case study 5.7.1) "seeks third-party certification to meet the highest standards of responsible recycling" and is certified to both of these standards.[36] The organization's CEO and President, Carl Smith, stresses that not all recycling processes are the same from an environmental perspective:

> What I see coming out of the EU now is all this comment about the circular economy. Anything that's recycling is deemed to be supporting the circular economy, but there are lots and lots of gradations on what constitutes good, better or best ways of recycling a product. You should not just look at whether something is put back into some sort of secondary use. You have to look at how something can be used not just a second time but a third or fourth time.[37]

---

34 McDonald's (2014). *Our Journey Together for Good: McDonald's Corporate Social Responsibility & Sustainability Report 2012–13*. Retrieved from http://www.aboutmcdonalds.com/mcd/sustainability.html

35 Crittenden, P., & Lewis, H. (2014). *The Business Case for Packaging Sustainability: Kathmandu*. Sydney: Australian Packaging Covenant. Retrieved from http://www.packagingcovenant.org.au/data/Resources/PackagingSustainability/Kathmandu.pdf

36 Call2Recycle (2015). *Annual Report 2014: 20 Years of Product Stewardship*. Atlanta, GA: Call2Recycle. Retrieved from http://www.call2recycle.org/2014-annual-report/, p. 2.

37 Personal communication (interview) with C. Smith, CEO and President, Call2Recycle, 3 September 2015.

The European Battery Recycling Association (EBRA) is developing a standard and certification programme for battery recyclers. This aims to overcome a lack of any EU-wide system to ensure that recyclers comply with the requirements of the EU Battery Directive, such as minimum recycling efficiency levels, and insufficient attention being paid to environmental, health and safety issues.[38]

The Australia and New Zealand Recycling Platform (ANZRP, Case study 4.7.3) seeks to ensure that all of its recycling partners comply with the voluntary Australian standard on e-waste, but do not believe that this has necessarily been the case for other approved co-regulatory arrangements. Reflecting on the policy development process, CEO Carmel Dollisson notes that this issue should have been better addressed:

> To commence without a standard was, in hindsight, folly. What it led to effectively was a price drive, which is poor for the recycling industry because the people with power and volume could negotiate prices down. So it wasn't in the best interests of the industry, or in any way a good outcome for recycling, because in some cases product went to landfill. Worse still, there are stockpiles of CRT glass around the country now because of a lack of standards and rates that did not cover the recycling cost.[39]

ANZRP lobbied the government for the standard to be mandatory for all scheme participants, an outcome that was achieved in 2015.[40]

6.3.4 Start small and learn as you go

Many of the recycling case studies described in this book started with a small pilot project and then evolved into a national programme. RED Group, for example, started by collecting plastic packaging in one city and through one major supermarket chain, before rolling out the programme nationally and extending it to another supermarket chain. This helped to attract the support of brand owners and retailers by showing that they had the capacity

38   Vassart, A. (2015). *The Why and How of the Certification Initiative for Recycling Plants. International Congress for Battery Recycling.* September 24–26, 2014, Hamburg, Germany.
39   Personal communication (interview) with C. Dollisson, General Manager, Australia New Zealand Recycling Platform, 6 August 2014.
40   Hunt, G. (2015). *Overhaul of E-waste Scheme Will Protect Jobs and Deliver 32,000 Tonne Recycling Boost.* Retrieved from http://www.greghunt.com.au/Home/LatestNews/tabid/133/ID/3320/Overhaul-of-e-waste-scheme-will-protect-jobs-and-deliver-32000-tonne-recycling-boost.aspx

to deliver a recycling service: "We didn't come to [the brands and retailers] from day one saying 'we're thinking of doing this'. We were already doing it. That's one of the things that was really important ..."[41] It also enabled them to "learn by doing":

> ... It's important to trial things instead of doing feasibility reports. I feel strongly that for these types of schemes you just have to get out and start doing something. You don't have to solve every single ... problem, just get started. It's really, really important.[42]

When they wanted to investigate the feasibility of a paint recycling project in New Zealand, Resene started with a trial in one store, one day a month for six months.[43] The lessons learned from the trial informed the development of a national take-back programme, which was gradually rolled out, region-by-region, over a few years.

Until a recycling programme is established, along with robust systems for data collection, it can be difficult to know how much material is available for collection or how consumers will respond to the availability of a recycling service. When ANZRP started its e-waste recycling programme, there was no reliable data on total e-waste quantities. The number of computers being exported for reuse, which is now known to be significant, made it harder for co-regulatory arrangements to meet the recycling target for computers. Carmel Dollisson believes that the scheme would have benefited from a more gradual roll-out:

> I have to say I'm losing confidence in consultants who write papers and model waste streams that turn out to be vastly different to reality. You need reliable data, so you probably need a pilot of some sort before you set targets to ensure a level playing field. If you know the size of the market and where is it generated; have tested the awareness campaign and consumer behaviour; and have an inkling of any issues for co-regulatory arrangements or recyclers ... [For example] if you know there is no market for leaded glass then "hello, we need to solve this before we go much further".[44]

These examples indicate that starting small, either by running a pilot project first or by rolling out a programme slowly, has a number of potential benefits:

41 Personal communication with L. Kasell (2014).
42 *Ibid.*
43 Personal communication (interview) with K. Warman, Marketing Manager, Resene, 21 November 2014.
44 Personal communication (interview) with C. Dollisson (2014).

- It can attract industry stewards by demonstrating that a project is feasible and that the organization is capable of delivering results

- It enables the organization to "learn by doing" and to fix any problems while the programme is still small

- Methods to calculate waste arising and recycling rates can be developed and refined before targets and other performance indicators are "locked in" to business plans or regulations.

6.3.5 Engage with consumers to promote more sustainable practices

Every successful recycling programme relies on the active participation of consumers. Rather than placing all of their unwanted products and materials into a single household waste bin, consumers are being asked sort recyclable from non-recyclable products. In most countries paper and packaging, for example, is sorted in the home and placed on the street for collection by the local municipality or their contractors. These programmes generally collect a high percentage of recyclable materials because of their convenience for consumers.

More knowledge and effort is generally required for consumers to recycle other products, such as plastic bags, e-waste, paint or batteries, which often need to be taken to different and geographically disparate drop-off sites. An individual consumer might have to drop their used plastic bags at a supermarket, their old computer and batteries at another retail store, and their leftover paint at a local council waste depot.

Successful recycling programmes put a lot of effort into consumer awareness and education. According to Call2Recycle's CEO, Carl Smith, encouraging consumers to bring their old batteries to a drop-off point is an ongoing challenge:

> Tip number one is that while the infrastructure is very important, it tends to be where there is too much emphasis. The emphasis ought to be on how you are going to communicate with and educate consumers on the behaviour you want them to embrace. I've had this strategy that says if you build it they still may not come. Building all these collection sites, transport and processes is great. But you have to find a way to create demand for that service to actually generate batteries.[45]

---

45   Personal communication (interview) with C. Smith (2015).

A focus on consumers is one of the three pillars of Call2Recycle's latest 5-year plan. In the annual report, Carl Smith highlights the importance of consumer convenience and access:

> Our focus will be on driving more consumers to recycle by improving the convenience and accessibility of our consumer-facing retail and municipal collection network ... our aspiration is to ensure that 95% of all US and Canadian consumers have access to a public battery recycling collection site within 10 miles of their homes.[46]

Motivating consumers to recycle and providing information on how to recycle are both essential to a successful take-back programme. In addition to promotion through its website, Call2Recycle provides information and a guide to finding the nearest drop-off location through a community website, Earth911.com. Social media is playing a more prominent role because it allows "real time" engagement with consumers on battery recycling and sustainability.[47]

The Australian Mobile Telecommunications Association (AMTA) uses regular market research surveys to guide their mobile phone recycling programme. These have found that consumer willingness to recycle is driven by value (consumer or community benefit), awareness (why, where and how) and access (convenience).[48] In the early years of the MobileMuster programme (Case study 4.7.4), AMTA members had become concerned about the lack of growth in the collection rate and decided to review the programme. It commissioned research that identified a low level of awareness of recycling options and a desire by consumers to store unused phones. To address these problems AMTA committed to:

- Promote and advertise the recycling programme nationally

- Educate mobile phone users, local councils, retailers, recyclers and students about why and how they can recycle mobile phones

- Offer incentives and rewards to those who collect and recycle

46   Call2Recycle (2015), p. 2.
47   *Ibid.*, p. 7.
48   AMTA (2015). *Australia's Mobile Decade: 10 Years of Consumer Insights into Mobile Use and Recycling.* Sydney: Australian Mobile Telecommunications Association.

6.3.6 Start voluntarily and then think about regulation

The success of many voluntary product stewardship initiatives, including the case studies described earlier, suggests that regulation is not always necessary to ensure that companies take action to address a particular issue. Companies such as Dell, HP, Canon, Kimberly-Clark, Nestlé and Unilever have product policies and targets and are working to reduce the life-cycle impacts of their products and packaging. Voluntary EPR programmes for polyethylene terephthalate (PET) and glass packaging in South Africa appear to have been more successful in stimulating recycling than mandatory requirements for plastic bags.[49] There may be many reasons for this, however, including the fact that plastic bags have a low value in secondary markets and are less amenable to recycling. It can also be argued that the PET and glass initiatives are not entirely voluntary, because they were established under threat of regulation: "mandatory plastic bag regulations actually provided a raison d'être for 'voluntary' initiatives in the glass and PET sectors".[50]

Regulation may be necessary to support collective industry take-back programmes, particularly if there are likely to be a significant number of free-riders. Feedback from industry practitioners suggests that the best approach may be to start voluntarily, for several reasons:

- Producers are likely to participate more willingly and be more enthusiastic than under a mandatory programme

- A voluntary programme, even with a high level of free-riders, may be less costly for industry participants than a mandatory programme, given that these tend to have higher targets and administration costs

- A voluntary programme allows the industry partners to design a programme that is efficient, based on solid data, and acceptable to all stakeholders (a government-led programme will impose mandatory conditions and targets that may be more onerous or costly)

Several of the people interviewed for this book believe that a voluntary scheme has significant benefits. Liz Kasell from RED Group, for example, argues that a voluntary programme is preferable because it changes the way that companies respond:

49   Nahman, A. (2009). Extended producer responsibility for packaging waste in South Africa: Current approaches and lessons learned. *Resource Conservation and Recycling*, 54(3), 155-162.
50   *Ibid.*, p. 161.

> The whole experience is so much more positive [when a programme is not regulated] ... That's really important for a programme like this because we're asking brand owners to dig into their pockets and support something they had never had to support in the past ... we were demonstrating the value and it was voluntary. I think that's really the reason they came on board. If they were told "you have to do this" there would be a certain amount of pushback. They support it because we could demonstrate the value ... not because they have to, but because there's real value here.[51]

A voluntary programme is more likely to succeed when companies see value that goes beyond environmental sustainability or corporate social responsibility. Steve Morriss from Close the Loop does not believe that regulation is necessary for recycling ink and toner cartridges in Australia because the programme already has strong support from brand owners.[52] While regulation would help to "create a level playing field" by ensuring that all OEMs contribute to the programme, he argues that the percentage of companies that have been identified as free-riders has fallen significantly. Originally the percentage of collected products that were not funded by a supporting partner was around 50%; by 2014 this had fallen to around 15%. The free-riders are primarily smaller OEMs and "clones" (replacement cartridges for major brands made by a third party).

Morriss believes that Close the Loop has "proven the case for voluntary programmes", and agrees with Liz Kassell's view that it changes the way that companies think about producer responsibility:

> I don't know about you but if you force me to do something I'm either not going to do it, or I'm going to be quite difficult to deal with if you force me into it. You force any company into anything and they're going to be prickly, they're going to do the minimal contribution. Voluntary programmes focus on the upside for the company. That's how the whole programme is designed.[53]

Resene manages a voluntary paint recycling programme in New Zealand (Case study 2.6.1). Marketing Manager Karen Warman argues that, while it would be beneficial if all consumers paid a levy to support recycling ("recycling is very expensive and some companies are getting a free ride"), she is wary of regulation:

51 Personal communication with L. Kasell (2014).
52 Personal communication (interview) with S. Morriss (2014).
53 *Ibid.*

> It's in the back of our minds but regulations can be high risk. In our view it's better if businesses work out what works for their industry, and run it, rather than being told what to do by someone who may not understand the best and most practical way to do it.[54]

While members of AMTA's MobileMuster programme constitute only 45% of the market for handsets (down from 90% when the programme commenced), they do not see the need for strong regulation at this stage. According to previous Recycling Manager Rose Read, there is really only one significant free-rider and AMTA would prefer to have them join voluntarily, rather than as a result of regulation:

> We've got a 50% collection rate, of available phones, there is very little going to landfill, [and] there is a strong reuse market now. So there is no real pressure on the industry from government to regulate. Our focus is on having the programme accredited by government as a voluntary scheme which we hope will encourage free-riders like Apple to join the programme. As well as set the benchmark for mobile phone recycling in Australia.[55]

Call2Recycle's Carl Smith suggests that there are several benefits from starting with a voluntary programme, even if regulation is eventually required to address free-riders:

> First of all, what is critical to understand is the infrastructure. Where are your collection sites? Knowing how best to transport from your collection sites. Knowing and getting used to the regulatory issues regarding safe transport.
>
> Second the industry itself needs to understand that this can be done economically. It's not far-fetched, that it's real.
>
> The third is it allows early movers—those who want to embrace sustainability, to get started and provide leadership, and distinguish themselves in the marketplace. That pulls the rest of the industry along. You don't get that same phenomena when it's mandatory across the board.
>
> The other thing is you can gear up over time. In highly regulated jurisdictions there are pretty strict expectations on collection rates, on dates, this and that, and it requires substantial upfront investment to meet that. You can ramp up more slowly over time when it's a voluntary programme rather than a prescriptive programme.[56]

---

54   Personal communication (interview) with K. Warman (2014).
55   Personal communication (interview) with R. Read, previously Manager Recycling, Australian Mobile Telecommunications Association (until February 2016), 1 November 2013.
56   Personal communication (interview) with C. Smith (2015).

6.3.7 Work with policy-makers on regulatory back-up

Successful stewardship programmes in the US have been developed in partnership with government regulators. By taking a leadership role, industry associations and stewardship organizations hope to achieve more cost-effective regulations and greater harmonization across jurisdictions.

The American Coatings Association (ACA) has been proactive in working with state regulators in the US to introduce EPR laws to support its take-back and recycling programme for used paint ("PaintCare"). Following a national stakeholder dialogue in 2003 facilitated by the Product Stewardship Institute (PSI), the association's board agreed to develop an industry-led paint stewardship programme. According to Alison Keane, ACA's Vice President, the business case at the time was clear: "we can do it ourselves or wait for state/local governments to do it". ACA felt that if it had to pay for recycling then it wanted to "own it, operate it, control it".[57] In its view legislation was needed for three reasons: to achieve a level playing field among all manufacturers and retailers; a sustainable funding system based on market share with anti-trust protection; and consistency across states.

ACA and PSI worked together on a model state programme that would be implemented across the country. Oregon passed the first paint stewardship law in 2009, requiring manufacturers to establish and fund a collection and recycling system for leftover architectural paint. By 2015 eight more states and the District of Columbia had passed similar laws.

Keane describes PaintCare as a "win–win" that other jurisdictions outside the US are monitoring closely with a view to introducing something similar. To date the programme has collected over 2 million gallons (9 million litres) of paint and 700 tons (635 metric tonnes) of plastic and metal paint cans. The industry has also benefited: "A primary purpose of the industry's pro-action on the issue was to ensure that the industry would not be facing 50 different state solutions to the issue, but rather one nationally coordinated approach".[58]

According to PSI's chief executive officer, Scott Cassel, other industries can learn from ACA's approach: "From the beginning, ACA helped to shape

57 Keane, A. (2013). *PaintCare Paint Stewardship Program*. Priority Product Stewardship Workshop. Global Product Stewardship Council. November 18, 2013, Melbourne, Australia, p. 6.
58 Keane, A. (2014, September 13). ACA and PaintCare: driving a post-consumer paint solution. *Global Product Stewardship Council Guest Blogs*. Retrieved from http://www.globalpsc.net/guest-blog-aca-and-paintcare-driving-a-post-consumer-paint-solution/

the program's development; when the bills were first drafted, ACA was in the driver's seat. The solution developed was an innovative funding model that worked for both industry and other stakeholders".[59]

The regulatory approach that seems to be preferred by industry associations and policy-makers in North America is a flexible, "light touch" regulation that provides the legal back-up for industry-led programmes. This is explored further in Chapter 7 (Section 7.2.5).

6.4 Conclusions

Over the past few decades industry leaders in many different sectors and jurisdictions have demonstrated how a strategic approach to product stewardship within their organization can deliver value for stakeholders and the business. These companies listen to stakeholders' concerns, practise life-cycle thinking, identify material issues and align product stewardship strategies with their business priorities. They look for multiple benefits, understand and promote the business case internally, and integrate product stewardship into existing business systems.

Effective product stewardship also requires partnerships with external stakeholders, particularly for recycling. Some of the common strategies for success that were identified through case studies include effective collaboration, a clear business case for industry partners, minimum performance and safety standards, and engagement with consumers to encourage participation. They often start voluntarily, and where back-up regulations are required industry groups work collaboratively with policy-makers to develop a model that works for the industry and its stakeholders.

---

59   Cassel, S. (2015, June 9). What big pharma can learn from the paint industry. *The PSI Blog*. Retrieved from https://productstewardshipinstitute.wordpress. com/2015/06/09/what-big-pharma-can-learn-from-the-paint-industry/

7
What's next? The future of product stewardship

7.1 Introduction

Community expectations and government regulations will continue to hold companies responsible for the environmental and social impacts of their products. This final chapter identifies some of the trends that are likely to influence the way that these responsibilities are defined and how companies respond.

The increasing focus on a "circular economy" for example, will add further weight to stakeholder calls for greater producer responsibility, while providing more intellectual rigour to debates about how products should be designed, used and managed at end of life. Consistent with this trend, increasing demand for resources in a growing global economy will help to drive recycling by increasing the value of secondary materials.

Regulations that mandate producer responsibility for recycling will extend to additional products and materials, and in more jurisdictions. Unlike the earliest extended producer responsibility (EPR) laws, many of these, particularly in North America, will regulate with a "light touch" by supporting rather than prescribing industry action.

Industry groups will play a stronger leadership role in the development of both voluntary programmes and regulations. Rather than waiting for governments to act, leading companies and associations are leading the development of programmes and supporting regulations that are acceptable to industry. One of their priorities is for nationally consistent regulations and programmes that improve efficiency and reduce compliance costs for producers. Harmonization within and between jurisdictions will continue to be a focus for producer responsibility programmes.

Finally, there is increasing recognition that product take-back laws and programmes, contrary to their original intention, do not provide producers with sufficient incentive to design recyclable and more sustainable products. Other complementary policy mechanisms and tools are likely to be introduced to influence design outcomes more directly.

7.2 Trends

7.2.1 The circular economy discourse

In Chapter 1 producer responsibility was rationalized as a social obligation, a response to stakeholder expectations or a source of competitive advantage. Another framework for producer responsibility is the concept of a "circular economy". This new sustainability discourse integrates many existing environmental goals such as cleaner production, waste reduction and recycling, but repositions them within an economic policy framework. It also takes a "total systems" approach by considering material flows and waste within the context of business models, technologies and consumption practices.

In December 2015 the European Commission (EC) adopted a comprehensive and ambitious "Action Plan for the Circular Economy" that aims to transform the economy:

> The transition to a more circular economy, where the value of products, materials and resources is maintained in the economy for as long as possible, and the generation of waste minimised, is an essential contribution to the EU's efforts to develop a sustainable, low carbon, resource efficient and competitive economy. Such transition is the opportunity to transform our economy and generate new and sustainable competitive advantages for Europe.[1]

The action plan takes a life-cycle approach, with measures to promote ecodesign, reduced impacts in production and less waste at end of life. Legislative proposals include the development of general operating requirements for EPR schemes. More ambitious targets will be adopted, including:

---

1   European Commission (2014). *Towards a Circular Economy: A Zero Waste Programme for Europe*. Brussels, Belgium, p. 2.

- A common EU target to reuse and recycle 70% of municipal waste

- A common target to recycle 75% of packaging waste by 2030

- A binding target to reduce landfill to a maximum of 10% of all waste by 2030[2]

The European Commission is not alone in its focus on economic drivers for materials efficiency and recycling. The Japanese Government has stated that its EPR laws are designed to create a sustainable economic system based on the "3Rs" (reduce, reuse, recycle).[3] There is also increasing recognition within China that the government's development targets will not be met without significant improvements in material efficiency.[4] The Chinese Government's Circular Economy Law, which is designed to support the "economic and social development of the state", places obligations on government agencies, producers and consumers, including reuse and recycling.

Business leaders also recognize that material efficiency and resource recovery are essential for future economic development. The US Chamber of Commerce Foundation has published an edited series of papers that outline the rationale for a circular economy and new business.[5] The Foundation's Jennifer Gerholdt argues that the linear economy, in which resources are extracted, transformed, used and thrown away, is no longer sustainable. Continuing with a "business-as-usual" approach will lead to increasing commodity prices and price volatility and a decline or depletion of critical material inputs. The "good news", according to Gerholdt, is that companies are actively pursuing alternative approaches that support a more circular economy: "This concept has captured the attention of many companies that see the economic opportunities of a viable model to successfully tackle sustainability challenges; drive performance, competitiveness and innovation; and stimulate economic growth and development".[6]

2   *Ibid.*, p. 1.
3   Ministry of Economy, Trade and Industry (2008). *Towards a 3R-oriented Sustainable Society: Legislation and Trends.* Tokyo: Ministry of Economy, Trade and Industry. Retrieved from http://www.meti.go.jp/policy/recycle/main/data/pamphlet/pdf/handbook2008_eng.pdf
4   Lowe, E. (2009). *China Seeks to Develop A "Circular Economy" (CE).* Indigo Development. Retrieved from http://www.indigodev.com/Circular1.html
5   US Chamber of Commerce Foundation (2015). *Achieving a Circular Economy: How the Private Sector is Reimagining the Future of Business.* Washington, DC: US Chamber of Commerce Foundation.
6   *Ibid.*, p. 4.

Unilever, for example, is repositioning its packaging strategy within a circular economy framework. The strategy includes both resource efficiency and "design for circularity": "We want to move to a circular economy, enabling more packaging to either remain in loops or have the best possible opportunity to be recycled".[7]

Five "circular business models" that provide benefits for individual businesses and the broader economy have been proposed by consulting group Accenture:

- A circular supply chain, in which scarce or environmentally destructive resources are replaced by renewable, recyclable or biodegradable materials that can be used in consecutive life-cycles to reduce costs and increase predictability and control

- The recovery and recycling model that eliminates waste—everything that used to be considered a waste is recovered for another purpose

- The product life extension model, in which the life-span of a product is extended as long as possible through repair, upgrades, remanufacturing or remarketing to capture value that would otherwise be lost

- The sharing platform model that allows consumers to make and save money by renting, sharing, swapping or lending under-utilized products

- The "product as a service" model, in which producers and retailers lease rather than sell products and have an incentive to improve longevity, reliability and reusability[8]

The circular economy discourse will help to strengthen the business case for producer responsibility by linking it to economic imperatives such as sustainable access to raw materials and less price volatility. Mark Buckley, Vice President Environmental Affairs for North American retailer Staples, has described EPR as the "highway to the circular economy".[9] Continuing

7   Unilever (2015). *Moving to a Circular Economy*. Retrieved from https://www.unilever.com/sustainable-living/what-matters-to-you/recycling-and-moving-to-a-circular-economy.html

8   Lacy, P., & Rutqvist, J. (2015). *Waste to Wealth: The Circular Economy Advantage*. Basingstoke, UK: Palgrave Macmillan.

9   Buckley, M. (2015). *Extended Producer Responsibility … The Highway to the Circular Economy*. In *2015 US Product Stewardship Forum* (unpublished). Boston, MA: Product Stewardship Institute.

the highway metaphor, Buckley suggests that EPR could provide "rules of the road" or "guardrails" that move materials and markets to a more sustainable, circular economy.

7.2.2 Resource scarcity and rising prices

Product stewardship policies will need to adapt to rising prices for many commodities, which will influence the operation of recycling markets. In the private sector recycling is driven by the value of commodities such as steel, lead, copper, precious metals and high quality plastics. As Adam Minter explained so well in *Junkyard Planet*, there are large and highly organized global markets for recycled commodities as diverse as computers, cars, plastic bottles and Christmas lights.[10]

Many producer responsibility (take-back) policies were introduced to facilitate recycling of used products and materials that have a negative value in the market, i.e. the value of recovered materials exceeds the total costs of collecting, transporting and reprocessing them. The rationale was that the costs of recycling should be borne, in part or in full, by producers. This is still the case for many plastics, reinforcing the case for EPR policies in order to minimize commercial risks to local government and more directly engage producers who are large consumers of recycled content. In 2015 the price of oil halved, reducing the value of baled plastic bottles and recycled PET (polyethylene terephthalate) materials. In South Africa, for example, the CEO of stewardship organization PETCO, Cheri Scholtz, noted that it was now more expensive to collect and recycle plastics than it was to use crude oil to make virgin plastic containers.[11] Similar problems have been experienced in North America and Europe.

While commodity markets are often volatile, the longer-term trend is for prices to increase, driven by a rising population, increasing demand for products and services, and a finite supply of non-renewable resources. In its report on accelerating the transition to a circular economy, the Ellen MacArthur Foundation notes that overall commodity prices increased by almost 150% between 2002 and 2010.[12] This has prompted some manufacturers,

---

10   Minter, A. (2013). *Junkyard Planet*. New York: Bloomsbury Press.
11   Scholtz, C. (2016, February 17). Message from CEO, Cheri Scholtz. *PETCO: PETRefresh: Spread the news*, Letter 19.
12   Ellen MacArthur Foundation (2014). *Towards the Circular Economy*. Prepared in collaboration with the World Economic Forum and McKinsey & Company. Geneva: WEF.

such as B&Q/Kingfisher, Renault and Ricoh, to take more control of their raw material supplies by sourcing secondary (recycled) materials.

Because rising commodity prices will drive demand for recycled materials, it has implications for product take-back policies. A report commissioned by the European Recycling Platform (ERP) concluded that the economic context has shifted over time, with some wastes now being viewed as a source of revenue rather than a cost, and EPR legislation has failed to adapt to the new paradigm.[13] The report notes that increased prices for metals used in electrical and electronic equipment in commodity markets have increased the diversion of e-waste into private markets "outside official EPR channels".[14]

It has been estimated that only 35% of e-waste discarded in Europe in 2012 ended up in official channels.[15] Most of the remaining 65% was exported, recycled under non-compliant conditions or scavenged for parts. These activities are driven by the market value of materials and components:

> The widespread scavenging of both products and components and the theft of valuable components such as circuit boards and precious metals from e-waste, means that there is a serious economic loss of materials and resources directed to compliant e-waste processors in Europe.[16]

This has caused a number of difficulties for producer responsibility organizations such as ERP, which were established by producers to meet their regulatory obligations under Waste Electrical and Electronic Equipment (WEEE) legislation. These include problems meeting recycling targets because material flows outside official channels are not accounted for, loss of valuable e-waste to other operators, and sub-standard recycling quality in some instances.[17] According to the authors of the ERP study, this has a number of implications for policy:

- Producers should only be responsible for the waste they control

---

13 Kunz, N., Atasu, A., Mayers, K. & van Wassenhove, L. (2014). *Extended Producer Responsibility: Stakeholder Concerns and Future Developments*. INSEAD Social Innovation Centre with support from European Recycling Platform.

14 *Ibid.*, p. 26.

15 Huisman, J., Botezatu, I., Herreras, L., Liddane, M., Hintsa, J., Luda di Cortemiglia, V., ... Bonzio, A. (2015). *Countering WEEE Illegal Trade (CWIT) Summary Report*. Lyon, France: Interpol, p. 6.

16 *Ibid.*

17 Kunz *et al.* (2014).

- Governments should be responsible for reaching collection targets, not individual producers

- All flows outside official channels should be reported and required to meet the same standards imposed on producer responsibility organizations (PROs)

- Legislation should specify requirements for actors operating outside official EPR channels[18]

7.2.3 More regulations, more products

The number of regulated producer responsibility programmes has increased significantly since the early 2000s. The first EPR laws were introduced in the European Union in the 1990s, providing the impetus for later initiatives in Asia, Oceania and North America (some examples are shown in Fig. 7.1).

A recent report from the OECD identified 395 "EPR policies" operating around the world, including take-back requirements, advance disposal fees, deposit/refund systems, upstream tax/subsidies, recycling standards and virgin material taxes.[19] Take-back requirements are the most common policy type (75%) and while some are voluntary the majority are mandatory. Over 70% have been implemented since 2001.[20]

The most common products covered by policies in the OECD survey were consumer electronics (35%), including mobile phones and rechargeable batteries, followed by packaging (17%) and vehicles and lead acid batteries (11%).[21] The "other" category (20%) includes used oil, paint, chemicals, large appliances and fluorescent light bulbs.

According to Scott Cassel from the Product Stewardship Institute (PSI), the number of take-back laws has increased significantly in the US over the past 15 years.[22] In 2000 there were a handful of laws applying to primary or rechargeable batteries. By 2015 this had grown to around 90 laws covering

---

18   *Ibid.*, p. 26.
19   Kaffine, D., & O'Reilly, P. (2013). *What Have We Learned about Extended Producer Responsibility in the Past Decade? A Survey of the Recent EPR Economic Literature.* Paris: OECD, p. 21. Retrieved from http://spot.colorado.edu/~daka9342/OECD_EPR_KO.pdf
20   *Ibid.*, p. 24.
21   *Ibid.*, p. 22.
22   Cassel, S. (2015). The state of EPR in the U.S. US Product Stewardship Forum, December 8–9, 2015, Boston, MA, http://www.productstewardship.us/?page=2015_ps_forum.

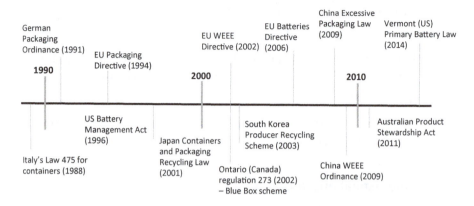

FIGURE 7.1   Key dates in the history of producer responsibility regulation

a wide range of products including appliances, batteries, carpets, mobile phones, electronics, mattresses, fluorescent lighting, mercury thermostats, used paint, pesticides and pharmaceuticals.

There are several trends in the producer responsibility regulations:

- The spread of regulations for packaging and e-waste to more jurisdictions

- The extension of e-waste laws to cover a wider range of products, particularly small appliances

- An increasing focus on hazardous products such as paint, batteries and mercury-containing lamps.

More regulations and voluntary take-back programmes are being introduced for the three product groups featured in previous chapters—packaging, e-waste and batteries. In Canada for example, EPR laws are being introduced by provincial and territorial governments in accordance with the Canada-wide Action Plan for Extended Producer Responsibility.[23] Most programmes are based on a shared responsibility model, with local government responsible for collection.

In the US there is a renewed push to introduce take-back laws at a state level for both packaging and printed paper, although several legislative proposals introduced between 2010 and 2014 failed to pass.[24] Garth Hickle,

---

23   CCME (2009). *Canada-wide Action Plan for Extended Producer Responsibility*. Winnipeg, MB, Canada: Canadian Council of Ministers of the Environment.

24   Cassel (2015).

Product Stewardship Team Leader from the Minnesota Pollution Control Agency, believes that EPR laws may be harder to introduce for these products because of the availability of an extensive collection system for paper and packaging and vested interests in local government.[25]

With regulations difficult to achieve, in 2016 California's Department of Resource Recycling and Recovery invited industry stakeholders to a workshop to explore voluntary stewardship proposals:

> What are product manufacturers and brand owners willing to do, on an industry-wide level, to recover their product packaging to help California reach the statewide goal of 75% source reduction, recycling, and composting by 2020? ... CalRecycle's Manufacturer's Challenge represents an opportunity for product manufacturers and brand owners to collectively come together and demonstrate their commitment to increasing the recovery of their product packaging in California by committing to achieve a goal of 50% reduction in packaging disposed in landfills by the year 2020 and proposing a voluntary plan to meet that goal.[26]

E-waste laws have been implemented or are being considered in a more jurisdictions. China (2009) and India (2011) have already introduced EPR laws that mandate producer responsibility for collection and recycling of e-waste. In 2015 the Vietnamese Government introduced an EPR law for e-waste, including fluorescent bulbs, televisions, computers, printers, fax machines, cameras, mobile phones, tablets, air conditioners and washing machines.[27] Hewlett-Packard Asia Pacific and Apple South Asia launched a pilot programme called "Vietnam Recycles", but had difficulty competing with informal recyclers that buy used electronics from consumers for reuse or recycling, often using unsafe or environmentally damaging processes.[28]

Some existing laws are also being amended to include a much wider range of electrical and electronic products. When the European Commission

---

25 Personal communication (interview) with G. Hickle, Product Stewardship Team Leader, Minnesota Pollution Control Agency, US, 5 February 2014.

26 CalRecycle (2015). Public Meeting Notice: *CalRecycle Packaging Workshop: Manufacturers Challenge 2015*. Retrieved from http://www.calrecycle.ca.gov/Actions/PublicNoticeDetail.aspx?id=1466&aiid=1335

27 Thanh Nien News (2015, October 13). Vietnam to start sorting electronic waste in 2015. *Thanh Nien News*. Retrieved from http://www.thanhniennews.com/business/vietnam-to-start-sorting-electronic-waste-in-2015-32475.html

28 McKay, Z. (2015, June 26). Vietnam searches for solutions to deal with domestic e-waste. *Ensia*. Retrieved from http://ensia.com/photos/vietnam%E2%80%8B-searches-for-solutions-to-deal-with-domestic-e-waste/

updated the WEEE Directive in 2012 its scope was broadened to include all electrical and electronic products. The Japanese Government has had an EPR law for large household appliances since 1998, and for personal computers since 2000 (the Law for the Promotion of Effective Utilization of Resources mandates recycling of computers discarded by businesses and encourages voluntary take-back of computers from households). A new law—Promotion of Recycling of Small Waste Electrical and Electronic Equipment (2013)—promotes voluntary separate collection of small electrical and electronic equipment by municipalities.[29]

Australia has EPR regulations for TVs and computers, but there are growing calls for these to be extended to other products. Carmel Dollison from the Australia New Zealand Recycling Platform (ANZRP) notes that consumers are starting to look for recycling solutions for products that they regard as similar to TVs and computers:

> People are now saying, "well if there is value in recycling my TV then why isn't there value in recycling my radio [and] microwave?" So while there are still people out there blind to recycling, there's lot of people out there who are thinking this has metal, it uses energy, it has some kind of circuit board, why can't I recycle this. There is a very slow but ground-up drive for expansion of product stewardship to a broader product selection.[30]

Regulations and programmes will also be introduced for many new product categories, particularly in Canada and the US. The Canada-wide Action Plan for Extended Producer Responsibility commits provincial governments to implement EPR laws or regulations to address a number of specified priority products and material, in two phases:

- **Phase 1** (within six years). Packaging, printed materials, mercury-containing lamps, other mercury-containing products, electronics and electrical products, household hazardous and special wastes (including batteries), and automotive products

- **Phase 2** (within eight years). Construction materials, demolition materials, furniture, textiles and carpet, and appliances[31]

29   Terazona, A., Oquchi, M., Lino, S. & Mogi, S. (2015). Battery collection in municipal waste management in Japan: challenges for hazardous material substance control and safety. *Waste Management*, 39, 246-257.

30   Personal communication (interview) with C. Dollisson, General Manager, Australia New Zealand Recycling Platform, 6 August 2014.

31   CCME (2009).

In the US the primary focus is on hazardous products such as paint, thermostats, batteries and pharmaceutical products. The American Coatings Association (ACA), for example, is continuing to work with state regulators to implement mandatory take-back programmes for used paint, with laws currently in place in nine states and the District of Columbia, and a further 12 states are pending. The aim is to roll the programme out nationally in all states. Battery producers are working with regulators to introduce a mandatory take-back programme for all consumer batteries, replacing the patchwork of current laws applying to selected rechargeable batteries.

EPR laws are also being developed for pharmaceutical products, driven primarily by concerns about the ecological impacts of unwanted pharmaceuticals being flushed into the sewerage system and waterways, and public health risks associated with unwanted drugs stored in the home. Mandated or voluntary take-back programmes are already in place in Belgium, France, Hungary, Portugal, Spain, Canada, Mexico, Brazil and Colombia.[32]

In 2012 Alameda County in California introduced the first mandatory take-back law for pharmaceutical products in the US, based on a similar law in British Columbia. San Francisco enacted its Safe Drug Disposal Stewardship Ordinance in 2015 and a number of counties have since followed. According to the executive director of the Californian Product Stewardship Council, Heidi Sanborn, "... a movement that started in California is spreading to the rest of the nation to ensure unused medications are properly disposed of in an effort to keep them out of the hands of children and out of our waterways".[33]

Activist group As You Sow has used its proxy voting power to lobby large US-based pharmaceutical manufacturers to take responsibility for used medicines:

> Lack of convenient disposal programs has been linked to poisoning of children and pets; misuse by teenagers and adults; seniors' health problems from accidentally taking the wrong or expired medicine; water pollution from flushed medications; and threats to sanitation workers handling improperly disposed needles. It's time for this growing public health concern to be addressed.[34]

32   Californian Product Stewardship Council (2016). *Pharmaceuticals: The Problem*. Retrieved from http://calpsc.org/products/pharmaceuticals/

33   Sanborn, H. (2016, February 19). Opinion: Safe and convenient medicine collection is good medicine for LA County. *Los Cerritos News*.

34   As You Sow (2015). *Waste Program Engages Big Pharma for Drug Take-back*. Retrieved from http://www.asyousow.org/2015-newsletter/waste-program -engages-big-pharma-for-drug-take-back/

Product stewardship consultant David Perchard has pointed out that the focus in Europe is very different from that of the US, for both historical and practical reasons:

> In North America the focus has been on hazardous wastes such as electronics, batteries and paints. We've tended not to do that. In Europe we've specifically focused on high quantity waste streams, whereas the Americans have focused on quality—"we'll take out the nasties". While there are some national EPR schemes for hazardous materials here there are no EU-wide schemes, and there won't be. Batteries are an exception as they were targeted for internal market reasons—to avoid member states adopting conflicting measures to limit heavy metals content.
>
> … The Commission is also finding it increasingly difficult to get legislation agreed. You have a meeting of member states in Brussels—they each give a 15-minute outline of their position—that's 7 hours. So no time to discuss possible compromises that day. So the working group meetings are held less and less, and if you hold them less and less you're going to get less agreed.[35]

While regulations will continue to be introduced for more products in more jurisdictions, in many cases the most appropriate solution will be a voluntary or co-regulated industry programme. This theme is explored further in Section 7.2.5 ("Industry control with regulatory oversight").

7.2.4 A greater focus on plastics

While most producer responsibility policies target specific products, there is also an increasing focus on plastics arising from concerns about recyclability and marine litter. The European Commission's circular economy package includes a strategy to address the "challenges" posed by plastics throughout their life-cycle.[36] This follows the Commission's *Green Paper on a European Strategy on Plastic Waste in the Environment* which outlined a number of issues of concern.[37]

The relatively low cost and versatility of plastics have contributed to exponential growth in their use over the past century; a trend that is set to continue. The quantity of waste being generated each year is also increasing. In 2008, an estimated 25 million tonnes of plastic waste were generated,

---

35   Personal communication (interview) with D. Perchard, Managing Director, Perchards Ltd, 2 October 2013.
36   European Commission (2014).
37   European Commission (2013). *Green Paper on a European Strategy on Plastic Waste in the Environment*. Brussels, Belgium: EC.

of which only 21.3% was recycled.[38] According to the Commission, approximately 10 million tonnes of litter end up in the oceans each year, and waste patches in the Atlantic and Pacific oceans may contain around 100 million tonnes of litter, of which around 80% is plastic.[39]

Studies have shown that plastics are durable and, once in the environment, particularly the marine environment, can cause widespread harm to aquatic life and seabirds.[40] This is mainly caused by ingestion or entanglement in products such as plastic bags and fishing line, but there is increasing concern about the toxicity effects of plastics and micro-plastics as toxic substances are transferred into marine organisms and enter the food chain. These include chemicals that are added intentionally to products (for example flame retardants or plasticizers) as well as pollutants that are absorbed by plastics in the environment. Solutions proposed in the literature include container deposit schemes[41] and EPR policies.[42]

Another issue raised by the European Commission is "technical difficulties" associated with new materials including nano-materials, micro-plastics and biodegradable plastics.[43]

Micro-plastics or "microbeads"—used in personal care products such as face washes, exfoliants and toothpastes—are already starting to be addressed through producer responsibility policies. Typically less than 5 mm in size, these tiny particles are designed to be washed down the drain, and end up in waterways and the marine environment. In 2015 the US Government introduced a law that bans the use of plastic or bioplastic beads in soaps, body washes, toothpaste and other personal care products from 1 July 2017, and the sale of personal care products containing microbeads from 1 July 2019. It won the support of the American Chemistry Council, which stated that "This new law reflects national product stewardship

---

38 *Ibid.*, p. 4.
39 *Ibid.*, p. 50.
40 See UNEP (2009). *Marine Litter: A Global Challenge.* Nairobi: United Nations Environment Programme (UNEP). Retrieved from http://www.unep.org/pdf/unep_marine_litter-a_global_challenge.pdf; Stevenson, S. (2011). *Plastic Debris in the California Marine Ecosystem.* Los Angeles: California Ocean Science Trust; Pors, J. (2013). *Plastic Marine Litter: One Big Market Failure.* Amsterdam, The Netherlands: IMSA Amersterdam; Hardesty, B.D., Wilcox, C., Lawson, T., Lansdell, M. & van der Velde, T. (2014). *Understanding the Effects of Marine Debris on Wildlife.* Report by CSIRO for Earthwatch Australia.
41 Hardesty *et al.* (2014).
42 Stevenson (2011).
43 European Commission (2013).

efforts by the personal care industry to phase out the use of solid plastic microbeads used in personal care exfoliating products".[44] Unilever is one of a number of global manufacturers who had already announced a global decision to replace plastic microbeads with alternative materials.[45] Australian environment ministers announced that they would work with industry on a voluntary phase-out by July 2018.[46]

Biodegradable plastics, particularly those manufactured from renewable materials such as cellulose or sugar cane, are regarded by many brand owners and consumers as a more sustainable alternative to conventional plastics, and their use is growing. The European Commission has raised a number of concerns about these materials including the fact that consumers are likely to understand the term "biodegradable" to mean that a product or package will break down in a home composting system.[47] In reality many of these materials only biodegrade under very specific conditions, such as those found in an industrial scale composting facility.

There are particular concerns about the impacts of conventional plastics, such as polyethylene, that contain an additive to promote faster degradation. These plastics, which are often marketed as biodegradable, are used in products such as shopping bags, bin liners and food packaging. However, their effectiveness and environmental impacts have been questioned. Research in the US, for example, concluded that the additives did not have any significant impact on degradation rates over a three-year period in conditions that simulated landfill disposal, composting or uncontrolled burial in soil.[48]

Biodegradable plastics are likely to come under greater scrutiny in future. Further research will clarify which polymers are beneficial from

44   Hardcastle, J. (2016, January 4). Plastic microbead ban signed into law, wins industry support. *Environmental Leader*. Retrieved from http://www.environmentalleader.com/2016/01/04/plastic-microbead-ban-signed-into-law-wins-industry-support/

45   Unilever (2015). *Micro-plastics*. Retrieved from https://www.unilever.com/sustainable-living/what-matters-to-you/micro-plastics.html

46   Department of Environment (2015). *Agreed Statement: Meeting of Environment Ministers*. Canberra, Australia. Retrieved from https://www.environment.gov.au/system/files/pages/4f59b654-53aa-43df-b9d1-b21f9caa500c/files/mem-meeting4-statement.pdf

47   European Commission (2013).

48   Doyle, C. (2015, March 25). "Biodegradable" plastics don't live up to manufacturers' claims. *ABC Environment*. Retrieved from http://www.abc.net.au/environment/articles/2015/03/25/4203912.htm

an environmental perspective and how these benefits can be optimized through appropriate design and management at end of life. The influential Sustainable Packaging Coalition (SPC), whose members include many large brand owners, packaging manufacturers and retailers, has taken a formal position against the use of degradation additives in petroleum-based plastics.[49] The SPC's position is based on several factors including the additives' inability to completely break down in composting conditions, potential negative impacts on recyclability, the release of greenhouse gas emissions when they break down, and the impacts of fragmented "micro-litter" if they break down in uncontrolled conditions.

7.2.5 Industry control with regulatory oversight

Russ Martin, chief executive of the Global Product Stewardship Council, has observed a trend in North America for new programmes to be driven by industry rather than government. This reflects both corporate commitments to product stewardship or corporate social responsibility, and a pragmatic approach to policy development:

> There's less debate about whether or not industry should fund something. It's more of an issue of businesses getting on board with an approach they can live with and wanting to have greater control over its design, or more flexibility in its implementation. So if the affected industry is going to be paying for something they want a say in how to control their costs to do it and how it's designed ...[50]

The case studies presented in previous chapters demonstrate that voluntary take-back programmes can be effective if there is strong industry leadership and commitment. Their financial sustainability depends, however, on their ability to share the costs equitably between brand owners. In many cases industry groups have implemented a recycling programme voluntarily and then sought back-up regulations to overcome a free-rider problem (companies benefiting from the availability of a service but not contributing to the cost).

An example is Call2Recycle, a take-back programme for rechargeable batteries in the US (Case study 5.7.1). Producer responsibility for recycling is

49   Sustainable Packaging Coalition (2015). *The SPC Position Against Biodegradability Additives for Petroleum-based Plastics*. Charlottesville, VA, US: GreenBlue. Retrieved from https://brandfolder.com/s/nyndc0-6aio5c-cq756b

50   Personal communication (interview) with R. Martin, CEO, Global Product Stewardship Council, 16 December 2013.

only mandatory in nine states, and generally only for nickel cadmium and sealed lead acid batteries, but Call2Recycle collects all rechargeable batteries through its national network. The programme has been running for over 20 years, but Call2Recycle is now convinced that regulations are needed to deal with an increasing number of free-riders.[51] The model EPR bill for portable batteries, developed by Call2Recycle with three other battery interest groups, is an example of a flexible approach to regulation.[52] Producers have to submit a plan to the government that outlines how a minimum collection rate for used batteries will be achieved, but it does not specify how this performance goal should be achieved. It also allows battery producers and stewardship organizations the right to bring a civil action to recover recycling costs from producers that are not meeting their recycling obligations (i.e. free-riders).

Under this model the role of the regulator is one of oversight rather than direction. It is typical of a trend in North America away from prescriptive laws to a more flexible, industry-driven approach. The Canadian action plan for extended producer responsibility describes the responsibilities of governments and producers under their preferred model:

- Governments determine the scope of producer responsibility programmes, establish measurable targets and ensure a level playing field. They are primarily interested in programme performance rather than operation.

- Producers and importers are responsible for programme design, operation and funding. They have an incentive to operate programmes efficiently and effectively while meeting performance targets set by the government.[53]

The model EPR programme that must be adopted by provincial governments includes a number of common elements.[54] Producers (or PROs

51 Smith, C. (2014). *Statement before the Senate Committee on Natural Resources and Energy H.695—An Act Relating to Establishing a Product Stewardship Program for Primary Batteries*. Retrieved from http://legislature.vermont.gov/assets/Documents/2014/WorkGroups/Senate%20Natural%20Resources/Bills/H.695/H.695~Carl%20Smith~Testimony~4-10-2014.pdf

52 Call2Recycle (2014). *Battery Industry Leaders Unveil the First Ever Model All Battery Recycling Bill*. Retrieved from http://www.call2recycle.org/all-battery-model-bill/

53 CCME (2009).

54 *Ibid.*

on their behalf) must submit a stewardship plan to the government for approval. This sets out how they will meet their obligations, including how products will be collected and recycled, key performance indicators and recovery targets. They must report to jurisdictions on programme outcomes, environmental benefits and waste diversion performance.

The EPR programme for waste electronics in Ontario is illustrative of the general policy approach to EPR in Canada.[55] The Waste Diversion Act (2002) authorizes the Minister of the Environment to designate a material for a producer responsibility programme, and in 2004 a regulation was developed for waste electrical and electronic equipment. This specified which products would be covered but did not include any performance goals. A producer responsibility organization, Ontario Electronic Stewardship, was established in 2007 and led the development of the stewardship plan. The plan, which was approved by the Minister in 2009, specifies performance goals including 5-year collection, reuse and refurbishment targets.[56]

Garth Hickle has observed that the Canadian approach is increasingly being adopted by state governments in the US.[57] Some existing EPR laws, such as the New York State e-waste law, are quite detailed and stipulate specific performance requirements such as recycling rates and convenience standards. This approach ensures a degree of accountability but lacks flexibility. The model EPR bills developed and championed by industry groups for products such as paint and batteries are much closer to the Canadian approach. These are characterized by industry-driven plans and a high level of flexibility, with much of the detail contained in stewardship plans rather than statutes or regulations.

This hybrid, co-regulatory approach combines an industry-driven plan with government oversight and enforcement. It has significant benefits for producers, including the ability to control costs (for example by determining their own targets) and to adapt the programme in response to changing circumstances. There are also benefits for government agencies with budgetary constraints. Russ Martin uses British Columbia as an example, noting that the requirement for verified public reporting makes it relatively easy for the Ministry of Environment to monitor compliance: "In BC you have five Ministry staff overseeing 25 very comprehensive industry-led product

55   Hickle, G. (2013). Comparative analysis of extended producer responsibility policy in the United States and Canada. *Journal of Industrial Ecology*, 17(2), 249-261.
56   *Ibid.*
57   *Ibid.*

stewardship approaches. This gives industry the flexibility to make their programmes work [and] reduce their costs, while minimizing government involvement".[58]

Producers are more likely to support producer responsibility programmes when they are part of the policy development process. Hickle notes "a growing awareness among some manufacturers that, if appropriately structured, EPR is a policy approach that they can live with".[59]

7.2.6 Greater policy harmonization

With the number of take-back laws increasing, both policy-makers and industry groups are aiming for greater policy harmonization both within and between jurisdictions.

The experience with e-waste in the US shows what can happen when there is a "patchwork" of state laws rather than a national approach. Between 2001 and 2004 the US EPA convened stakeholder meetings to design a system to pay for e-waste collection and recycling. This failed when industry groups could not reach agreement on how such a scheme would be financed, and television manufacturers opposed any form of EPR.[60] State governments took action instead, and by 2015 there were 25 laws that mandate producer responsibility for e-waste.[61] These laws vary widely in scope (which products are covered), how producer responsibility is defined, and what happens if producers fail to meet their obligations.[62]

Hickle has argued that achieving consistency between policies in different states has been particularly difficult in the US, partly because of a perception that policies need to be tailored to unique state circumstances and partly (as with e-waste) because of a lack of agreement between affected companies.[63] The role played by the affected companies is critical: "Another consideration is that achieving consistency requires strong consensus among the impacted brand owners with the ability to translate that

58   Personal communication with R. Martin (2013).
59   Hickle (2013).
60   Nash, J., & Bosso, C. (2013). Extended producer responsibility in the United States: Full speed ahead? *Journal of Industrial Ecology*, 17(2), 175-185.
61   Cassel (2015).
62   Nash, & Bosso (2013).
63   Hickle, G. (2014). Moving beyond the "patchwork": a review of strategies to promote consistency for extended producer responsibility in the U.S. *Journal of Cleaner Production*, 64, 266-276.

consensus into policy leadership and ability to navigate the political landscape in multiple states".[64]

Leadership is evident in other sectors, where brand owners and industry associations are developing a national approach to take-back laws for products such as paint, batteries, mattresses, thermostats and mercury lamps. The primary mechanism for consistency is the development of a "model bill" in consultation with stakeholders. Following a series of meetings convened by PSI with the National Paint and Coatings Association (now American Coatings Association), recyclers, retailers and government officials, an agreed "work plan" become the basis for legislation in Oregon (2009), California (2010) and Connecticut (2011).[65] Producer responsibility laws for used paint are now in place in nine states.[66]

A model bill for mercury thermostats was negotiated by PSI in 2006 to strengthen the voluntary programme established by manufacturers. The model bill, which included a "menu of options" that states could use, was first adopted by Maine (2006), followed by eight other states. More recently the Corporation for Battery Recycling (CBR), the National Electrical Manufacturers Association, the Rechargeable Battery Association and Call2Recycle unveiled an all-battery model recycling bill. These industry groups are actively engaged with policy-makers in several states including Maine, Connecticut and Texas.

In Canada harmonization between the provinces is being achieved through its national action plan for EPR.[67] Within the jurisdictions, "framework regulations" are commonly used to ensure consistency for different products. In British Columbia, for example, the legal framework for EPR is provided by the province's Recycling Regulation which outlines programme principles and a schedule for product categories that will be subject to industry-led stewardship plans.[68]

National harmonization makes it easier for industry stewardship organizations to operate across provincial borders. The Canadian Stewardship Services Alliance (CSAA), for example, offers "a one-stop-shop for packaging and printed paper stewards to fulfil all of their stewardship obligations,

64   *Ibid.*, p. 269.
65   Nash & Bosso (2013).
66   Cassel (2015).
67   CCME (2009).
68   Hickle (2014).

doing away with costly replication province-by-province" and runs five programmes across the country.[69]

Legislation to provide a similar "framework" approach to EPR has been introduced in nine US states, but only one of these (Maine) was enacted.[70] In Australia, the Product Stewardship Act (2011) provides the framework for mandatory, co-regulatory and voluntary producer responsibility programmes.[71] Regulations were established under the Act for a national television and computer recycling scheme, which mandates producer responsibility, and for certification of voluntary schemes.

Harmonization is also on the agenda in Europe, where there are inconsistencies between the waste directives as well as marked differences in the way that each directive has been transposed in member states. According to Russ Martin "many people think that because there are EU directives that there's a more consistent approach in Europe, and that couldn't be further from the truth".[72] This increases complexity for producers, and some are concerned that they may inadvertently break the rules.[73]

A recent review of five EU waste directives—for packaging, end-of-life vehicles (ELV), batteries, PCB/PCT (polychlorinated biphenyls and polychlorinated terphenyls) and sewage sludge—evaluated their effectiveness, efficiency, coherence and relevance.[74] The coherence check aimed to "ensure that policies complement each other, are coordinated, and do not contradict one another".[75] A number of inconsistencies were identified, for example:

- Only the batteries and ELV recycling directives (and not the packaging directive) legally enshrine the producer responsibility principle

---

69   CCSA (2013). *Introducing Canadian Stewardship Services Alliance (CCSA)*. Toronto, Ontario, Canada, p. 1. Retrieved from http://www.cssalliance.ca/wp-content/uploads/2013/09/intro-to-cssa.pdf

70   Hickle (2014).

71   Australian Government (2011). *Product Stewardship Act 2011*. Department of the Environment and Energy. Retrieved from https://www.environment.gov.au/protection/national-waste-policy/product-stewardship/legislation

72   Personal communication with R. Martin (2013).

73   Kunz *et al.* (2014).

74   Bio Intelligence Service, Arcadis, & Institute for European Environmental Policy (2014). *Ex-post Evaluation of Certain Waste Stream Directives*. Report to the European Commission—DG Environment.

75   *Ibid.*, p. 13.

- Targets are treated differently, for example the batteries directive distinguishes between collection and recycling targets while the other directives do not

- There are inconsistencies in the way that key terms such as recycling are defined

In response the European Commission has announced that it will introduce a series of measures to achieve "simplification and better implementation of waste legislation" as part of its broader circular economy programme.[76] Measures will include legislative changes to harmonize waste targets and definitions, and minimum operating conditions for EPR schemes that could be further developed at a national level or in EU guidance documents.

A similar process is under way in the UK, where the government is seeking to improve coherence across its four producer responsibility regimes—for packaging, e-waste, batteries and ELV. The objective is to maximize their overall effectiveness and reduce administrative burdens on businesses.[77]

7.2.7 Revisiting the design objective

The principle of extended producer responsibility was originally intended to achieve two objectives:

- To shift responsibility (physical and/or financial) upstream to the producer and away from local government

- To provide incentives to producers to incorporate environmental considerations in the design of their products[78]

In practice EPR policies appear to have been effective in promoting the first objective but not the second. One of the common criticisms of the WEEE Directive, for example, is that implementation through collective responsibility does not give producers sufficient incentive to design

---

76   European Commission (2015). *Closing the Loop: An EU Action Plan for the Circular Economy*. Brussels, Belgium: EC, p. 9.

77   DEFRA (2013). *Review of Producer Responsibility Regimes*. Department for Environment Food & Rural Affairs, Department for Business Innovation & Skills, Department of the Environment, Welsh Government and the Scottish Government.

78   OECD (2001). *Extended Producer Responsibility: A Guidance Manual for Governments*. Paris: Organisation for Economic Cooperation and Development, p. 4.

products for repair or recycling.[79] Some laws in developing and emerging economies that focus on financial aspects, for example WEEE laws in China and Taiwan, provide even less incentive.[80] In both China and Taiwan producers pay a fee or tax to the government to subsidize recycling of e-waste.

A major review was undertaken for the EC to identify best practice guidelines for EPR programmes. Based on a detailed evaluation of 36 case studies and extensive stakeholder consultation, the authors concluded that "there is no clear evidence of a strong positive impact of EPR on the eco-design of products".[81] This is attributed to the lack of targets or indicators for ecodesign and the development of collective rather than individual takeback schemes. The economic reasoning behind EPR is to make producers internalize treatment and disposal costs so that they have an incentive to design products that last longer and are more easily recycled. By averaging costs among a large number of different producers, collective programmes provide no incentive for individual producers to implement ecodesign.[82]

This shortfall could be addressed by changing the funding mechanism to provide companies with an incentive to "design for recycling".[83] The EU report on guiding principles for EPR includes the "true cost" principle: "The fees paid by the producer to an EPR scheme should reflect, as far as possible, the true end-of-life management costs of his own products".[84]

In theory the true cost principle would be implemented through differentiated fees that reflect the actual costs of collecting, transporting and recycling each company's products. While there was broad support for the idea of differentiated fees based on true costs, industry stakeholders identified significant challenges, including the "enormous and recurring effort to establish such a cost" and the difficulties involved in determining the recyclability of a product.[85] In its circular economy package the European

---

79   Kunz *et al.* (2014).
80   Tong, X., & Yan, L. (2013). From legal transplants to sustainable transition. *Journal of Industrial Ecology*, 17(2), 199-212.
81   Bio Intelligence Service (2014). *Development of Guidance on Extended Producer Responsibility (EPR)*. Report to European Commission—DG Environment, p. 23.
82   *Ibid.*
83   Mayers, K., Lifset, R., Bodenhoefer, K. & van Wassenhove, L. (2012). Implementing individual producer responsibility for waste electrical and electronic equipment through improved financing. *Journal of Industrial Ecology*, 17(2), 186-198.
84   Bio Intelligence Service (2014), p. 125.
85   *Ibid.*, p. 208.

Commission is proposing differential fees that reflect true end-of-life costs as a way of encouraging design for reuse and recycling.[86]

Some EPR schemes have already introduced modulated fees, although not necessarily to the extent proposed by a "true cost" principle. The two PROs for consumer batteries in France are required, as part of the approvals process, to introduce "eco-modulated fees" for members. Fees are based on the environmental impacts for each battery chemistry using five criteria:

- An estimation of "eco-cost" for each battery chemistry, including key impacts on the environment, human health and non-renewable resources

- Energy capacity (efficiency)

- The number of recharge cycles

- Risks, including the risk of explosion or fire from short-circuits

- An adjustment to the eco-cost based on the relative impact at end of life[87]

When fees are adjusted for environmental impact the differences can be significant. In 2013, for example, fees were €0.039/kg for alkaline batteries and €0.184/kg for nickel cadmium batteries.[88]

In France modulated fees have also been introduced by packaging take-back programmes, Eco-Emballages and Adelphe. Both organizations provide members with training and tools to help them reduce the environmental impacts of packaging and design for recycling.[89] Additional fees are charged for "disruptive" packaging, including:

- A 50% surcharge for materials including glass packaging with a ceramic or porcelain cap, liquidpaperboard packaging less than 50% fibre, and PET bottles with aluminium in labels, caps, inks, etc.[90]

86   European Commission (2015).
87   Hedouin, F. (2013). *French Battery CRO's: Implementation of an Eco-modulated 2013 Price List*. International Congress for Battery Recycling. September 11–13, 2013, Dubrovnik, Croatia.
88   *Ibid.*
89   Bio Intelligence Service (2014). *Development of Guidance on Extended Producer Responsibility: Case Study on Packaging in France*. Report to European Commission—DG Environment. Brussels, Belgium.
90   Bell, V. (2015). *How Recycling Markets Impact EPR Programs*. In *PSI Product Stewardship Forum*. Boston, MA: Product Stewardship Institute.

- A 100% surcharge for non-recoverable packaging with sorting instructions but no recycling stream, such as stoneware or PLA (polylactic acid, a compostable resin)

An alternative approach is to use complementary policies to address the design objective. In their action plan for EPR, Canadian environment ministers acknowledge that, as a relatively small country, their ability to influence design decisions through government policy will be limited.[91] Instead they propose that EPR policy be supported and reinforced by complementary measures to address specific design issues. These include eco-labelling, restrictions on toxic substances, recycled content standards and regulations, green procurement policies, environment performance/voluntary agreements and other standards, bans, guidelines and educational tools.

If the objective is to reduce or eliminate hazardous substances it may be more effective to use direct regulation or enforceable standards rather than the indirect approach of a take-back policy. In Europe a series of "Essential Requirements" for packaging to be placed onto the market are specified in the Directive on Packaging and Packaging Waste. These include minimizing weight and volume, reducing the impact of noxious and other hazardous constituents, and designing packaging for reuse, recycling, energy recovery or composting.[92] While there is insufficient data to determine the direct impacts of the Essential Requirements on improved recycling rates and packaging weights, it is estimated that increased implementation will lead to further environmental improvements and cost reductions.[93]

Other regulatory instruments are already being used to control the use of hazardous substances in products. These include the EU's Directive 2011/65/EU on the Restriction of the Use of Certain Hazardous Substances in Electrical and Electronic Equipment ("the RoHS Directive"), which has inspired similar regulations in China and elsewhere. The EU's Directive 2006/66/EC on Batteries and Accumulators and Waste Batteries and

91   CCME (2009).
92   Commission of the European Communities (1994). *European Parliament and Council Directive 94/62/EC of 20 December 1994 on Packaging and Packaging Waste*. Retrieved from http://eur-lex.europa.eu/legal-content/EN/ALL/?uri=CELEX%3A31994L0062
93   Bio Intelligence Service (2011). *Awareness and Exchange of Best Practices on the Implementation and Enforcement of the Essential Requirements for Packaging and Packaging Waste*. Brussels, Belgium: European Commission—DG Environment. Retrieved from http://ec.europa.eu/environment/waste/packaging/pdf/packaging_final_report.pdf

Accumulators (2006) (the "Battery Directive") places strict controls on the use of mercury, cadmium and lead.

There is increasing recognition that take-back policies are just one of the options available to producers and policy-makers to influence the life-cycle impacts of a product. According to John Gertsakis, a product stewardship advocate and practitioner in Australia, "It's time to go back to the original intent of EPR":

> Go back to EPR and what [Thomas] Lindhqvist tried to do. ... What can we do to adjust and recalibrate to achieve that? How can we get information feedback? Is that something we regulate for? How do we internalize externalities? ...[94]

Gertsakis argues that product stewardship and EPR policies are not the only tools available to influence product outcomes:

> ... The time is right to acknowledge that we need to use life-cycle thinking, and think about the circular economy when looking at product stewardship and EPR. We need to be a little bit grown up and say there is a toolbox here and it's called environmental management or sustainable futures; product stewardship is one tool. Another tool might be LCA, or environmental management systems, or stakeholder engagement. [We need] to acknowledge that [product stewardship is] not a silver bullet; it's one tool or policy approach of several that must be used coherently depending on the problem. These things don't work in isolation.[95]

The European Commission's circular economy package is a clear example of a more holistic approach to product policy. The Commission is integrating waste management and producer responsibility policies with other initiatives that directly influence the design, production and use of products. Some successful projects that could be scaled up and applied more widely include sustainable sourcing standards, voluntary schemes led by manufacturers and retailers, information on how products can be repaired or recycled, and collaborative consumption projects based on lending, swapping, bartering or renting products.[96]

94   Interview with J. Gertsakis, 14 May 2014.
95   *Ibid.*
96   European Commission (2014).

7.3 Conclusion

These are just some of the trends that are already influencing government policy and corporate efforts to manage the environmental and social impacts of products.

New issues are always emerging in the public arena with implications for product design and corporate social responsibility. They can be as diverse as risks to children ingesting lithium coin-shaped batteries,[97] sugar levels in soft drinks linked to rising levels of obesity,[98] and personal wipes marketed as "flushable" clogging sewerage systems.[99] An issue that starts as a news report or social media campaign can lead to a loss of corporate reputation, a fall in sales or costly regulations if not managed effectively.

As explored in Chapter 2, companies need to take a systematic and knowledge-based approach to product stewardship. Rather than basing their strategy on instinct, personal values or a response to public pressure, managers should take the time to understand the issues, the perceptions and interests of their stakeholders, and how both of these interact with the company's products and business interests. This approach has the most potential to reduce product impact while creating value for the business.

The principle of product stewardship is, either explicitly or implicitly, being institutionalized by industry leaders in their sustainability policies, relationships with suppliers, product development processes and systems to reuse or recycle products at end of life. The question is no longer *if* companies have responsibility for the social and environmental impacts of their products, but rather *how they should respond*. The answer will vary depending on the individual circumstances of each business, including their strategic goals, core products, geographic location and external relationships.

The examples and case studies presented in this book show that there is a business case for action.

Companies that are proactive, either by implementing voluntary initiatives or by negotiating acceptable regulations with government, can protect their social licence to operate and achieve multiple business benefits.

97   The Battery Controlled (2016). *The Facts*. Retrieved from http://thebattery controlled.com.au/the-facts/

98   Triggle, N. (2016, March 16). Sugar tax: how will it work. *BBC News*. Retrieved from http://www.bbc.com/news/health-35824071

99   Power, J. (2016, March 6). Sydney Water threatens legal action as wipes block drains. *Sydney Morning Herald*. Retrieved from http://www.smh.com.au/ nsw/sydney-water-threatens-legal-action-as-wipes-block-drains-20160304 -gnax4u.html

Glossary

Accumulator	Rechargeable battery
Batteries	In this book the term "batteries" is used in a general sense to refer to all batteries, accumulators and cells (single use and rechargeable)
CO_2	Carbon dioxide
Design for environment (DFE)	Considering the environmental impacts of a product or packaging over its entire life-cycle, and opportunities to reduce these impacts, during the product development process
Design for sustainability	Considering the environmental, social and economic impacts of a product or packaging over its entire life-cycle, and opportunities to reduce these impacts, during the product development process
Ecodesign	See Design for environment
EC	European Commission
EEE	Electrical and electronic equipment
EPR	Extended producer responsibility
EU	European Union (Austria, Belgium, Bulgaria, Croatia, Republic of Cyprus, Czech Republic, Denmark, Estonia, Finland, France, Germany, Greece, Hungary, Ireland, Italy, Latvia, Lithuania, Luxembourg, Malta, Netherlands, Poland, Portugal, Romania, Slovakia, Slovenia, Spain, Sweden and the UK)

EU-15	The number of member countries in the EU prior to the accession of ten candidate countries in 2004 (Austria, Belgium, Denmark, Finland, France, Germany, Greece, Ireland, Italy, Luxembourg, Netherlands, Portugal, Spain, Sweden and the UK)
EU-27	EU-15 plus Bulgaria, Cyprus, Czech Republic, Estonia, Hungary, Latvia, Lithuania, Malta, Poland, Romania, Slovak Republic and Slovenia
EU-28	EU-27 plus Croatia (joined 2013)
Li-ion	Lithium ion
NiCd	Nickel cadmium
NGO	Non-government organization
OEM	Original equipment manufacturer
PPWD	Packaging and Packaging Waste Directive (European Union)
PRO	Producer responsibility organization: a collective entity set up by producers voluntarily or through legislation to meet the recycling obligations of individual producers
PET	Polyethylene terephthalate, a type of plastic
PRO	Producer responsibility organization
PVC	Polyvinyl chloride, a type of plastic
R2	The responsible recycling standard for electronics recyclers
SLAB	Sealed lead acid batteries
UK	United Kingdom
US	United States of America
WEEE	Waste electrical and electronic equipment

About the author

Helen Lewis has been involved in product stewardship for many years in industry, academic and government roles. Her previous roles have included CEO
of the Australian Battery Recycling Initiative and
Director of the Centre for Design at RMIT University.
Combined with extensive experience as a product
stewardship consultant, these have given her unique
insights into the value of life-cycle thinking and prod-
uct stewardship across different sectors.